W9-CPF-775

Intellectuals Don't Need

GOD

& OTHER MODERN MYTHS

Building Bridges To Faith Through Apologetics

ALISTER E. McGRATH

ZondervanPublishingHouse
Academic and Professional Books
Grand Rapids, Michigan

A Division of HarperCollinsPublishers

INTELLECTUALS DON'T NEED GOD
Copyright © 1993 by Alister E. McGrath

Published in the United Kingdom under the title *Bridge Building* by InterVarsity Press, 1992.

Requests for information should be addressed to:
Zondervan Publishing House
Academic and Professional Books
Grand Rapids, Michigan 49530

Library of Congress Cataloging in Publication Data

McGrath, Alister E., 1953-
    [Bridge-building]
    Intellectuals don't need God and other modern myths: building bridges to faith
through apologetics / by Alister McGrath
        p.   cm.
    Originally published: Bridge-building. Leicester: InterVarsity Press, 1992.
    Includes bibliographical references and index.
    ISBN 0-310-59091-4
    1. Apologetics—20th century. I. Title.
BT1102.B428 1993
239—dc20   92-39362
                                                                       CIP

Edited by Ed M. van der Maas
Cover design by Ron Kadrmas

Printed in the United States of America

93 94 95 96 97 98 / CH / 10 9 8 7 6 5 4 3 2 1

Contents

Acknowledgments

This book had its origins as a series of lectures at the University of Oxford, and it was developed during speaking tours of the United States and Australia. I am grateful to the student audiences who provided much-appreciated comments on those lectures. A number of individuals, among whom I must single out Professor Gordon R. Lewis (Denver Seminary) for special mention, read this work in typescript and made invaluable suggestions for improvements. I hope that this book will help equip and encourage the people of God in the years ahead. Their task is great, and they need every resource they can lay their hands on.

Introduction

Like every significant discipline, apologetics has a long and respectable pedigree. Christians have been defending their faith against all sorts of criticisms and misunderstandings ever since the New Testament period.[1] But the situations that writers such as Athenagoras and Justin Martyr addressed are usually of relatively little apologetic relevance today (whatever their attractions may be to historians of thought). Second-century Alexandria, thirteenth-century Paris, and seventeenth-century Cambridge—to note some outstanding periods in the history of Christian apologetics—lie firmly in the past. Their situations do not necessarily bear much relation to our own. Textbooks on Christian apologetics often indulge in extensive historical analysis simply because this is expected. But experience suggests that all too often the historical section is simply skipped over: "Who cares what Justin Martyr had to say when this is of purely antiquarian interest? It is the situation of *today* that demands attention!"

For the situation has indeed changed. The debate has shifted radically away from the universities and from the academic approaches to apologetics. It is in the marketplace of ideas, not the seminar rooms of universities, that Christianity must fight for its life. The television studio, the national press, the university cafeteria, and the local shopping mall are the new arenas in which the truth claims of Christianity are tried and tested. Christianity must commend itself in terms of its relevance to life, not just its inherent rationality.

Today we must realize that apologetics is more than a commendation of the cerebral attractions of Christianity. Classical apologetics has tended to treat Christianity simply as a set of ideas, meeting a series of intellectual barriers that can be neutralized, or perhaps even overcome, by judiciously deployed arguments. It has focused its sights firmly on the great intellectual riddles which each and every age has regarded as posing obstacles to faith in God—such as the enigma of human suffering, or the difficulties encountered in proving that God really exists. By refining its arguments and deploying ever more

9

sophisticated distinctions and subtleties, apologetics has sought to ensure that the Christian voice remains heard in an increasingly secular intellectual world.

Traditional apologetics has served the church well through the ages and will continue to do so in the future. But too often, traditional apologetics has sought to commend Christianity without asking why it is that so many people are not Christians.[2] It seems relatively pointless to extol the attractiveness of the Christian faith if this is not accompanied by a deadly serious effort to discover why it is so obviously *un*attractive to so many people. There is a reluctance to listen to those outside the community of faith to learn why they *are* outside that community. Those who have yet to discover Christianity and those who have rejected it, whether unconsciously or deliberately, often do so for reasons that totally escape the dragnet of traditional apologetics.

What sort of reasons? History often conspires against Christianity by pointing to unacceptable past associations between the Christian church and political or social oppression. Culture often brings its weight to bear against the gospel by implying that it is not acceptable to be a Christian, since to be a Christian often means adopting a set of values that run counter to those of the prevailing culture. As a result, Christians are cast in the role of cultural outsiders.

At one level, these sorts of pressures are not intellectual in nature. They are not "arguments," in the sense of a rationally justified case against the Christian faith. But such pressures and many others undoubtedly exist. They affect people. They shape their attitudes toward faith, prejudicing them against it.[3] They are part of a wider matrix of arguments, attitudes, and values that collectively build up to provide a cumulative climate that is hostile to faith. To exclude them from reference or consideration results in a truncated apologetics, incapable of meeting the full seriousness of the contemporary challenge to faith. Yet that challenge must be met in all its fullness. A challenge demands an *apologia*.

Traditional apologetics, which was conceived as a science, with timeless questions and timeless answers, seems to have become stranded in a backwater, bypassed by the real debate and ignored by the opinion-makers. It often seems sadly irrelevant to the real debates and arguments of the modern age. It has become marginalized in the great debate within modern society, precisely because it makes its appeal to an increasingly marginalized element inside this society—the academically minded. The cutting edge of faith now lies elsewhere— with the preacher whose sermons aim to reassure the committed and challenge the outsider, the business executive who shares his faith with his colleagues at work, or the student who explains her faith on campus. Apologetics needs to be revitalized—creatively and effectively. A new situation means that a traditional resource needs to be adapted to its needs and opportunities. The *science* of apologetics needs to be complemented by the *art* of apologetics.

This book does not seek to discard or discredit traditional approaches to apologetics—it seeks to supplement them. It aims to make available different ways of thinking about and doing apologetics—ways that complement the more traditional approaches. This book is not especially academic in tone, although it rests on rigorously academic foundations. It is not committed to a single theory of apologetics, nor to a single approach, nor to the writings of a single outstanding apologist. Rather, it tries to bring the resources of the Christian apologetic tradition and of Christian theology to bear on the people and the situations of greatest relevance within modern society.

Above all, this book seeks to stimulate its readers to explore and develop approaches to the defense of the gospel that are appropriate to their own special needs and opportunities. While recognizing the strengths of the *science* of issue-based apologetics, it commends the art of a people-based approach. Responsible apologetics is based on a knowledge of both the gospel and its audience. People have different reasons for not being Christians. They offer different points of contact for the gospel. An apologetics that is insensitive to human individuality and the variety of situations in which people find themselves is going to get nowhere—fast.

The apologist must make the connections with the lives of real people in the modern world. Without those connections, theories remain theories—abstract ideas hang in mid-air rather than being grounded in the realities of life. But the history of Christian apologetics demonstrates that these connections *can* be made, just as the history of the church shows that they *must* be made.

The effective apologist is one who listens before speaking and who makes every effort to link the resources of the Christian apologetic tradition both to the needs of that person and to the level of that person's ability to handle argumentation and imagery. The art of effective apologetics is hard work. It simultaneously demands a mastery of the Christian tradition, an ability to listen sympathetically, and a willingness to take the trouble to express ideas at such a level and in such a form that the audience can understand them and respond to them.

Effective apologetics also requires creativity, unless apologetics is to be relegated to the dust-laden pages of textbooks, suitable for philosophy of religion examination papers instead of preparing the ground for changing the hearts and minds of the people in our cities.

Effective apologetics demands both intellectual rigor and pastoral concern, for when all is said and done, apologetics is not about winning arguments—it is about winning people.

PART 1

Creating Openings for Faith

CHAPTER ONE

The Theological Foundations of Effective Apologetics

Awareness of a sense of emptiness resonates throughout secular culture. One thinks of Boris Becker, the noted tennis player, who came close to taking his own life through being overwhelmed by this sense of hopelessness and emptiness. Even though he was enormously successful, something was missing.

> I had won Wimbledon twice before, once as the youngest player. I was rich. I had all the material possessions I needed: money, cars, women, everything. . . . I know that this is a cliché. It's the old song of the movie and pop stars who commit suicide. They have everything, and yet they are so unhappy. . . . I had no inner peace. I was a puppet on a string.

Or one thinks of Jack Higgins, a highly successful thriller writer at the top of his profession, author of best-selling novels such as *The Eagle Has Landed*. He is reported to have been asked what he now knew that he would like to have known when he was a boy. His reply: "That when you get to the top, there's nothing there."

Becker and Higgins are excellent witnesses from the world of secular culture to the fact that most people are aware that something is missing from their lives, even if they are not able to put a name to it or may not be able to do anything about it. But the Christian gospel is able to interpret this sense of longing, this feeling of unfulfillment, as an awareness of the absence of God—and thus to prepare the way for its fulfillment.

A. APOLOGETICS IS GROUNDED IN THE DOCTRINES OF CREATION AND REDEMPTION

Through the grace of God, the creation points to its Creator. Through the generosity of God, we have been left with a latent memory of him, capable of stirring us toward a fuller recollection of him. Although there is a fracture between the ideal and the empirical, between the realms of fallen and redeemed creation, the memory of that connection lives on, along with the intimation of its restoration through redemption.

If there is some point of contact already in existence, then apologetics can make use of a God-given starting point in the very nature of the created order itself. The witness to God within his creation, the "signals of transcendence" (Peter Berger) in human life, can act as a trigger, stimulating people to ask questions about the meaning of life or the reality of God. Those points of contact are meant to be there—and they are meant to be used.

A point of contact is a God-given foothold for divine self-revelation. It is a catalyst, not a substitute, for God's self-revelation. It is like the advance guard of an army, preparing the ground for the major force that follows it. It is like the prestrike of a bolt of lightning, in which a conductive path is established from the earth to the sky so that the massive energy of the lightning can discharge itself fully into the waiting earth. God gives himself in the act of revelation; there is, however, a sense in which he has prepared the ground for that giving: not to preempt it, nor to make it unnecessary, but simply to make it more effective when it finally happens.

But we must be careful. Points of contact are not in themselves adequate to bring people into the kingdom of God. They are merely *starting points*. Nor are they adequate in themselves to bring people to a specifically *Christian* faith. They might well point toward the existence of a creative and benevolent supreme being. The connection with "the God and Father of our Lord Jesus Christ" (1 Peter 1:3) remains to be made. The apologist must still show that the Christian gospel is consistent with these points of contact, that it is able to explain them, and more than that it is able to deliver all that they promise, turning hints into reality.

Christian apologetics cannot go beyond the boundaries of the biblical insights concerning the revelation of God in his creation, but it must feel able to press on toward those full limits authorized by Scripture. It must do this cautiously, wary of the dangers that lie in the path of an uncritical appeal to creation. Among those dangers, the following may be noted as especially significant.

a. There is a limit to what human reason can discern about God by an appeal to nature.[1] Sin brings with it a propensity for distortion, by which God's revelation in creation is easily changed into an idol of our own making. The egocentricity of human sin, grounded in the fallen human will, expresses itself in the fatal wish of fallen humanity to create God in its own image and likeness, rather than to respond obediently to the self-revelation of God. This disobedience is without excuse (Rom. 1:18–2:16). Yet this flagrant abuse of God's revelation in nature does not discredit a cautious and responsible appeal to nature as pointing beyond itself to the one who created it and who will one day recreate it in glory—that is, God himself.

There is thus a fracture within creation. Fallen human nature can only reflect on a fallen creation. The fallenness of both the beholder and that which is beheld thus introduces a twofold distortion. This is most emphatically not to say that no knowledge of God may be had. Rather, we must admit that this knowledge is imperfect, broken, confused, and darkened, like a cracked mirror or a misty window. Anything that reveals less than the complete picture potentially presents a distorted picture. A "natural knowledge of God" is thus a distorted knowledge of God. But as a *starting point* it has real potential and value.

And responsible Christian apologetics makes no claim greater than this: That our perceptions of God from nature can be taken up and transfigured by the Christian revelation, in Christ and through Scripture.

b. How can the infinite ever be disclosed through the finite? How can God, who is infinite, reveal himself through or in nature, which is finite? Early Christian writers were fond of comparing our ability to understand God with looking directly into the midday summer sun. The human mind can no more cope with God than the human eye can handle the intense glare and heat of the sun. So how can a finite and weak creature ever comprehend the Creator?

The most thorough-going response to this question relates to the "principle of analogy," an idea deeply grounded in Scripture and given sophisticated theological development in the writings of such individuals as Thomas Aquinas and John Calvin. The basic idea can be stated as follows. In creating the world, God leaves his trace upon it. Just as an artist might sign a painting to draw attention to the fact that it is his or her creation, so God has left the imprint of his nature upon the created order. This is no historical accident; it is the self-expression of

God in his world. And just as the eye can cope with the brilliance of the sun by looking at it through a piece of dark glass, so God wills to make himself known in a manageable way in his creation. As Calvin states this point:

> The most suitable way of seeking God is not to attempt, with arrogant curiosity, to penetrate to the investigation of his essence (which we ought to adore, rather than to seek it out meticulously), but for us to contemplate him in his works, by which he makes himself near and familiar to us, and in some manner communicates himself to us.[2]

This is not to say that nature is God. The Creator and creation are not one and the same. We are not talking about the totality of God in this matter. We are talking about pointers, hints, rumors and signposts—the sort of things that point to God, but are not God in themselves.

c. *Wrongly understood, natural theology could be seen as an attempt by human beings to find God.* It implies that the initiative lies with fallen humanity, rather than with the revealing and redeeming God. This concern runs throughout the writings of the Swiss theologian Karl Barth and must be taken with the utmost seriousness. Barth scathingly dismisses those who construct theological towers of Babel in an attempt to make a name for themselves; their initiatives must fail, because the initiative does not lie with them. There is a gulf between ourselves and God that can never be bridged from our side. (This theme recurs in the later writings of Cornelius van Til; see Appendix B.) Even in his more irenic works, Barth is stridently insistent:

> [God] cannot be known by the powers of human knowledge, but is apprehensible and apprehended solely because of his own freedom, decision and action. What man can know by his own power according to the measure of his own powers, his understanding, his feeling, will be at most something like a supreme being, an absolute nature, the idea of an utterly free power, or a being towering over everything. This absolute and supreme being, the ultimate and most profound, this "thing in itself," has nothing to do with God.[3]

Nothing? This is clearly rhetorical exaggeration. The principle of the point of contact allows us to suggest that such notions are hints of something better, and intimations of Someone who is yet to come into our thinking.

Barth's point may have been overstated, but experience suggests that overstatement is occasionally necessary to gain a hearing. To imagine that we can conjure up everything that needs to be said about God by looking at nature or at ourselves is quite unrealistic. The old-fashioned idea of "the human quest for God" is misguided: Christianity is about God's quest for us, in which the Son of God went into the far country to bring us sinners home.[4]

"True knowledge of God" (Calvin) can only derive from revelation; yet God, in his mercy, has provided anticipations and hints of such saving knowledge in the world. A natural knowledge of God serves its purpose well when it intimates both the necessity and possibility of a fuller knowledge of God than that hinted at by the natural order. It is a traitor to itself when it allows itself to be seen as that knowledge in all its fullness.

B. APOLOGETICS IS GROUNDED IN GOD'S ABILITY TO COMMUNICATE HIMSELF THROUGH HUMAN LANGUAGE

God is able to communicate with humans through human language. This belief is fundamental, to the point of being axiomatic, to Christian apologetics. Even though human words are inadequate to do justice to the wonder and majesty of God, they are nevertheless able to point to him—inadequacy does not imply unreliability. Human words possess a capacity to function as the medium through which God is able to disclose himself and to bring about a transformational encounter with the risen Christ.

The biblical idea of the "word of God" itself bears witness to the creative and transformative character of words. In commenting on the importance of language for the self-revelation of God within the biblical tradition, a leading Old Testament scholar observed that "the word"

> . . . is a distinct reality charged with power. It has power because it emerges from a source of power which, in releasing it, must in a way release itself. . . . No-one can speak without revealing himself; and the reality which he posits is identified with himself. Thus the word . . . confers intelligibility upon the thing, and it discloses the character of the person who utters the word.[5]

The "word of God" is powerful and dynamic. It is no mere "articulate sound or series of sounds which, through conventional association with some fixed meaning, symbolizes and communicates an idea" (*Webster's Dictionary*). It is the living reality of God, making itself available in, through, and under what we so cheaply call "words."

One of the most important exponents of the ability of God to accommodate his majesty and glory in the poverty of human language is John Calvin. Beneath the surface of Calvin's assertions concerning the ability of human words to convey the reality of God lies a remarkably sophisticated theory of the nature and function of human language.

In Scripture, Calvin argues, God reveals himself verbally, in the form of words. But how can words ever do justice to the majesty of God? How can words span the enormous gulf between God and sinful humanity? Calvin develops what is usually referred to as the "principle of accommodation."[6] The term *accommodation* should here be understood to mean "adjusting or adapting to meet the needs of the situation."

In revelation, Calvin argues, God adjusts himself to the capacities of the human mind and heart. God paints a portrait of himself which we are capable of understanding. The analogy behind Calvin's thinking here is that of a human orator. The parables of Jesus illustrate this point perfectly: they use language and illustrations (such as analogies based on sheep and shepherds) perfectly suited to his audience in rural Palestine. Paul also uses ideas adapted to the situation of his hearers, drawn from the commercial and legal world of the cities in which the majority of his readers lived.[7]

Similarly, Calvin argues, God has to come down to our level if he is to reveal himself to us. God scales himself down to meet our abilities. Just as a human mother or nurse stoops down to reach her child, by using a different way of speaking than that appropriate for an adult, so God stoops down to come to our level.[8]

Examples of this accommodation are the scriptural portraits of God. God is often, Calvin points out, represented as if he has a mouth, eyes, hands, and feet.[9] That would seem to suggest that God is a human being. It might imply that somehow the eternal and spiritual God has been reduced to a physical human being. (This being portrayed in human form is called *anthropomorphism.*) Calvin argues that God is obliged to reveal himself in this pictorial manner because of our limited intellects. Images of God that represent him as having a mouth or hands are divine "baby-talk," a way in which God comes down to our level and uses images we can handle.

To those who object that this is unsophisticated, Calvin responds that it is God's way of ensuring that no intellectual barriers are erected against the gospel; all—even the simple and uneducated—can learn of, and come to faith in, God.[10] For Calvin, God's willingness and ability to condescend, to scale himself down, to adapt himself to our abilities, is a mark of God's tender mercy toward us and care for us.[11]

It must be stressed from the outset that Calvin does not believe that it is possible to reduce God or Christian experience to words.

Christianity is not a verbal religion; it is experiential.[12] It centers on a transformative encounter of the believer with the risen Christ. From the standpoint of Christian theology, however, that experience comes before the words that generate, evoke, and inform it. Christianity is Christ-centered, not book-centered; if it appears to be book-centered it is because it is through the words of Scripture that the believer encounters and feeds upon Jesus Christ. Scripture is a means, not an end; a channel, rather than what is channeled. Calvin's preoccupation with human language, and supremely with the text of Scripture, reflects his fundamental conviction that it is here, through reading and meditating on this text, that it is possible to encounter and experience the risen Christ. To suggest that Calvin—or, indeed, anyone why pays high regard to God's self-revelation in and through Scripture—is a "bibliolater," one who worships a book, is to betray a culpable lack of insight into Calvin's concerns and methods. It is precisely because Calvin attaches supreme importance to the proper worship of God, as he has revealed himself in Jesus Christ, that he considers it so important to revere and correctly interpret the only means by which full and definitive access may be had to this God—Scripture.

Apologetics, then, does not rest on finding the right form of words, as if that were an end in itself. It is grounded in the ability of God to make himself known and available through words. It is one of the many merits of the writings of C. S. Lewis that they take seriously the way in which words can *generate* experience. In his autobiography, *Surprised by Joy*, he comments on the effect of a few lines of poetry on his imagination. The lines were from Longfellow's *Saga of King Olaf:*

> I heard a voice that cried,
> Balder the beautiful
> Is dead, is dead—

These words had a profound impact on the young Lewis:

> I knew nothing about Balder; but instantly I was uplifted into huge regions of northern sky, I desired with almost sickening intensity something never to be described (except that it is cold, spacious, severe, pale and remote) and then . . . found myself at the very same moment already falling out of that desire and wishing I were back in it.[13]

Words, Lewis discovered, have the ability to evoke an experience we have not yet had. In his essay *The Language of Religion*, Lewis made this point as follows:

> This is the most remarkable of the powers of Poetic language: to convey to us the quality of experiences which we have not had, or

perhaps can never have, to use factors within our experience so that they become pointers to something outside our experience— as two or more roads on a map show us where a town that is off the map must lie. Many of us have never had an experience like that which Wordsworth records near the end of *Prelude* XIII; but when he speaks of "the visionary dreariness," I think we get an inkling of it.[14]

Apologetics shares this characteristic of poetic language (not *poetry* per se but the *language used in poetry*). It tries to convey to us the quality of the Christian experience of God. It attempts to point beyond itself, to rise above itself, straining at its leash as it rushes ahead, to point us to a town beyond its map—a town which it knows is there, but to which it cannot lead us.

Apologetics is able to use words in such a way that they become pointers for those who have yet to discover what it feels like to experience God. It uses words that try to explain what it is like to know God, by analogy with words associated with human experience. For example, "forgiveness"—if you can imagine what it feels like to be forgiven for a really serious offense, you can begin to understand the Christian experience of forgiveness. Or "reconciliation"—if you can imagine the joy of being reconciled to someone who matters very much to you, you can get a glimpse of what the Christian experience of "coming home" to God is like.

But how can apologetics use words in this way? How can we take the human experience of reconciliation and dare to say that it somehow echoes the experience of reconciliation with God?

It is here that the Christian doctrine of creation undergirds our theological affirmations. The analogy is given, not invented. It is, so to speak, built into the order of things. To speak of "redemption," "forgiveness," "reconciliation," or "liberation" is indeed to speak of situations within the human world. But it is also, through the grace of God, to speak of the entry of God into his world and of his ability to convey himself through our words. He who was rich beyond splendor became poor for our sakes—and that selfsame willingness and ability to become poor is demonstrated in the kindness that allows human words to be signposts to him. The ordinariness of human words can be transfigured by grace.

The apologist thus relies, not on a human verbosity that invents new words to speak of God, but on the grace of God that uses old words in new ways. The drabness of our words is transfigured by grace, and their poverty turned into power by the presence and purpose of the Holy Spirit. Word and Spirit are joined together in the final stage of this gentle divine persuasion, when the Holy Spirit applies those words to our minds and our lives, causing faith to be born from understanding. This, in the famous words of the *Westminster Shorter Catechism,*

> is the work of God's Spirit whereby, convincing us of our sin and misery, enlightening our minds in the knowledge of Christ, and renewing our wills, he doth persuade and enable us to embrace Jesus Christ freely offered to us in the gospel.[15]

C. APOLOGETICS IS THEOLOGICALLY INFORMED

In the eighteenth century, Isaac Newton made an important discovery in his rooms at Trinity College, Cambridge. He noticed that a beam of white sunlight, entering through a narrow slit in the shutters of his darkened rooms, could be split into its constituent colors—red, orange, yellow, green, blue, indigo, and violet—by a glass prism. The colors of the rainbow could be reproduced by a piece of glass in the laboratory.

The glass prism did not *impose* these colors on the white light; it allowed them *to be discerned.* What had hitherto been taken to be a simple color—white—was now shown to be a complex unity of different colors.

The same is true of responsible Christian theology. The message of the cross is a unity—but it is a *complex* unity. It is by examining its individual components individually that the whole message can be better appreciated and understood. Theology does not invent these components; it merely uncovers them. They are not the product of some overactive theological imagination. They are already present, awaiting our analysis, in the "message of the cross." All that the theologian does is isolate them, so that each can be studied individually.

To illustrate this process, we may pass the Christian doctrines of the cross and resurrection of Christ through a theological prism very briefly and examine the spectrum of images that is produced.[16]

a. Images from a battlefield. Christ has gained a victory over sin, death, and evil through his cross and resurrection. Through faith, believers may share in that victory and claim it as their own.

b. Images from a court of law. Through his obedience on the cross, Christ has obtained forgiveness and pardon for sinners. Those who are guilty can be washed clean of their sin and be justified in the sight of God. They are acquitted of punishment and given the status of being righteous before God.

c. Images from a relationship. As sinners, we are alienated from God. God was in Christ reconciling the world to himself; just as an alienated man and woman can draw together again through the process of forgiveness and reconciliation, so we who are far from God can draw close to him through the death of Christ.

d. Images from a prison. Those who are imprisoned by the oppressive forces of evil, sin, and the fear of death can be liberated by the gospel of the cross of Christ. Just as Christ broke free from the prison of death, so believers can, by faith, break free from the bonds of sin and come to life in all its fullness.

e. Images from a hospital. Those who are ill on account of sin can be made whole again through the ministrations of the wounded physician of Calvary. Through his cross and resurrection, Christ is able to bind up our wounds and heal us, restoring us to wholeness and spiritual health.

Newton's experiments with white light and prisms did not stop with his observation that white light could be broken up into its constituent parts. He soon discovered that the same prism that split the white light up into its components could recombine those colors and reproduce the original beam of white light. An experiment was devised which proved this neatly. A beam of white light, passed through one prism, splits up into a glorious multicolored spectrum, which, when passed through a second prism, identical to the first, produces a second beam of white light.

The same is true of theology. After analyzing the message of the cross and identifying the images of grace within it in order that they can be better understood, the theologian recombines them to give the message of the cross. It is the same message as before—but it is a message that is now far better grasped and appreciated.

So what is the relevance of all this to apologetics? The answer is as simple as it is important: because we need to relate the message to its audience. We need to ensure that the message of the cross is as effectively proclaimed as possible. While all the components of the message of the cross are relevant to the human situation, individual human beings will have different specific needs.

For example, someone who is conscious of a deep sense of moral guilt, which prevents him or her from drawing near to God, may find the components of the "word of the cross" drawn from the court of law deeply relevant. The proclamation of forgiveness could transform her life. But that does not mean that the message of the cross has been reduced to that theme. It simply means that the theologian enables the apologist to discern what his or her resources are in order to connect

Gospel proclamation   Apologetic possibilities

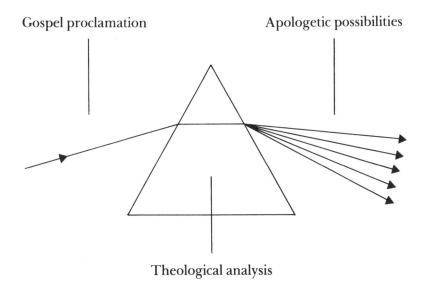

Theological analysis

Figure 1.1
The relation of theological analysis and apologetics

up as effectively as possible with the needs of the individual to whom he or she is ministering.

Someone else may have a genuine fear of dying. The gospel needs to be particularized for that person, tailored to his situation. The image of victory over the fear of death may well be profoundly important to that person. Does that mean *reducing* the gospel? No. It is to recognize that this is where the rubber hits the road in this particular life. This is a point of contact for the gospel. It is a Trojan horse that enters the camp of unbelief before throwing open its gates to the full resources of the gospel. The rest can, and will, follow in its wake.

The remainder of the message of the cross remains to be experienced by that person. He has discovered it in part; its fullness will gradually break in on him in that glorious process of exploration that attends good Christian discipling. And, as many discover, the best wine of the gospel is sometimes kept to the end; the aspect of the gospel that attracts someone to faith is often overshadowed in later Christian life as another aspect of the gospel comes to be understood and appreciated fully.

D. APOLOGETICS ADDRESSES ITSELF TO SPECIFIC AUDIENCES

It follows from the foregoing that at its most effective, Christian apologetics is *responsive*. It presents the divine initiative of the gospel in terms with which its hearers can identify. "There is an obligation to strive for the presentation of the Christian faith in terms and modes of expression that make its challenge intelligible and related to the peculiar quality of reality in which they live."[17]

The sixteenth-century reformers discovered that it was pointless trying to preach the gospel in the high cadences of Ciceronian Latin to the peasants of Germany—they just couldn't understand what was being said. The Reformers were forced to use the vernacular instead. We too must avoid using a cultural framework and vocabulary unfamiliar to our audiences. C. S. Lewis, unquestionably the greatest apologist of his time,[18] made this point perfectly:

> We must learn the language of our audience. And let me say at the outset that it is no use laying down *a priori* what the "plain man" does or does not understand. You have to find out by experience. . . . You must translate every bit of your theology into the vernacular. This is very troublesome . . . but it is essential. It is also of the greatest service to your own thought. I have come to the conclusion that if you cannot translate your own thoughts into uneducated language, then your thoughts are confused. Power to translate is the test of having really understood your own meaning.[19]

We must communicate clearly and effectively. Barriers to communication represent barriers to the gospel. But there is a deeper issue. There is a sense in which the gospel will always be alien to the world. It provides a powerful challenge to prevailing secular standards, outlooks, and ideas. That means it is going to encounter difficulties. It is going to confront prejudice, ignorance, and confusion. Why make the gospel seem even more alien by presenting it in forms that immediately declare it to be an outsider to any given culture? The gospel is too easily—and unnecessarily—made to seem middle class to a working class audience, or Western to an Asian audience. The pervasive role of the United States and Great Britain in evangelization during the nineteenth and early twentieth centuries has led to a widespread perception in many African and Asian cultures that Christianity is a Western creed. This distortion is introduced through the careless presentation of Christianity, in which the cultural norms of the apologete have been unthinkingly—and unjustifiably—projected onto the gospel proclamation itself.

Classic presentations of the gospel are often superbly tailored to the cultural situation the gospel preacher addresses. We have much to learn from them. The suspicion that the gospel is an outsider to a culture can be disarmed through the use of words, ideas, events, and values familiar to that culture.

The parables of Jesus are a superb example of the way in which the gospel is presented in terms of the common life of the people. The parables are stories about particular people who lived at a given time in history in a specific cultural setting—first-century Palestine. The Palestinian audience for these parables instantly recognized their own cultural situation. Here was an insider talking to them as one of them and explaining new ideas in such a way that their strangeness was minimized. The ideas may have been new or unsettling; the language and imagery in which they were expressed were reassuringly familiar. An important potential obstacle to the gospel was brilliantly circumvented.[20]

How unsettling those ideas were at the time is perhaps lost on modern Western audiences. For example, we read of the father of the prodigal running to meet his returning son (Luke 15:20). For a village patriarch to *run* is unheard of. The more important you are, the more slowly and pompously you walk.[21] The fact that the father runs to meet his son thus brings home visually and dramatically his care and love for his son. He sacrifices his honor in order to show his love.

Jesus' preaching thus begins where people actually are—in the everyday world of rural Galilee.[22] He told stories that reflected the world of his audience. He spoke of traders making business deals, of the hiring of laborers, of the failings of vineyards, of weeds growing among wheat, of the wasted seed strewn along the ground, of sheep wandering away from their flock, and of children playing in the street.

But the familiarity of this world is disturbed by unexpected twists in the story. The father runs to meet his son, even before the delinquent youth has had a chance to apologize for his behavior. Those who worked for one hour are paid the same as those who worked a full day. It is the sinful publican, not the pious Pharisee, who is justified. Here is "heaven in ordinary"—the transcendent and holy gospel revealed and embodied in the flow of everyday life.

We see a similar pattern in Paul's letters. Whereas Jesus spoke to a rural Palestinian audience, Paul wrote to a Greek-speaking constituency in the cities of the Roman Empire. The images he uses to make sense of the Christian life are firmly grounded in that urban world of his readers. A specific example is found in his letter to the Philippians.

Philippi was founded as the city of Krenides by an Athenian

exile, Callistratus. After Anthony and Octavian defeated Brutus and Cassius there in the famous battle of 42–41 B.C. that marked the end of the Roman Republic—made immortal by Shakespeare's famous lines in *Julius Caesar*, "I will see thee at Philippi then"—the city was refounded as a Roman colony. After the defeat of Anthony's forces at Actium eleven years later, Octavian reconstituted the colony once more. The city thus developed a decidedly Italian atmosphere due to both the permanent presence of Italian settlers and the large numbers of Roman troops regularly passing through the city because of its strategic location in Macedonia.[23] The language, imagery, and outlooks of a Roman colony would thus be part of the everyday thought-world of Paul's audience in the city. Philippi was conscious of its ties with Rome, including its language (Latin seems to have been more widely spoken than Greek) and laws. Roman institutions served as the model in many areas of its communal life.

Paul uses the image of a "colony (*politeuma*) of heaven" (Phil. 3:20) to bring out several aspects of Christian existence. By speaking of the Christian community in this way, Paul naturally encourages his readers to think along certain lines. Those strands of thought would include the following. The Christian church is an outpost of heaven in a foreign land. It speaks the language of that homeland and is governed by its laws—despite the fact that the world around it speaks a different language and obeys a different set of laws. Its institutions are based on those of its homeland. And one day its citizens will return to that homeland to take up all the privileges and rights that that citizenship confers. This image thus lends dignity and hope to the Christian life, especially the tension between the "now" and "not yet" and the bittersweet feeling of being outsiders to a culture, "in" the world and yet not "of" the world.

Again, we see a similar pattern in Paul's Areopagus sermon (Acts 17:22–31), which has rightly been hailed as an object lesson in apologetics. There is a sense in which this sermon illustrates Paul's desire to "be all things to all people." The religious and philosophical curiosity of the Athenians shaped the contours of his theological exposition.[24] The "sense of divinity" present in each individual is here used as a powerful apologetic device that enables Paul to base himself on acceptable Greek theistic assumptions while at the same time going beyond them. Paul shows a clear appreciation of the apologetic potential of Stoic philosophy, portraying the gospel as resonating with central Stoic concerns while extending the limits of what might be known. What the Greeks held to be unknown, possibly unknowable, Paul proclaims to have been made known through the resurrection of

Christ. The entire episode illustrates the manner in which Paul is able to exploit the situation of his audience without compromising the integrity of faith.

The Areopagus sermon also illustrates the New Testament tendency to mingle the proclamation of the gospel message (the kerygma) and its reasoned defense (apologetics) as two aspects of a greater whole. The rigid systematization of theology, which has been so damaging in recent Christian history, leads to a radical separation of *kerygma* and *apologia*. Kerygmatic theology has been detached from apologetics for methodological reasons—yet both are essential components of the New Testament conception of the proclamation of Christ. The New Testament brings the two together in a creative and productive interplay: to proclaim the gospel is to defend the gospel, just as to defend the gospel is to proclaim the gospel.[25]

The basic point to emerge from this discussion is simple. Effective Christian apologetics is grounded in a knowledge of its audience. This audience is not static and predictable. It is not the same irrespective of its age, social location, country of origin, or language. Rather, it is dynamic and changing. The apologist needs to know his or her audience, speak its language, and share its common flow of life. The best apologists are always found within a society. Those who live in a society know its hopes and its fears. They share its outlook and its images. And they can sense, almost intuitively, the points of contact that exist for the gospel.

Jesus spoke in Aramaic, and Paul and the later evangelists spoke and wrote in the everyday Greek (*koine*) of the Roman world of that age. This observation has enormous apologetic importance. Christ and Paul spoke and wrote in the language of their people. They used the idioms of their people. They did not in any way seek to isolate themselves from their people—for example, by using an arcane religious vocabulary, a mystic set of symbols, or an ecstatic language whose meaning was denied to all save a few.

Ordinary language was deemed to have the dignity of grace—to have the God-given ability to become the medium of his revelation. Our everyday language can do the same—if we bother to take the trouble over it and ground it in the God-given and God-authorized matrix of Scripture.

CHAPTER TWO

Points of Contact

In the last chapter we explored the theory of the point of contact. In this chapter we will supplement theoretical considerations with practical application and discuss in more detail a number of specific points of contact and suggest how they may be used.

A. A SENSE OF UNSATISFIED LONGING

We are made in the image of God. We have an inbuilt capacity—indeed, an inbuilt *need*—to relate to God. Nothing that is transitory can ever fill this need. To fail to relate to God is to fail to be completely human. To be fulfilled is to be filled by God. Nothing that is not God can ever hope to take the place of God. And yet, because of the fallenness of human nature, there is a natural tendency to try to make other things fulfill this need. Created things are substituted for God, and they do not satisfy.

This phenomenon has been recognized since the dawn of human civilization. In one of his dialogues,[1] Plato compares human beings to leaky jars. Somehow we are always partly empty—and for that reason experience a profound awareness of a lack of fullness and happiness. "Those who have endured the void know that they have encountered a distinctive hunger, or emptiness; nothing earthly satisfies it."[2]

Paul Elmer Moore, one of America's greatest Platonist philosophers, eventually became a Christian. Moore had always been fascinated and deeply satisfied by the world of beautiful Platonic forms, the world of the purely ideal. But gradually, disillusionment set in. He began to experience a sense of unutterable bleakness and solitariness. He was driven to search for God "by the loneliness of an Ideal world without a Lord." He longed for those impersonal forms to become personal—to turn into a face. "My longing for some audible voice out of the infinite silence rose to a pitch of torture. To be satisfied I must see face to face, I must, as it were, handle and feel—and how should this be?"[3] Moore demonstrates superbly the basic need that the Christian doctrine of the incarnation addresses and meets. Dissatisfaction can set us firmly on the road that leads to the discovery of a personal God—a God with a face, a God we can handle, feel, and name (note 1 John 1:1–3).

The Marxist analysis of human experience recognizes this feeling of dissatisfaction and claims to cure it. When the revolution comes, this sense of emptiness (which is a direct result of capitalism) will disappear. But in those parts of the world where the revolution came, the sense of alienation and dissatisfaction remained. More recently, Jean-Paul Sartre persistently pointed out the disconcerting truth that we cannot find happiness in anything human or created—but beyond that the innate human desire to deny our inability to find satisfaction in the world. It is almost as if we could not bear to live with the idea that fulfillment will permanently elude us.

This feeling of dissatisfaction is one of the most important points of contact for gospel proclamation. In the first place, that proclamation interprets this vague and unshaped feeling as a longing for *God*. And second, it offers to fulfill it. There is a sense of divine dissatisfaction with all that is *not* God. This divine dissatisfaction has its origin in God and ultimately leads to God. Sartre is right: the world cannot bring fulfillment. Here he echoes the Christian view. But the Christian view goes on to affirm that here, in the midst of the world, something that is ultimately beyond the world makes itself available to us. We do not need to wait for eternity to experience God; that experience can begin, however imperfectly, now. One of the greatest expressions of this longing and its answer is found in the famous words of Augustine of Hippo: "You have made us for yourself, and our hearts are restless until they rest in you."[4] The same theme recurs throughout Augustine's reflections, especially in the *Confessions*. We are doomed to remain incomplete in our present existence. Our hopes and deepest longings will remain nothing but just that: hopes and longings.

This bittersweet tension remains real, even for the Christian who becomes increasingly aware of the wonder of God and of the inadequacy of our present grasp of that wonder. There is a sense of postponement, of longing, of wistful yearning, of groaning under the strain of having to tolerate the present when the future offers so much.[5] Perhaps the finest statement of this exquisite agony is found in Augustine's cry, "I am groaning with inexpressible groanings on my wanderer's path, and remembering Jerusalem with my heart lifted up towards it—Jerusalem my homeland, Jerusalem my mother."[6] We are exiled from our homeland—but its memories haunt us. Like Augustine, C. S. Lewis was aware of deep human emotions that point to a dimension of our existence beyond time and space, a deep and intense feeling of longing that no earthly object or experience can satisfy. Lewis calls this emotion "joy." It is "an unsatisfied desire which is itself more desirable than any other satisfaction . . . anyone who has experienced it will want it again."[7]

Lewis describes this experience (better known to students of German Romanticism as *Sehnsucht*) in his autobiography. He relates how, as a young child, he was standing by a flowering currant bush, when—for some unexplained reason—a memory was triggered.

> There suddenly rose in me without warning, as if from a depth not of years but of centuries, the memory of that earlier morning at the Old House when my brother had brought his toy garden into the nursery. It is difficult to find words strong enough for the sensation which came over me; Milton's "enormous bliss" of Eden . . . comes somewhere near it. It was a sensation, of course, of desire; but desire for what? Not, certainly, for a biscuit tin filled with moss, nor even (though that came into it) for my own past . . . and before I knew what I desired, the desire itself was gone, the whole glimpse withdrawn, the world turned common-place again, or only stirred by a longing for the longing that had just ceased. It had only taken a moment of time; and in a certain sense everything else that had ever happened to me was insignificant in comparison.[8]

Lewis here describes a brief moment of insight, an overwhelming moment of feeling caught up in something that goes far beyond the realms of everyday experience. But what did it mean? What, if anything, did it point to?

Lewis addressed this question in a remarkable sermon entitled "The Weight of Glory." There is something self-defeating about human desire: that which is desired, when achieved, seems to leave the desire unsatisfied.

> The books or the music in which we thought the beauty was located will betray us if we trust to them; it was not *in* them, it only came *through* them, and what came through them was longing. These things—the beauty, the memory of our own past—are good images of what we really desire; but if they are mistaken for the thing itself they turn into dumb idols, breaking the hearts of their worshippers. For they are not the thing itself; they are only the scent of a flower we have not found, the echo of a tune we have not heard, news from a country we have not visited.[9]

Human desire, the deep and bittersweet longing for something that will satisfy us, points beyond finite objects and finite persons (who *seem* able to fulfill this desire, yet eventually prove incapable of doing so). It points *through* these objects and persons toward their real goal and fulfillment in God himself.

The paradox of hedonism—the simple fact that pleasure cannot satisfy—is another instance of this curious phenomenon. Even in our contentment we still feel in need of something that is indefinably missing. It is as if God leaves us with a certain weariness with nature that can be satisfied only by pressing on beyond nature to its source and goal in God himself. If meditation on the goodness of God does not drive us to him, perhaps weariness with the pleasures of the world will have the intended effect.

Pleasure, beauty, personal relationships: all seem to promise so much, and yet when we grasp them we find that what we were seeking still lies beyond them. There is a "divine dissatisfaction" in human experience that prompts us to ask whether there is anything that may satisfy the desires of the human heart.

Lewis argues that there is. Hunger, he suggests, is an excellent example of a human sensation which corresponds to a real physical need. This need points to the existence of food by which it may be met. Simone Weil echoes this theme and points to its apologetic importance when she writes: "The danger is not lest the soul should doubt whether there is any bread, but lest, by a lie, it should persuade itself that it is not hungry. It can only persuade itself of this by lying, for the reality of its hunger is not a belief, it is a certainty."[10]

Any human longing, Lewis argues, points to a genuine human need, which in turn points to a real object corresponding to that need. This sense of longing points to its origin and its fulfillment in God himself.

Lewis's less perceptive critics—sadly, more numerous than one might hope—maintained that his argument rests on an elementary fallacy. Being hungry does not prove that there is bread at hand; the feeling of hunger does not necessarily correspond to a supply of food. But this objection, Lewis replies, misses the point.

> A man's physical hunger does not prove that man will get any bread; he may die of starvation in a raft in the Atlantic. But surely a man's hunger does prove that he comes of a race which repairs its body by eating and inhabits a world where eatable substances exist. In the same way, though I do not believe (I wish I did) that my desire for Paradise proves that I shall enjoy it, I think it a pretty good indication that such a thing exists and that some men

will. A man may love a woman and not win her; but it would be
very odd if the phenomenon called "falling in love" occurred in a
sexless world.[11]

So how can this point of contact be applied? Here is what an apologetic
sermon exploiting this point of contact might look like.

> Have you ever noticed what happens when you want something
> very badly, and then you get it? A new job? A marriage partner?
> An important qualification? A pay raise? You begin by longing for
> it. "When I get this, I shall be satisfied, and ask for nothing
> more." But it doesn't work out like that at all. When you finally
> get your heart's desire, it doesn't seem to satisfy. You want more.
> You want something else. The old proverb that says, "it is better
> to journey in hope than to arrive," makes just this point. The
> paradox of hedonism, which is that the pursuit of pleasure is self-
> defeating, rests on this very observation. It seems that nothing
> finite can satisfy some deep sense of longing within us. But where
> does that sense of longing come from? And is there any way in
> which this bittersweet yearning *could* be satisfied?[12]

The remainder of the sermon is left to you. The point of contact is for
real; it is up to you to make the most of it.

B. HUMAN RATIONALITY

Something about human nature prompts it to ask questions
about the world. And there seems to be something about the world
that allows for answers to those questions. This seemingly trivial
observation is actually of considerable importance.

> We are so familiar with the fact that we can understand the world
> that most of the time we take it for granted. It is what makes
> science possible. Yet it could have been otherwise. The universe
> might have been a disorderly chaos rather than an orderly cosmos.
> Or it might have had a rationality which was inaccessible to us . . .
> There is a congruence between our minds and the universe,
> between the rationality experienced within and the rationality
> observed without.[13]

The fact that there is a congruence between human rationality and the
rationality—the *orderedness*—which we observe in the world around
us raises a major question: Why? Why is it, for example, that the
abstract structures of pure mathematics—a free creation of the human
mind—provide such important clues to understanding the world?
Suppose the same master creator fashioned both the world and
the human mind. Would one not expect that the world should show
traces of divine ordering and that human minds should be capable of
discerning this order and grasping its possible significance? This

simple supposition puts a highly suggestive question mark behind the statements of those who dismiss God on scientific grounds.

> What is behind the universe is more like a mind than it is like anything else we know. That is to say, it is conscious, and has purposes, and prefers one thing to another. . . . It made the universe, partly for purposes we do not know, but partly, at any rate, in order to produce creatures like itself . . . to the extent of having minds.[14]

The resonance of reason with God is thus a harmony of rationality, hinting that human nature is still marked with the *imago Dei*. Given the Christian understanding of who God is and what he is like, our knowledge of both our rational selves and the rational world ties in with belief in his rational and creative existence.

It would seem to follow that the same human reason that can investigate nature and uncover its ordering should also prove capable of grasping something—however slight—of God himself. The resonance of reason is grounded in the creatorship of God. This point was developed at length by the thirteenth-century theologian Thomas Aquinas, who proposed five arguments that suggest that the Christian belief in God is completely consistent with the world as we know it.[15]

Aquinas's arguments, known as the "Five Ways," are sometimes referred to as "proofs of the existence of God." This is not correct. Aquinas did not try to prove the existence of God by rational argument, but to provide a rational defense of an already existing faith in God. His primary reason for believing in the existence of God is God's revelation of himself. Aquinas expects his readers to share his faith in God. He does not expect that he will have to prove it to them first. Nevertheless, Aquinas believes that it is proper to identify pointers toward the existence of God, drawn from outside Scripture. But these arguments or pointers are *supports*, not *proofs*, for the existence of God. They serve to reinforce a faith that already exists, not to bring that faith into existence.

This is an important point, for many critics of the Christian faith accuse believers of grounding their faith in outdated or unconvincing arguments—such as Thomas Aquinas's Five Ways. It is proper to respond to such criticisms by pointing out that they are based on a superficial reading of Thomas Aquinas and on a serious misunderstanding of how individuals come to faith. The ultimate grounds of faith lie in God's self-revelation in Christ through Scripture.

The basic concept guiding Aquinas throughout his discussion is the principle of analogy: the world as we know it mirrors God, its creator. In exploring the Five Ways briefly, it will soon become obvious that the structure of each of Aquinas's arguments is rather similar. Each depends on tracing a causal sequence back to its ultimate origin and identifying this ultimate origin with God.

a. The first way begins with the observation that things in the world are in *motion or change*. The world is not static, but dynamic. But how did nature come to be in motion? Why isn't it static? Aquinas argues that everything that moves is moved by something else. For every motion, there is a cause. But each cause of motion must itself have a cause. And *that* cause must have a cause, and so on. But unless there is an infinite number of these causes, Aquinas argues, there must be a single cause right at the origin of the series from which all other motion is ultimately derived. And this ultimate cause, he concludes, is God himself.

b. The second way begins from the idea of *causation*. Aquinas notes the existence of causes and effects in the world. One event (the effect) is explained by the influence of another (the cause). The idea of motion is a good example of this cause-and-effect sequence. Using a line of reasoning similar to that used above, Aquinas argues that all effects may be traced back to a single original cause—God himself. (This argument, as has often been pointed out, depends on the highly questionable assumption that an infinite regression of causes is impossible.)

c. The third way concerns the *existence of contingent beings*. The world contains beings (such as ourselves) which aren't there by necessity. Aquinas contrasts this type of being with a necessary being (one who is there as a matter of necessity). God, Aquinas says, is a necessary being, and we are contingent beings. The fact that we *are* here needs explanation.

Aquinas then argues that a nonnecessary or contingent being comes into existence because something which already exists brought it into being. In other words, our existence is caused by another being. We are the effects of a series of causations. Tracing this series back to its origin, Aquinas declares that this original cause of being can only be someone whose existence is necessary—in other words, God.

d. The fourth way begins with *human values*, such as truth, goodness, and nobility. Where do these values come from? What causes them? Aquinas argues that there must be something that is in itself true, good, and noble, and that this brings into being our ideas of truth, goodness, and nobility. The origin of these ideas, Aquinas suggests, is God, who is their original cause.

e. The final way is usually known as the teleological argument. Aquinas notes that the world shows obvious traces of intelligent *design*.

Natural processes and objects seem to be adapted with certain definite objectives in mind. They seem to have a purpose. They seem to have been designed. But things do not design themselves—they are caused and designed by someone or something else. Arguing from this observation, Aquinas concludes that the source of this natural ordering must be conceded to be God himself.

On the basis of these considerations, Aquinas concludes that it is rational to believe in God. Not for one moment does he suggest that these arguments constitute *proofs* for the existence of God. Rather, he is concerned to demonstrate that reason is capable of pointing in the direction of God and lending its support to those who already believe in him.

Reason, then, provides an important point of contact for the gospel. Though fallen, reason still possesses the ability to grasp and point, however darkly, toward the reality of God. It is a valuable ally— and a dangerous foe—for the apologist. How significant is the fact that reason *is* fallen for apologetics? Reason has been taken captive by sin, like a town captured by an enemy, and is no longer fully able to play its role as God's viceroy within us. While it retains an ability to recall the "loving memory" of God (Augustine), it has become the servant of sin. Its natural tendency is thus to keep us in that same captivity, rather than to enable us to escape from it. Through the Fall, that which was meant to lead us to God actually draws us away from him. Rationalism—that is, a system of thought based entirely upon reason, deliberately excluding any ideas based upon divine revelation—is thus locked into the sinful human situation. It is trapped within its confines, as one might be within the walls of a city held by an enemy.

To be liberated from this bondage, reason needs to recover its awareness of its being grounded in the nature of God himself. True rationality rests on the congruence between reason and the nature of God himself. Empirical reason—that is, reason as we know it—must become aware of its limitations if it is to transcend them. In his work *Escape from Reason*, Francis Schaeffer makes the following point, which merits close consideration:

> Christianity has the opportunity, therefore, to say clearly that its answer has the very thing modern man has despaired of—the unity of thought. It provides a unified answer for the whole life. True, man has to renounce his rationalism; but then . . . he has the possibility of recovering his rationality.[16]

Christianity is in no sense irrational; indeed, its own system of rationality is perfectly coherent. The difficulty is that this system of rationality does not happen to agree with a rationalistic approach to the world, which holds that the world can be known totally by reason alone. As we shall see,[17] the widely acknowledged fatal defects in the rationalistic worldview should encourage us to reexamine the rationality of Christianity itself. For reason does not merely point toward God; once it has found God—only to discover that it was actually found by God first—it is itself transfigured into a God-centered unity.

C. THE ORDERING OF THE WORLD

Modern science has demonstrated that the world is ordered. But its disclosure of an intelligible and delicately balanced structure raises questions that transcend the scientific and provide an intellectual restlessness that seeks adequate explanation. Perhaps the most fundamental of these questions can be summarized in a single word: Why?

It was once thought that there were certain gaps in scientific understanding, that could never be filled by scientific investigation. It therefore seemed to make apologetic sense to invoke God to explain such gaps. But these gaps kept getting filled through scientific inquiry, with the result that God gradually got squeezed out of a series of steadily decreasing gaps.

A more credible approach, increasingly adopted in Christian apologetics, is to concentrate on the scientifically "given" rather than the scientifically "open." In other words, science discloses the world as having a tightly knit and intricately interconnected structure that must be explained. Yet, paradoxically, the natural sciences are unable to provide such explanations, even though this would appear to be an essential aspect of the project of understanding the world.[18]

The central question is, Where does the ordering of the world come from? An obvious answer might be that there is no order in the world except that which we impose on it. It is a construct of the human mind that has no adequate basis in reality. Attractive though this belief might initially seem, it rests on a series of historical improbabilities. Time and time again, the neat and ordered theories of human beings have come to grief against the sheer intractability of the observational evidence. The ordering which the human mind seeks to impose on the world proves incapable of explaining it, forcing the search for a better understanding. The ordering imposed by the human mind is thus constantly being compared with that disclosed in the world, to be amended where it is inadequate.

One feature of the ordering of the universe that has attracted special attention recently is what is known as the *anthropic principle*. In order for creation to come into being, a very tightly connected series of conditions had to apply. John Polkinghorne, formerly Professor of Mathematical Physics at the University of Cambridge, who resigned his chair to become a Christian minister, speaks of

> our increasing realization that there is a delicate and intricate balance in its structure necessary for the emergence of life. For example, suppose things had been a little different in those crucial first three minutes when the gross nuclear structure of the world got fixed as a quarter helium and three quarters hydrogen. If things had gone a little faster, all would have been helium; and without hydrogen how could water (vital to life) have been able to form?[19]

After listing other aspects that indicate a significant degree of fine-tuning, Polkinghorne points to the way in which such considerations lay the foundations for the Christian belief in God. They do not necessarily give rise to that belief, but they are consistent with it and raise important and disturbing questions the apologist can exploit.

A full treatment of the apologetic possibilities offered by the natural sciences lies beyond the scope of this book, largely because of the complexity of some of the notions requiring explanation. The apologist operating on university campuses, with regular interaction with students studying the natural sciences, will find that study of such themes can be productive and valuable.

D. HUMAN MORALITY

Most humans have a sense of moral obligation, or at least an awareness of the need for some kind of agreement on morality. This is, in itself, an important point of contact for the gospel. It used to be thought that morality had no bearing on anything to do with religion. For example, in his *Ethics Without God*, Kai Nielsen argued that the human sense of morality and the specific moral systems that are built on it are quite independent of God. A closer examination of Nielsen's arguments, however, raises serious doubts about the strengths of his case.[20] There is a new sympathy toward reconsidering the religious foundations of ethics in the postmodern age, now that rationalism—with its ludicrous and unfulfilled promises of a totally rational ethic—has been discredited.

To explore the potential value of this point of contact, we may consider its most popular exposition—the opening pages of C. S. Lewis's *Mere Christianity*. Lewis begins his case for Christianity by appealing to a commonplace of experience. People argue. "They say things like this: 'How'd you like it if anyone did the same to you?'— 'That's my seat, I was there first'—'Leave him alone, he isn't doing you any harm.' "[21] As they argue, they make an unconscious appeal to moral standards. When people disagree about moral issues, they behave as if there is an underlying agreement about what is right and wrong:

> It looks, in fact, very much as if both parties had in mind some Law or Rule of fair play or decent behaviour or morality or whatever you like to call it, about which they really agreed. And they have. . . . Quarrelling [sic] means trying to show that the other man is in the wrong. And there would be no sense in trying to do that unless you and he had some sort of agreement as to what Right and Wrong are; just as there would be no sense in saying that a footballer had committed a foul unless there was some agreement about the rules of football.

Unless you and the person you are arguing with have the same presuppositions about right and wrong, the argument is unlikely to get very far. "Right" would quickly become "right for me, regardless of what anyone else thinks."

It is, of course, clear that there are differences between various understandings of right and wrong. Lewis's point, however, is that there is a core of moral constants underlying human civilization. He asks us to imagine a country "where a man felt proud of doublecrossing all the people who had been kindest to him," adding that we "might just as well try to imagine a country where two and two made five." (Lewis does not ask us to think of a single man who is proud of deceiving those who were kind to him. He asks, rather, that we try to imagine a society in which this behavior is regularly and unconditionally thought of as being a virtue. The single individual we are asked to imagine reflects the morality of his society as a whole.)

Where the laws of science describe the way things are, Lewis suggests that morality prescribes the way things ought to be. But where does this come from? What basis does this moral law have? Lewis argues that the only explanation of morality lies with God. If Lewis's line of argument is followed, a syllogism along the following lines could be constructed as follows:

    a. Unless there is a God, there cannot be objectively binding moral obligations.
    b. Objectively binding moral obligations exist.
    c. Therefore there is a God.

A number of writers are unhappy with the bold claims that Lewis makes, however, and prefer to adopt a probabilistic approach. While it cannot be demonstrated with certainty that morality depends on God, they argue, this is nevertheless its most probable or plausible explanation. The syllogism then becomes:

a. Unless there is a God, there probably cannot be objectively binding moral obligations.

b. Objectively binding moral obligations exist.

c. Therefore there probably is a God.

While this approach lacks the knock-down certainty of Lewis's, it has the undoubted advantage of seeming more reasonable to some, given the difficulties in demonstrating that there is a firm and unbreakable link between morality and the existence of God. The probabilistic conclusion that the existence of God is the most likely explanation of the way things are may at first seem modest. But apologetics is not concerned with this single conclusion. It is concerned with the accumulation of pointers, of which this is but one, which eventually build up to give a credible, persuasive, and attractive case for God.

The approach, however, has its critics, and we must look at one criticism in some detail. Part of the secular case against the appeal to God in matters of ethics rests on what has become known as the "Euthyphro dilemma," which is first clearly stated in Plato's dialogue *Euthyphro*. The dilemma, which would appear to imply that God is totally irrelevant to ethics, is usually stated as follows:

a. Is something good because God commands it?

b. Or does God command something because it is good?

If the first option is correct, goodness becomes something arbitrary, dependent on the whim of God. If God were to command us to torture the innocent or exterminate an entire race of people, then that action would be good—despite the fact that it is so obviously evil. Yet the fact that we would recognize such acts as evil implies that it is actually we, and not God, who decide what is good and what is evil.

If the second option is correct, God is irrelevant to ethics. All he does is endorse what is already good. And so he does not need to be brought into the discussion at all. God can be left out, and it would not make the slightest difference to morality.

The Euthyphro dilemma has force if, and *only if*, human and divine ideas of justice or goodness are understood to be two completely independent entities—a perfectly reasonable assumption for Plato, given the polytheism of his period in ancient Greek cultural history. But the Christian doctrine of God destroys the dilemma by insisting upon an inbuilt and indissoluble link between human and divine ideas of goodness, which persists even in fallen human nature. We recognize that what God does is right, because we have been created in the image of divine ideas of righteousness. Human and divine ideas of goodness resonate; the disharmony presupposed by Plato is an irrelevance, given the Christian understanding of God and human nature. Euthyphro poses no dilemma to the Christian.

The approach we have been considering here is based on using the idea of moral perception as a point of contact for the gospel. The sense of moral obligation need not necessarily point to God. But it is highly suggestive. It is an invaluable discussion starter. It does not necessarily *prove* anything; but it suggests that the existence of God provides the most plausible or probable explanation of the existence of moral obligation.

E. EXISTENTIAL ANXIETY AND ALIENATION

Every now and then I get the impression that English is not a very expressive language. It seems to have to rely on the richness of foreign languages to express even quite basic ideas. Gradually, these foreign words become assimilated into English. People stop printing them in italic type and start pronouncing them as if they were ordinary English words. This will probably eventually happen to two words that have become increasingly common during the last generation—the German term *Angst* and the French word *anomie*. They both refer to a basic disorder in human existence, a flaw, an anomaly, that while it expresses itself at every level of our existence, often appears to possess a peculiar power at the existential level. This feeling of existential anxiety—usually referred to simply as *Angst*—is a significant point of contact for the gospel.

What is this existential anxiety? How do we describe it and how can we exploit its apologetic potential? Modern existentialist writers, from Martin Heidegger to Jean-Paul Sartre, have explored the various aspects of *Angst,* drawing especially on the experience of alienation which became significant in Western Europe and North America in the decades following the Second World War. We shall consider the basic features of this experience before moving on to deal with its potential use.

The word *existence* comes from the Latin verb *existere,* which seems to have the basic meaning of "standing out." To exist, in the full sense of the word, means to stand out from your environment. There is a sense in which stones and inanimate objects do not exist; they are there, but they do not stand out from their background. There is a useful comparison here between the two Greek words commonly used to describe the idea of "life": *bios,* which has the basic sense of life at the biological level of existence; and *zoe,* in the sense of *real* life. For men and women, to exist does not mean to limp along at a purely biological level of being; it means to live an authentically human existence, in which we fully stand out from the world and achieve our full human potential.

But all kinds of dehumanizing forces in the world threaten to reduce us to the level of the impersonal. We are in danger of "falling into the world" (Heidegger), collapsing into the background, and losing our distinctiveness. We run the risk of being reduced to a statistic, our individuality denied. A deep-seated threat of meaninglessness can be discerned in much existential literature: either we will discover that life has no meaning, or we will lose sight of the meaning that is already there. *Angst* is the collective name given to fears of these kinds—anxiety about losing our way in the vastness of an impersonal world and being reduced to cosmic insignificance. *Angst* reflects a deeply rooted fear of meaninglessness and pointlessness, a sense of the utter futility of life, even sheer despair at the bewildering things that threaten to reduce us to nothing more than a statistic—ultimately a mortality statistic.

Such anxieties are already there in your audiences. Often, such feelings are heightened during middle age. The energy and enthusiasm of youth often allow us to overlook, perhaps even to deny, such anxieties. But they emerge from their suppression as if they had gained new strength from their enforced hibernation. While it seems trite to talk about "the meaning of life," it is a question that lingers at the edges (and sometimes squarely in the center) of reflective human existence.

The apologist may address this anxiety and bring it to the level of conscious articulation. It is a real point of contact for the gospel. We do not feel secure in the world. This awareness is a powerful stimulus to look for some grounds of assurance. Where Luther asked, "Where may I find a gracious God?" many today ask, "Where can I find security and peace of mind?" Yet, paradoxically, both questions are the same: the first is that of a theologically articulate individual who has yet to find a gracious God; the second is that of an insecure person, lacking any spiritual insight or theological intuition, whose questioning may well set him or her on the road to finding a gracious God. This human sense of anxiety is ultimately grounded in the absence of the presence of God. The apologist has the task of correlating the gospel with this sense of profound unease, interpreting it and fulfilling it with the presence of the living God. To paraphrase Augustine: our hearts are restless because they have yet to find a resting place, yet alone to discover that the only resting place that grants true rest is God himself.

F. AWARENESS OF FINITUDE AND MORTALITY

When I was about twelve or thirteen, I used to lie in my bed on winter evenings, gazing out through my bedroom window at the night sky. I had become interested in astronomy and knew the names of most of the major constellations, as well as facts about some of their stars. Although I was always impressed by the beauty of the night sky, it nevertheless made me feel rather melancholy. Why should something so beautiful make me feel so sad? Because I knew that the light from some of those stars had taken thousands of years to reach the earth. And I knew that I would be dead and gone long before the light now leaving those stars would ever reach earth. The night sky seemed to me to be a powerful symbol of my own insignificance and mortality. I found it unbearable.

When my daughter was seven, she began to think about death and human transience after we had visited a medieval castle in Cheshire, in northwestern England. My daughter was greatly impressed with the age of the building. "The people who used to live here must be very old now," she remarked. We told her that they had all died long ago. She was stunned.

Other people discover mortality in different ways. Police officers are reminded of human mortality every time they are called to a fatal crash. Death is a routine part of life in our major hospitals. And at some point, the personal reality of death hits home. Death does not just happen to other people. It is going to happen to me.

In part, *Angst* owes its origins to the deep-rooted and pervasive human fear of death. Much of modern Western society prefers to ignore death. In his famous study *The Denial of Death*, Ernst Becker points out how, time and time again, modern Westerners attempt to evade the issue of death. Hospitals speak of "negative patient care outcome" (meaning that the patient died). Death is sanitized, wrapped up in the language of sleep. The cremation oven is euphemistically referred to as "the slumber chamber." Euphemisms have constructed a worldview in which the bleak reality of death is denied.

Yet the fear of death, often voiced in terms of a radical inability to cope with the brute fact of human transience, runs deep in human nature. "I'm not frightened of dying. I just don't want to be there when it happens" (Woody Allen). The trauma of transience seems unbearable. It is hardly surprising that the seduction of humanity, described so powerfully in Genesis 3, is linked with the false hope of evading death: "You will not die . . . you will be like God" (Gen. 3:5).

Death is a threat because it challenges the reassuring set of beliefs that we have woven around ourselves that the world, in which we have invested so much time and effort, will one day pass beyond us. It is so much more reassuring to believe that we and the world will go on for ever—that we will be able to hold on to all the glittering prizes we win during life.

But the reality is very different. Suffering strips away our illusions of immortality. It causes anxiety to rear its ugly, revealing head. It batters down the gates of the citadel of illusions. It confronts us with the harsh facts of life. And it makes us ask those hard questions that have the power to erode falsehood and propel us away from the false security and prizes of the world and toward God.

Yet this intimation of mortality, along with the dreadful anxiety it often brings in its wake, is a real point of contact for the gospel. The hunger for something that death cannot take away; the yearning for immortality; the hope of transcending the final frontier—all are intimately linked with the Christian doctrines of creation and redemption. Anxiety over death is a symptom of the emptiness that comes from being separated from God—and it is precisely this anxiety that is an intimation of the possibility of fulfillment of our sin-broken being. Anxiety, in the context of the Christian doctrines of creation and redemption, is both a disclosure of our fallenness and an intimation of the possibility of redemption.

This is a classic instance of what Luther termed the dialectic between the "strange and proper works of God."[22] Sometimes God works in a way that is obviously consistent with his nature, a way that Luther calls "the proper work of God" (*opus proprium Dei*). At other times God works in a way that initially seems to contradict his nature yet on further reflection is seen to be totally consistent with it. Luther refers to this as "the strange work of God" (*opus alienum Dei*).

As an example, Luther suggests we think about God's condemnation of sinners, which initially seems to contradict what we know of God. Is not God merciful and compassionate? But then we realize how shallow and superficial this idea of God is. It treats God as a sentimental being who ignores the whole question of sin. Knowing that we are condemned alerts us to the reality of our situation—that we are sinners, that we stand under the wrath of God, that we have no claim whatsoever to mercy and forgiveness. And as a result we turn in our hopelessness and helplessness to God and receive forgiveness and mercy. God uses means that seem to be out of line with his nature in order to bring about a goal that is obviously true to his nature.

The disclosure of our mortality is the "strange work" of God; the finding of eternal life through that disclosure is his "proper work."

Anxiety about death proves the gateway to eternal life. It forces us to ask the questions to which the gospel has the answers. The physical reality of death acts as a pointer toward the spiritual necessity to die to oneself, to be crucified with Christ, and to rise to new life with Christ. The noted Oxford apologist Austin Farrer put his finger on the point at issue:

> God desires that we should grow, live, expand and enrich our imaginations, become splendid creatures. He also desires that we should die, should be crucified on the cross of Christ Jesus, should surrender all we have and are to him; and he desires that we should die that death spiritually before we die it physically.
>
> Well, now, what after all are we to say about our dear, delightful, unconverted friends? We must say that so far as their lives are wholesome or truly human, they are splendid manifestations of the power to live; but that they have not yet learned to die. They have not made even the first step along that more difficult path which Jesus Christ opened up for us.[23]

The sense of fear that assaults human nature may itself be regarded as God gently knocking at the door of our life, reminding us that we are but tenants on a short-term lease. We have to come to terms with the inevitable; God, in his grace, has allowed the fear of death to lead to the joy of forgiveness, the discovery of Jesus Christ, and the hope of eternal life. From the nettle of human fear we are allowed to pluck the flower of God's peace.

G. THE POINT OF CONTACT AND EVANGELISTIC PREACHING

How can the point of contact we have discussed be used in preaching or teaching?

The basic image to bear in mind here is that of a dragnet. The evangelistic preacher must not confine his or her presentation of the gospel to a single point of contact, thus excluding a substantial part of the congregation from involvement in the sermon. Rather, the preacher should allow his or her "coat to trail along the ground" like a dragnet in order to "pick up" people at different points. One point of contact may relate especially well to certain members of the congregation, where another will capture the imagination of a different section of that same group. Within the limits of time, it is helpful to provide as many points of entry as possible in order to involve the congregation in the task of correlating human needs—*their* needs—and the gospel proclamation.

How this is done can be determined only by the preacher in the light of his or her knowledge of the local situation and the nature of the congregation. Here, by way of example, is a shortened extract from an apologetic address I gave to a student audience at Ormond College, University of Melbourne, Australia.[24]

> I remember once going to a fairground. I walked into what they called a "Hall of Mirrors." And in these mirrors I saw myself as I had never seen myself before. I was distorted. Everything seemed to be wrong and out of alignment. And that feeling of distortion often comes back to me as I think about life. The way things are seems to be all wrong. We try to pretend that everything is fine. But deep down, we know it's not. Many are frightened about dying. They may not want to talk about it. But the fear is there. Some find it unbearable. And deep in the night, they wonder about death. They wonder if its fear could ever be overcome. Others find themselves longing for something—something which they can never quite define, and which anyway never seems to happen. They thought that this career move, that academic qualification, this relationship, would satisfy their deepest desires. But they don't. There is this deep sense of yearning for something that somehow never seems to come along. And people wonder: Is there any way in which this deep and unsatisfied longing could ever be satisfied? Yet there always seems to be another mountain to climb, another river to cross. Something seems to be wrong. And we wonder: can anything be done about it?

This example shows how two points of contact were presented to a student audience, aiming to capture their interest and their imagination, and to lead them on to see how their anxieties and needs were met by Christ. These ideas drew some students in that audience to reflect on the great themes of the Christian faith. They lodged the gospel in the experiential reality of the lives of a substantial part of that audience (to judge by reaction afterwards), allowing my subsequent presentation of the gospel itself to be seen as relevant.

There is much more that needs to be said and that would be said during the subsequent process of Christian discipling. But the creative and responsible use of points of contact goes a considerable way toward ensuring that the gospel gets a sympathetic hearing. It is simply the thin end of the apologetic wedge. But it is a powerful tool which the evangelist can use to great effect.

CHAPTER THREE

From Assent to Commitment

How does assent to the truth of the Christian faith become a living faith in God, leading to the forgiveness and renewal of the sinner? How is truth related to transformation? The apologist and evangelist must be able to give an account of how a conviction of the truth of the gospel can become the bridge by which the transforming and refreshing presence of God may enter into the life of believing human beings. The apologist must be aware of the real constraints he or she will confront. Apologetics is at its best when it is aware of its goals on the one hand and its limitations on the other. With this point in mind, we may turn to an analysis of the manner in which apologetics functions in the overall process of a person's coming to faith.

A. THE NATURE OF FAITH

Most people outside Christianity regard faith as some kind of belief. It is intellectual assent. It is accepting that certain things are true. To believe in God is to believe that God exists. To believe in Christianity is to believe that the ideas of Christianity are correct. In everyday English, which is still heavily influenced by the ideas of the Enlightenment, the word *faith* means something like "a lower form of knowledge." The well-known story has the preacher declaring in his sermon, "That there is a congregation out there is a matter of fact; that they are listening to me is a matter of faith."

But behind the word *faith* lies a host of vital ideas, deeply embedded in both the Hebrew and Greek languages and the Christian experience of God's dealings with his people. And this means that the deceptively simple word *faith*, used in a Christian context, actually means far more than that same word used in an everyday context. We must ask our audience to set aside secular ideas of what faith is and listen to the Christian understanding of the word.

To someone outside the Christian faith this might at first sight seem to mirror the attitude of Humpty-Dumpty in Lewis Carroll's *Through the Looking-Glass*, who said, "When *I* use a word, it means just what I choose it to mean—neither more nor less." But this is a shallow reaction to a serious issue in linguistics. The point at issue here is familiar from twentieth-century philosophical debates, such as that arising out of the writings of Ludwig Wittgenstein. "To imagine a language means to imagine a form of life. . . . The speaking of language is part of an activity, or form of life."[1] Modern linguistics, from Ferdinand de Saussure onward,[2] has stressed the importance of communities.[3] Dictionary definitions of words are not divine mandates, establishing the permanent and unique meaning of a word; rather, they are generalizations about the ways (plural) in which the word is used in the real world of human living, not prescriptions for the way it ought to be used in some ideal world.[4]

This applies also to the word *faith*. It has one meaning in everyday English and another in the language of Christianity. These meanings are recognizably related to one another—but they are different. We can begin to identify the similarities and differences by comparing the "everyday" and Christian meanings of the word.

a. Faith is about believing that certain things are true. Thus when we say that we believe in God, we are at the very least believing in his existence. Or if we say that we believe in the promises of God, we could mean simply that we recognize or accept that the promises really are there. In this sense, faith is basically assent. "I believe in God" means something like "I believe that there is a God," or "I think that God exists." Faith assents to belief in the existence of God and his promises. This is an essential starting point. Before we can begin to say anything about what God is like, we need to assume that there is a God in the first place.

Many people outside the Christian faith have the understandable, yet misleading impression that there is nothing more to Christian faith than this assent to God's existence. To them, Christian belief is little more than running through a checklist of propositions—such as those contained in the creeds. But faith is more than assent.

b. Faith is trust. When I say that I believe in the promises of God, I am declaring that I trust them. It is more than a recognition that these promises exist; it is an awareness that they can be trusted and relied on. Faith is not something purely intellectual, enlightening the mind while leaving the heart untouched. Faith is the response of our whole person to the person of God. It is a joyful reaction on our part to the overwhelming divine love we see revealed in Jesus Christ. It is the simple response of leaving all to follow Jesus. Faith is both our recognition that something wonderful has happened through the life, death, and resurrection of Jesus Christ, and our response to what has happened. Faith realizes that God loves us, and it responds to that love. Faith trusts in the promising God.

The idea of "trust" is naturally linked with that of "faith" in everyday English. I can have faith in a friend, meaning that I trust him or her. Or I can have faith in the skill of an airplane pilot, meaning that I am prepared to entrust myself to him when I cross the Atlantic Ocean. Or I can have faith in the promise of a political party to bring about certain much-needed changes in society, as a result of which I will vote for its candidates in the next election. But there is still more to the Christian idea of faith than this. Christian faith has a component that is quite without parallel in everyday language.

c. Faith is entry into the promises of God, receiving what they have to offer. Having recognized that the promises exist and that they can be trusted, it is necessary to act upon them—to enter into them, and benefit from them. I may *believe* that God is promising me forgiveness of sins; I may *trust* that promise; but unless I *respond* to that promise, I shall not obtain forgiveness. The first two stages of faith prepare the way for the third; without it they are incomplete.

An analogy may make this point clearer. Consider a bottle of penicillin, the antibiotic responsible for saving the lives of countless individuals who would otherwise have died from various forms of blood poisoning. Imagine that

a. this bottle is sitting on my bedside table and that

b. I am suffering from blood poisoning.

What are my options?

a. I may *accept* that this bottle of penicillin exists.

b. I may *trust* that it is capable of curing my illness, which otherwise will probably kill me. But I shall never cure my blood poisoning, unless

c. I *act* upon that trust and take the penicillin. If I do not, I shall die, accepting and trusting, but having failed to benefit at all from the resource which could have saved me.

It is this third element of faith that is of special relevance today. Just as faith links a bottle of penicillin to the cure of blood poisoning, so faith forges a link between the cross and resurrection of Jesus Christ and the tragic human situation in which we find ourselves. Conceptual truth guides us to trust God, by reassuring us of the *reliability* of that commitment of faith. Faith then unites us with the risen Christ and makes available to us everything that he gained through his obedience and resurrection—such as forgiveness, grace, and eternal life. These "benefits of Christ"—to use Philip Melanchthon's admirable phrase[5]—become ours through faith. They are not detached from the person of Christ, as if we could have them in isolation; rather, they are given together with his real and redeeming presence within us, brought about by faith.

Faith, then, is not just assent to an abstract set of doctrines. Rather, it is a "wedding ring" (Luther), pointing to mutual commitment and union between Christ and the believer. It is the response of the whole person of the believer to God, which leads in turn to the real and personal presence of Christ in the believer. Faith makes both Christ and his benefits—such as forgiveness, justification, and hope—available to the believer.

Christ, Calvin says, is not "received merely in the understanding and imagination. For the promises offer him, not so that we end up with the mere sight and knowledge of him, but that we enjoy a true communication of him." Both the person of Christ and the benefits he won for us by his obedience on the cross and through his resurrection from the dead are made available to us by faith. Faith is like a channel that allows both the person and the benefits of Christ to flow into our lives. It is like an open mouth that feeds on Christ and his work in order that we might be nourished. It is like an empty, open hand, reaching out in order to grasp and hold the precious treasure of the risen Christ and his benefits.

Martin Luther draws the analogy between the quintessentially *Christian* understanding of the nature of faith and the marriage bond uniting husband and wife:

> Faith unites the soul with Christ as a bride is united with her bridegroom. By this mystery, as the Apostle teaches us, Christ and the soul become one flesh (Eph. 5:31–32). And if they are one flesh, and there is between them a true marriage—indeed, the most perfect of all marriages, since human marriages are but poor examples of this one true marriage—it follows that everything that they have they hold in common, the good as well as the evil. Accordingly the believing soul can boast of and glory in whatever Christ possesses, as though it were his or her own; and whatever the soul has, Christ claims as his own. Let us compare these and we shall see inestimable benefits. Christ is full of grace, life and salvation. The soul is full of sins, death and damnation. Now let

faith come between them and sins, death and damnation will be Christ's, while grace, life and salvation will be the soul's.[6]

A human marriage is no legal fiction—it is a real and vital relationship between two persons that involves mutual commitment, a common life, and a sharing of goods. Precisely this relationship is established between the believer and the risen Christ through faith. The believer comes to be in Christ. A dynamic bond is forged between the believing human being and the redeeming Christ, bringing in its wake a partaking of all that he won for us by his obedience. Yet, to go back to our original point, this vital aspect of the Christian understanding of faith is completely missing from everyday English. The apologist must supply and explain it.

How does faith relate to the science of apologetics?

B. APOLOGETICS DOES NOT CREATE FAITH

The aim of apologetics is to create an intellectual and imaginative climate favorable to faith; it does not itself create that faith. Having stressed the potential value of a point of contact to effective Christian apologetics, it is now necessary to sound a note of caution. Apologetics is an excellent servant of the church; it can, however, too easily be allowed to become its master. An authentically Christian apologetics is an apologetics of reserve. That is to say, it is aware of its limitations and rigorously upholds the central Christian insight that it is none other than God himself who creates justifying faith.

How does the discipline of apologetics relate to each of the three components of faith discussed in the preceding section?

First, apologetics aims to persuade people that Christianity is true, whether this takes the form of total assurance through a watertight argument from first principles, or a recognition that Christianity is probably true through an inferential analysis of the world. In this sense of the word, apologetics has a major contribution to make to the birth of faith in that it can help people to believe that certain things are true.

But truth is no warranty of relevance or acceptance, nor is existence a guarantee of trustworthiness. The second task of apologetics is to create a climate of trust in which God can be seen as worthy of faith and commitment. And while apologetics can go some way toward creating this climate, its resources are limited. For example, part of the warranty of the trustworthiness of God lies in the personal experience of those who have already put their trust in him, and this experience itself must be regarded as brought about, at least in part, by God himself.

Third, faith concerns entering into the promises of God and receiving all that they offer. And here apologetics finds itself at the limits of its tether. It has, so to speak, led us to the door of faith. Now it must draw back and allow us to enter in. It is like Virgil in Dante's *Divine Comedy:* although able to guide Dante through much of his journey, Virgil eventually has to be left behind for its final stages. It is like John the Baptist, who points to Christ, showing us where he may be found. But we must find him ourselves. Apologetics assures us that there is a God to be found and that he is profoundly worth finding— then points us to where God may be met in Jesus Christ. Paradoxically, we then realize that all along it has been God who has been searching for us and God who finally comes to meet, greet, and accept us.

C. THE LIMITATIONS OF APOLOGETICS

The recognition that apologetics does not create faith raises the question whether there might be other limitations placed on its value. In practice, this turns out to be the case. To illustrate the kind of limitations we have in mind, consider one of the most important forms of Christian apologetics—historical evidentialism.

Historical evidentialism can minimize a significant obstacle to faith—the feeling that the New Testament is "made up," lacking any real historical roots. It poses a powerful challenge to those who argue, usually on rather flimsy grounds, that Christianity is just some kind of wish fulfillment, by stressing the historical events that *forced* the birth of Christian ideas.

Historical evidentialism fulfills a vital and distinct function in the arsenal of the Christian apologist. An appeal to history is far less demanding than an appeal to reason; it is far more interesting, and it avoids the sense of abstraction that makes the more theoretical types of apologetics so dull. Historical evidentialism serves to reinforce confidence in the historical foundations of faith. It reassures insiders of the reliability of the gospel accounts of the great historical events on which faith rests. But what role does an appeal to historical evidence have to persons outside the faith? Will it enable them to come to faith?

It is here that historical apologetics is vulnerable. It describes events; the gospel concerns interpretations of events. Historical apologetics asks, "Did it really happen?" Yet the big questions of life concern meanings, not events. Indeed, it is fair to suggest that historical events continue to be remembered because of what they mean rather than what they are in themselves. The historical evidentialist approach tends to imply that facts anchor meaning, where the reverse appears to hold true. Suppose it was conceded that a man called Jesus of Nazareth really did live and die, and that there are inescapable reasons for supposing that he rose again. Would that constitute proof of the gospel? It would certainly eliminate a significant objection to the gospel. It would undoubtedly create an intellectual atmosphere favorable toward faith. Yet it would not prove the gospel, in that the gospel rests on a specific interpretation of those historical facts.

The complexity of the interaction between event and meaning has been well brought out by philosophers of history such as Raymond Aron, who wrote: "The brute fact of the assassination [of Caesar] would not interest anyone, unless it is put in its place within the totality brought about by the crisis of the Roman power, the resistance of the senatorial aristocracy to personal power, and so on."[7] Similarly, the meaning of the Crucifixion and Resurrection depends on their being seen within the totality of Old Testament messianic expectations and certain patterns of divine activity in history.

An incident earlier in Caesar's career illustrates the point rather well. In 49 B.C., Caesar led an army southward from modern-day France. At one point they had to cross an insignificant river—the Rubicon. Crossing it posed no particular difficulties and required no particular heroism. It was not like crossing a wide and raging torrent, such as those encountered by the American settlers as they moved westward. The act of crossing the Rubicon, in itself, was of no historical significance. But that river happened to mark the border of the territory governed directly by the Roman senate. As a result, crossing this international boundary was nothing less than a declaration of war by Caesar against Rome.

It is the "totality brought about by the crisis of the Roman power," as Aron put it, that gives the crossing of the Rubicon its fully merited place in history.

We must therefore establish not just what happened, but also how the event should be interpreted. The totality that gives the event its meaning must be ascertained. Whether we are dealing with Caesar crossing the Rubicon or Jesus dying on the cross and rising again from the dead, the principle is the same. The historical significance of the event needs to be settled. It is at this point that purely historical apologetics, dedicated to establishing what happened, begins to falter. Events need to be supplemented with interpretation.

There is a significant gap to be bridged if we are to move from historical events to a specific interpretation of those events. That Jesus died and rose again might well be a matter of history; but that Jesus died and rose again in order that we might be reconciled to the living and loving God is the heart of the gospel itself. There is a clear link between historical fact and Christian faith—but that link needs to be firmly established by the apologist. It is not given; it needs to be made. Historical evidentialism thus lays the foundations for creating an intellectual environment favorable to faith in the "God of the Christians" (*Deus Christianorum*), to use Tertullian's phrase. It does not, however, prove that such a God exists.

Related problems arise in other approaches to apologetics. For example, the five arguments Thomas Aquinas develops in support of belief in the existence of God go some way toward suggesting that it is reasonable to believe in a creator of the world or in an intelligent being who is able to cause effects in the world.[8] Nevertheless, a decision to believe—what Kierkegaard called "a leap of faith"—is still required. We still have to show that this creator or intelligent being *is* the God whom Christians know and worship.

Indeed, Aquinas's arguments could lead to some form of theist belief, that is, faith in the existence of a god rather like that favored by the Greek philosopher Aristotle, an Unmoved Mover, who is distant from and uninvolved in the affairs of his world. This point was made forcefully by the French writer Blaise Pascal, who was profoundly aware of the limitations of philosophical ways of thinking about God. Pascal believed passionately that philosophy had squandered the insight that the God of the Bible is intensely personal. After his death, a crumpled piece of paper was found sewn inside his shirt. The words on this piece of paper have become legendary; they are intensely relevant to our theme. "God of Abraham, God of Isaac, God of Jacob, not of philosophers and scholars, God of Jesus Christ, my God and your God. Your God shall be my God."

As Pascal intuitively grasped, the philosophical idea of God bears little relation to the God of Jesus Christ—*our* God. Somehow, the philosophical idea of God seems bleak and dreary, both in itself and in comparison with the joyful Christian experience of God. It reminds me of Mr. Edwards' celebrated remarks to Samuel Johnson: "You are a philosopher, Dr. Johnson. I have tried too in my time to be a philosopher, but I don't know how; cheerfulness was always breaking in."

Of course, philosophy has its uses, provided its limitations are recognized. To the Christian reader of Aquinas, his arguments are useful backup material for faith. While they do not prove that God exists, in terms likely to be treated as conclusive proof by those outside the Christian faith, they go some considerable way toward showing the internal consistency of the Christian faith and its ability to mesh with the real world of experience. But to someone outside the bounds of the Christian faith, they may well seem to point to less than this. Perhaps there is indeed a prime mover. Maybe there are reasons for thinking that there might well be a god of some sort or other behind the universe. But is this the same god as the God we find in the New Testament? Maybe there is a creator. But is that creator also the redeemer? (After all, gnosticism argued for the existence of two gods, one responsible for the creation of the world, and the other for the more significant work of redeeming it.)

Apologetics thus has its limitations. The responsible apologist will recognize this fact. You cannot argue people into the kingdom of God. Apologetics creates a climate favorable to faith; it does not create faith. It establishes a framework, making the "leap of faith" easier than it might otherwise be. But that step of faith eventually has to be made. The next section explores how the point of contact with the world becomes a point of departure from the world.

D. THE POINT OF CONTACT AS POINT OF DEPARTURE

A central question of relevance to apologetics concerns how the transition is made from a secular to a Christian worldview. Three main accounts of this may be offered.

The *classical* view is grounded in the notion of a universal rationality, of which Christianity is a part. Because Christianity is itself rational, it can be shown that it belongs within the sphere of reason. Thomas Aquinas is an excellent representative of this tradition with his repeated appeal to the writings of Aristotle to undergird his theological arguments. We could summarize this view diagrammatically as in figure 3.1. No conflict between Christianity and reason occurs. To be a Christian is to take up a specific place within a general rational worldview that places stress on such matters as the explanatory power of the hypothesis of the existence of a creator God.

The *presuppositional* view, associated especially with Cornelius van Til,[9] stresses the utter discontinuity between secular and Christian conceptions of rationality. It must be stressed that van Til does not suggest that Christianity is irrational, as some of his less perceptive interpreters have claimed. Rather, Christianity possesses its own

Secular rationality

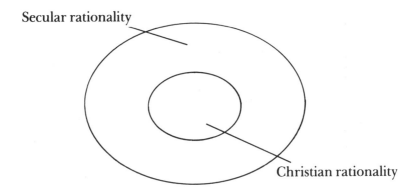

Christian rationality

Figure 3.1
The point of contact in classic apologetics

distinct rationality that does not overlap with secular rationalities. Judged from the standpoint of those secular rationalities, Christianity indeed seems irrational. But "irrational" here means "not conforming to secular rationality" rather than "devoid of reasoned consistency."[10] We could summarize van Til's approach diagrammatically as in figure 3.2. There is no point of contact between secular and Christian rationalities.[11] To be converted is to leap from the secular to the Christian outlook.

The *creative* approach, based on the notion of the point of contact, argues that secular and Christian rationalities, although distinct, overlap at points. Sin has a noetic influence in that it disrupts the continuity between secular and Christian outlooks; it does not, however, destroy their contiguity. The task of the apologist is to identify the areas of overlap in order to facilitate the transition from a secular to a Christian worldview. We could represent this diagrammatically as in figure 3.3.

It is thus possible to make the transition from a secular to a Christian outlook through the points of contact that act as bridges between the two. There is not so much a "no man's land," as an area of shared possibilities, a region in which there is room for ambiguity.

Secular rationality

Christian rationality

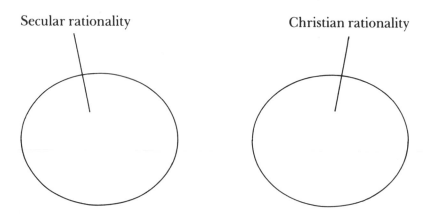

Figure 3.2
The point of contact in presuppositionalist apologetics

Secular rationality

Christian rationality

Point of contact

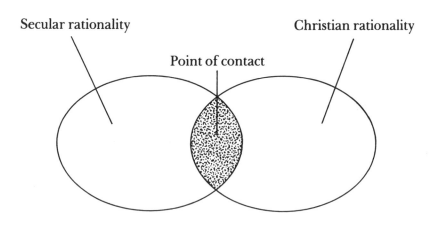

Figure 3.3
The point of contact in creative apologetics

The creative apologist will direct attention to this region with a view to exploring it and emerging within the context of a Christian worldview. This region could prove the vital bridge between a secular and Christian worldview, enabling someone previously committed to the former to make the critical transition to the latter.

But this transition still involves a step of faith. How are we to understand this?

E. THE DECISION TO BELIEVE

Throughout this book I have stressed that Christianity makes sense. I have been concerned to commend its attractiveness as well as its credentials and its credibility. Yet, in the end, a step of faith has to be made. But why?

Let's look at a situation taken from real life, centering on Sheldon Vanauken, who studied English Literature at Yale and Oxford, where he came to faith in the spring of 1951, with some friendly guidance from C. S. Lewis. Vanauken's dilemma was this: Christianity seemed probable; it seemed to have "a sort of *feel* of truth," but there was a gap between the probable and the proved. How could that gap be bridged?[12]

Vanauken describes with stunning clarity the kind of thoughts that go through many people's minds about the "leap of faith":

> There is a gap between the probable and the proved. How was I to cross it? If I were to stake my whole life on the risen Christ, I wanted proof. I wanted certainty. I wanted to see him eat a bit of fish. I wanted letters of fire across the sky. I got none of these. And I continued to hang about on the edge of the gap. . . . It was a question of whether I was to accept him—*or reject*. My God! There was a gap *behind* me as well! Perhaps the leap to acceptance was a horrifying gamble—but what of the leap to rejection? There might be no certainty that Christ was God—but, by God, there was no certainty that he was not. This was not to be borne. I could not reject Jesus. There was only one thing to do once I had seen the gap behind me. I turned away from it, and flung myself over the gap toward Jesus.[13]

Vanauken here provides a brilliant statement of the dilemma the creative Christian apologist addresses, while at the same time solving it in a highly personal and memorable manner.

Note the decision to believe. There is no contradiction here. Justifying faith is a decision to believe in God, trusting that the gospel promises are for real and that one day they will be *seen* to be for real.

The decision to believe breaks the paralysis of indecision that otherwise hovers around the gap of faith. Vanauken puts it like this:

> I *choose* to believe in the Father, Son and Holy Ghost—in Christ, my Lord and my God. Christianity has the ring, the *feel*, of unique truth. Of *essential* truth. . . . [But] a choice was necessary; and there is no certainty. One can only choose a side. So I—I now choose my side: I choose beauty; I choose what I love. But choosing to believe *is* believing. It's all I can do: choose. I confess my doubts and ask my Lord Christ to enter my life. I do not *know* God is, I do but say: Be it unto me according to Thy will. I do not affirm that I am without doubt, I do but ask for help, having chosen, to overcome it. I do but say: Lord, I believe—help Thou my unbelief.[14]

Vanauken here appears to have stumbled on one of the most powerful insights of Christian theology. Justifying faith rests on *our decision to believe*—at least, what seems to us, from our human standpoint, to be our decision. Theology, with its more reflective standpoint, is able to discern the decision of God behind our decision; the movement of God toward us in advance of our movement toward him; God's search for us beneath what we discern as our quest for him. Theology prevents us from rushing into the seductive conclusion that the way things seem to us is the way things really are. It affirms the prevenience of grace at every point in the apologist's efforts. It insists that we discern and respect the guiding hand of God in every aspect of our journey to faith.

But apologetics is not actually concerned with the detailed unfolding of the theological drama that underlies an individual's coming to the brink of faith. It is concerned with addressing the situation as perceived by the one standing on that brink. The theology can come in later. The apologist has but one thing to say: "Choose to believe! Make that choice! Decide for Christ!" And with that decision, the gap of faith is bridged. The task of apologetics is completed; that of theology has now begun.

PART 2

Overcoming Barriers to Faith

CHAPTER FOUR

What Keeps People from Becoming Christians?

Having laid the foundations for apologetics, we must now turn to deal with the problems that the apologist can expect to encounter in the great marketplace of ideas. What stops people from coming to faith? A central task of apologetics is to identify the general pressures that persuade people *not* to believe. These problems are not simply intellectual. They include cultural pressures, historical memories, and personal feelings—all of which vary enormously from one situation and one individual to another.

Furthermore, the question needs to be particularized: "What stops *this person* from coming to faith?" After all, the response to the first question is the aggregate of responses to the second. Effective apologetics is oriented toward individual situations—whether of persons or of communities. Instead of trying to give an exhaustive account of the issues that have prevented people from coming to faith in the past, it asks specific and focused questions. What is it that stops *this person* from coming to faith? What factors prevent this group of people from responding to the gospel?

Michael Green makes this point with characteristic clarity, drawing upon his considerable experience as an evangelist. He also points to the close relationship of apologetics and evangelism:

> I think of one of the atheists I met who became one overnight through the death of the father whom he idolized. . . . I think of another celebrated atheist, with whom I was due to debate. During the dinner beforehand, it became evident that the cause of her atheism was a series of terrible experiences in a Catholic school as a youngster. Another was a survivor of Auschwitz. Another was

brought up in a strongly anti-religious home, and had imbibed his
parents' attitude uncritically. . . . We must be people-centered in
our approach and discover, if possible, what lies behind the atheist
front. It may of course be sheer reasoning, but I have found that
rarely to be the case. Whatever the cause, we need to find it out
before we can hope to deal with the person appropriately.[1]

Effective apologetics rests on knowing, or being willing to discover,
what the real problems are. Once the specific difficulty has been found,
it may be addressed directly. Experience suggests that eight main
groups of problems may be identified, each demanding a different
approach.

A. INTELLECTUAL BARRIERS TO FAITH

Some people have difficulty in accepting Christianity because
they see real intellectual obstacles in their path. Many of these are
familiar to anyone involved in apologetics. "How can I believe in God,
in the face of human suffering?" "Science has made Christianity
irrelevant." "The idea of Jesus Christ being divine is a logical
contradiction."

It must immediately be recognized that some of these intellectual
barriers are more imagined than real. "I could never be a Christian
because of the problem of suffering" can mean two quite different
things:

a. Having thought the matter through carefully, it seems to me
that there is a real problem posed to the intellectual coherence of the
Christian faith because of the existence of human suffering.

b. I don't want to get involved in a discussion about Christianity,
which could get very personal and threatening. But I don't want to
admit this, as it might seem to imply that I lack intellectual courage,
stamina, or honesty. I can save face by letting it be understood that
there are good grounds for my rejection of Christianity. So let me
select a problem . . . suffering will do very nicely. Anyway, it will stall
the efforts of this guy who's trying to convert me.

For the apologist to launch into a sustained defense of Christianity over the issue of suffering would be of genuine interest to the first
person, but not to the second. It might alter the first person's mind; it
would probably make no difference to the situation of the second. The
questions that the discerning apologist must learn to ask here are the
following:

a. Which is the *real* barrier—the presenting intellectual
difficulty, or something else?

b. If it isn't the intellectual problem that keeps this person from coming to faith, what is? Quite possibly the real problem nestles somewhere amid the remaining difficulties noted in this chapter.

For some, then, throwing intellectual problems at the Christian evangelist is like a warplane ejecting flares to divert heat-seeking missiles. It is a decoy meant to divert a deadly attack. But intellectual difficulties nevertheless constitute a real problem for some people, and answers must be given to their difficulties. The following major intellectual difficulties will be dealt with in the rest of this book.

a. "Christianity is a hangover from the intellectual dark ages. It no longer has any place in the modern world. It is impossible to live in the modern world and be a Christian." This sort of attitude is expressed well in a comment made by the anthropologist Max Müller in 1878:

> Every day, every week, every month, every quarter, the most widely read journals seem just now to vie with each other in telling us that the time for religion is past, that faith is a hallucination or an infantile disease, that the gods have at last been found out and exploded.[2]

The worldview that led to this attitude has long since been discredited. However, we give full consideration to the issues as follows:

• Enlightenment rationalism (see pp. 147–55).
• The scientific worldview (see pp. 160–66).

b. "The idea of 'a god' is simply some kind of wish fulfillment. Because we feel the need for a god, we promptly invent one. The entire Christian faith thus rests on a simple delusion." We shall consider this objection on pages 94–100.

c. "The existence of suffering makes nonsense of the idea of a loving God." This is often a real difficulty for people who have faced bereavement or who know suffering firsthand. This is then no mere intellectual riddle—it is a perfectly proper question about life. We shall consider this objection on pages 100–108.

d. "There are many religions, all making truth-claims. Christianity is just one among many. Why should I pay attention to it, rather than to them?" This question is not "modern"—it is as old as Christianity itself. It has been a fact of life for Christians in India and the Arab nations for more than a millennium, even if Western culture has only recently discovered it. This difficulty is especially obvious in a multicultural society such as Britain, Australia, or the western seaboard of the United States and Canada, and it clearly demands an answer. We shall consider this problem on pages 108–19.

e. "Christianity rests on a series of unjustifiable, outdated, and objectionable ideas that cannot be taken seriously in the modern world." The three such groups of ideas that are usually singled out are:

- the Resurrection (see pp. 119–23);
- the doctrine of the Incarnation (see pp. 123–33);
- the ideas of sin and salvation (see pp. 133–143).

A point should be made before proceeding further. Of all the world's religions, it is Christianity that has been subjected to the most intense, persistent, and critical examination over the last three hundred years. It has survived in the most hostile of cultural and intellectual climates. Aggressively secularizing publications—such as *The Myth of God Incarnate* (1977)—often give the impression that something has recently happened to make Christianity unbelievable. The word *modern* is bandied around as if the very word discredited Christianity. But modernity is over. Although this fact has yet to permeate into the darker recesses of the Enlightenment, the Western world has entered into a postmodern situation (see pp. 175–81). And this development has brought exciting new possibilities for Christianity as well as new difficulties. But one thing is clear. The idea that Christianity is obsolete has itself become obsolete. It has a curiously dated feel to it, like a relic of a bygone era. The person who mechanically repeats the parrot cries of earlier generations—"science has disproved Christianity"; "Christianity is irrelevant in a world come of age"—has become stranded in a time warp. It may take some time for this fact to filter down from the opinion-makers to popular writing, but it has happened. There has been a major shift of ideas, which we shall be exploring further in this book. It is a shift in favor of faith.

B. THE HISTORICAL ASSOCIATIONS OF CHRISTIANITY

History holds the key to understanding the present by asking how the present came into being. Attitudes within the present are shaped by past forces. To understand the past is thus to cast light on the present. We live in the present, learn from the past, and look to the future. And some of the barriers to faith in the present have their origins in the past of an individual or community.

One of the most common historical barriers to faith relates to the institution of the church. The growth of anticlericalism in Europe on the eve of the sixteenth-century Reformation is a case in point.[3] There can be no doubt that there were some very dedicated and effective priests in the late medieval church, faithfully dedicated to ministering to their people and their needs. But they were more than outnumbered by others who brought the institution of the church and its ministers into disrepute. Case after case can be listed. But two common themes underlie them.

First, priests became alienated from the communities they were meant to serve. To give but one example, in early sixteenth-century France, the upper clergy tended to be drawn from noble families who were immune from the social and financial pressures facing ordinary folk. The clergy were exempt from taxation, from prosecution in the civil courts, and from compulsory military service. As a major landowner, the church had no difficulty in providing for its clergy, even in periods of severe economic recession and food shortages that plagued the feudal French economy at the time. The result was perhaps inevitable. A large section of the community—what we would probably refer to as the middle class—became disaffected with the church. They were receptive to the new and radical ideas of the Reformation partly because of their alienation from their own church.

Sadly, this is not something restricted to the sixteenth century. My own church—the Church of England—seems to be suffering from more or less the same thing today. It is seen as being very white and middle class. It does not seem to relate naturally to the concerns of other groups. Independent black-led churches have sprung up to fill this vacuum. The charismatic movement is making inroads into working class areas, being able to relate better to their experiential needs. The Church of England, with its very "bookish" liturgy, often gives the impression of being ill-prepared to interact favorably with this culture. This reminds us of the need to ground our ministry firmly in the needs, hopes, and abilities of the communities we serve.

But second, the events on the eve of the Reformation show up a disturbing tendency: Christianity tends to get identified with the institutional church. The truth and relevance of the gospel become dependent on the quality of its institutions and ministers. In theory, people were merely protesting the shortcomings of the medieval clergy and the fallibilities of the church. In practice, they ended up rejecting medieval Catholicism. Ideas were judged, not on the basis of whether they were right or wrong, but on the basis of the quality of the individuals and institutions who embodied them.

Much the same thing may be seen during the French Revolution, when Catholicism was rejected in favor of secularism largely because of a popular hatred of the church and its clergy. The French church has still not recovered from its eighteenth-century reputation. And, to take a more modern example, consider the fate of Marxism in Europe in recent years. Is Marxism *true?* Most modern Europeans would probably answer, Who cares? We have seen the effects it has on individuals and institutions. Whether it is true or not, we do not want anything to do with it.

Experience suggests that people can cope surprisingly well with many of the intellectual problems raised by Christianity—for example, the problem of evil. But when they have to face up to a Christian leader who preaches fervently against certain practices, only to indulge in them himself, their faith can be severely undermined. It is not internal theoretical problems that really bother most people—it is the way in which Christianity relates to life in general and to individuals and institutions in particular.

Classical apologetics, which aims to demonstrate the rationality of the Christian faith, often conveys the impression that Christianity is a set of ideas that some people accept and others reject. Yet Christianity is about ideas incarnated in history, about the embodiment of values in real life.

I do a lot of work on university campuses, and very often I hear comments like this. "Christianity can't be much good. A friend of mine is a Christian, and it hasn't done much for her. She's not an especially nice person." Now part of me wants to respond by saying, "Well, just think how dreadful she would be if she wasn't a Christian!" But the remainder of me responds by registering how the gospel is being evaluated, not on the basis of its ideas, but on the basis of its effects on people and institutions.

This is an excellent example of "condemnation by association." The gospel is being rejected, not because of any problems with its rationality, but because of its past associations. The institution of the church and the Christian faith itself are very easily amalgamated in people's minds. The failings of the church thus come to be projected onto Christianity itself. Take the remark "Christianity is oppressive." In fact, the gospel is profoundly liberating. But historically, the institution of the church has indeed often been deeply oppressive toward certain people, such as German peasants at the time of the Reformation.

The apologist thus needs to become aware of the associations that may linger, unidentified and unchallenged, in the subconscious memory of an individual or community, and that occasionally rise to the surface in a consciously articulated anti-Christian form. Christianity may have undesirable associations in the minds and memories of certain people, which may be entirely restricted to these individuals and have no validity outside those specific lives. These associations are personal, not universal. They need to be identified and disarmed—a process that demands knowledge of, and commitment to, that person.

The task confronted by the apologist here is that of exorcising the past. The associations that Christianity possesses for people need to be brought to conscious articulation. People need to be helped to see how their attitudes toward the gospel are being shaped by other people and events, rather than by the gospel itself. There is a need to confront the past and to end its negative influence over the present. But how?

First, we need to stress that historical and personal associations do not have any necessary or direct bearing on whether a position is true or not. It may be that a friend of mine, who is utterly charming and caring, believes passionately that the world is flat, whereas another, whom even the most generous critic would regard as combining the charm of Attila the Hun with the intellectual ability of a frog, believes with equal passion that the world is spherical. The latter friend's view is correct, even if he is something of a pain. Negative personal or historical associations do not necessarily mean that a belief is wrong.

But then it might reasonably be objected that Christian faith *ought* to make people nice. It ought to elevate them above their former selves. It ought to change them and lead to positive historical and personal associations. The existence of bad Christians thus raises a question, not so much about the intellectual credibility of Christianity, as about its moral and spiritual power and relevance. If Christianity is so good, why doesn't it make Christians nicer than they are?

This is an important objection, and it needs to be taken seriously. I shall respond to it by drawing on the resources of a neglected minor classic of modern English theology—D. R. Davies' *On to Orthodoxy*,[4] the personal reflections of a disillusioned liberal. The idea that Christianity is basically a religion of moral improvement, to be judged by its positive moral effects on individuals and society, has its roots in the liberal Protestantism so characteristic of the late nineteenth century and early twentieth century.

This version of Christianity tended to emphasize the perfectibility of human nature and the ability of the gospel to achieve this perfection. It inculcated the notion of human evolution toward moral perfection with such force that the idea of Christianity as a moral improving agent for human society became widely accepted inside and outside Christian circles and continues to have influence today.

But then came the First World War, which shattered the idea of human perfection. As Davies puts it:

> The Great War caught Liberal Christianity unawares. It was an
> event for which it was totally unprepared. It administered a nasty
> jar to its whole scheme and outlook. It broke in on it like a

gangster in a drawing room full of old maids sipping their afternoon tea. It took the lid off that human nature of supposed fundamental goodness, and there emerged something which couldn't be squared with the roseate dream of an inevitable progress into perfection. Something had gone wrong somewhere![5]

What had gone wrong was that the idea of sin had been abandoned by liberal Christianity as some kind of unnecessary hangover from an earlier and less enlightened period in Christian history. "The idea that there was in human nature an element of deliberate defiance and rebellion against God, against the good, fell out of the scheme of modern life. The traditional Christian idea of the sinfulness of man . . . was abandoned."[6] As Davies witnessed the development of Fascism and Communism in Europe, his conviction of the radical grip of sin on human nature intensified. His personal statement of faith opens as follows:[7]

(1) I believe that man is radically evil, that sin is of the very texture of human nature.

(2) I believe that, owing to that original, inherent sin, man is incapable of creating a just society . . . that he is cursed by a fatal contradiction which ordains that the power by which he advances in civilization nullifies and destroys his progress.

(3) I believe that, if left to his own resources, man is doomed to destruction.

For Davies, this was an entirely realistic and entirely Christian estimation of the situation. It corresponds well to the classic Augustinian presentation, given new directions by the sixteenth-century reformers such as Luther and Calvin. For Luther, human nature is *incurvatus in se,* "bent in on itself." There is a radical deformity in human nature on account of sin—and that deformity expresses itself at the social, political, religious, and personal levels. Sin causes sins—not merely personal sins, but structural sin, built deep into the very fabric of human institutions and agencies.

Academic theologians, who have generally provided liberal Christianity with its intellectual resources, have found it relatively easy to overlook human sin, largely because they are shielded from many of the harsher realities of that sin. For them, sin might express itself in minor, irritating lapses of manners: plagiarism of ideas, the irritability of colleagues in the faculty lounge, or the unreliability of publishers and editors. Sin in the ivory tower is a petty affair—but in the grim and ugly world of corrupt city councils, tyrannical governments and genocidal armies, sin is real. It is significant that the people who have tried to put sin back on the Christian agenda have been pastors—

people who experienced the darker side of life, such as Reinhold Niebuhr's experiences in the automobile plants of Detroit. Christianity thus has to contend with sinful people. As Martin Luther put it, Christians are *simul iustus et peccator*—righteous yet sinners at one and the same time. We are like ill people under the care of a competent physician: although we believe passionately that we shall one day be cured, the fact remains that we are ill at the moment.

It is the intractability of human sin, rather than any deficiency in the gospel, that underlies the fact that there are bad Christians. Sadly, sin is so pervasive that the Christian church tends to obscure Christ as much as she reveals him. It is only by the grace of God that the attraction of Christ and his gospel breaks through the tainted witness of the institutional church. That there are Christians who are not especially good is a testimony to the reality and power of human sin; that there are Christians who are especially good is a testimony to the reality and power of divine grace.

These observations apply especially to Christian leaders—a point made powerfully in Anthony Trollope's Barchester Chronicles, or, more recently, in Susan Howatch's novels *Glittering Images* and *Ultimate Prizes*. Richard Holloway, a bishop in the Scottish Episcopal Church, comments perceptively on the impact of sin and human frailty on the public representatives of the gospel:

> Professional Christians, church leaders or preachers, become terribly aware that they are walking contradictions, licensed frauds. On the one hand, as public figures we represent the Christian message, and people project on to us their own expectations and longings. . . . And yet we know that we are, in fact, not anything like the stained glass window that some people imagine us to be, want us to be, or think we ought to be. Inside we are just as full of doubts, fears, anxieties, lusts, longings, as everyone else.[8]

Holloway stresses how easy it is to assume that admiration of an ideal implies an ability to conform to it. Yet experience suggests that many of the ideals that we most admire lie beyond us and cannot be achieved by our frail and fallen human nature.

> We are here in the middle of all this confusion, knowing how inappropriate we are as vessels of God's disclosure and yet also knowing that in all sorts of ways that is precisely what we are. God *does use* these frauds, these very flawed and confused creatures, to address, comfort, challenge and console people. Back we come again to the ambiguity, the ambivalence. We are still very much flesh, blood and galloping neuroses, yet through all that God reaches people.[9]

Grace does not abolish sin, in individuals or institutions; it enables God to work through that sin. Grace does not destroy our frailty, making us into spiritual superheroes; it transfigures that frailty, enabling God to make his treasure available through our earthen vessels. Sin is for real, crippling our efforts to become like Christ; grace is equally for real, allowing God to achieve wonders through what little we have to offer him in the way of self-improvement.

Since sin is a pervasive and perennial feature of human existence—including Christian existence—it is helpful to approach negative personal or historical associations from this standpoint. They are a witness to the power of sin in the world and in Christian believers and institutions. They are a demonstration of our need for grace and forgiveness: "*All* have sinned and fall short of the glory of God" (Rom. 3:23). The real test is whether Christianity makes a difference— whether the "after" is superior to the "before." And it is your task, as an apologist, to make sure that you do not unintentionally cause anyone to make negative connections between you and your Christian faith. Your lifestyle as much as your message are part of your case for Christianity.

There is, however, another point that must be made. I make it with a degree of sadness and reluctance. At least some of what passes for Christianity in the world is a pathetic distortion of the real thing. Nominal Christianity—a form of Christianity that retains its outward beliefs, while its life-force has been spent—is among the worst enemies of the Christian apologist. The spiritual and moral deadness that often lingers around such forms of Christianity can be deeply oppressing and cause the most negative associations in the minds of individuals. And sadly, these associations are often imprinted on young peoples' minds at a most impressionable age. If I could draw on my own experience as an apologist, there seems to be nothing like Roman Catholic boarding schools for turning out committed atheists.

Inoculation against dangerous diseases such as polio and typhoid involves the introduction of a harmless or dead form of the bacteria of an otherwise deadly disease into the human bloodstream. This causes the body to produce antibodies that will defend it against future attacks by the virulent form of the disease. Christianity is a disease against which it is very easy to become inoculated. There are many dead and decaying versions of it that build up people's resistance against the real thing. There is much truth in the old Latin proverb, *corruptio optimi pessimum est,* "there is nothing worse than the corruption of the best."

If this seems to be a genuine difficulty for the person to whom you are speaking, you will probably have to be quite honest with them and tell them that they may well have been unfortunate enough to encounter a dead and unrepresentative form of Christianity. To judge Christianity by this standard would be to condemn falling in love on the basis of watching a tired and failing marriage in which the partners are simply going through the motions of living together, all love and loyalty having long since deserted them. Ask them for another chance—and show them the real thing.

C. THE PROBLEM OF RELEVANCE

A common response to rational justifications of Christianity runs like this. "What you say may well be reasonable. It may well be true. But it lacks any real relevance to life. Why should I be interested in such irrelevant ideas, even if they are true?" This problem highlights a deficiency in classical apologetics that is primarily concerned with the rational justification of faith. Truth is no guarantee of relevance.

A colleague of mine is a dedicated philatelist with a most impressive collection of postage stamps. He is perfectly capable of telling me everything I could possibly want to know about the watermarks of stamps issued during the reign of Queen Victoria by the Caribbean islands of Trinidad and Tobago. And while I have no doubt about the truth of what he is telling me, I cannot help but feel that it is an utter irrelevance to my life.

Many people feel the same way about Christianity. Two matters give rise to this difficulty: A failure to grasp what the "benefits of Christ" actually are, reflecting a failure on the part of the apologist to *particularize* the gospel in the situation of that person or community, and a serious misunderstanding of the nature of faith.

First, the apologist cannot be content to mumble vague generalities about the gospel, adopting a "to whom it may concern" approach that blunts the force of the gospel. The specificity of the gospel to the life of an individual is too easily compromised through a failure to think through its relevance in a given situation. The gospel does indeed talk about—and offer!—liberation. But from what does a person need to be liberated? From bondage in Egypt? From the fear of death? From slavery in the Old South? From famine? From the paralyzing power of guilt? If the gospel seems irrelevant it is because of our failure to take the trouble to *make* it relevant. There is nothing wrong with the gospel; the weak link in the chain lies with those whose task it is to contextualize it, to anchor it in the situations of real life. We shall explore this further on pages 189–211.

Second, there has been a failure to explain what that deceptively simple word *faith* actually means. As we saw earlier,[10] faith has three main elements.

a. Faith is about believing that certain things are true.

b. Faith is about trusting in the promises of God.

c. Faith is about entering into the promises of God, receiving what they have to offer.

It is only the first of these three components that immediately suggests itself to those outside the Christian faith—and which thus prompts the question, "How can believing that something is true totally change you?" The apologist must be prepared to explain the Christian language and the spiritual realities to which it points.

The relevance of Christianity can be grounded in a number of key areas of life:

a. *The need to have a basis for morality* (see pp. 39–42). Moral values reflect an understanding of the nature and purpose of the world and of the human beings in it. As the moral philosopher Basil Mitchell observed, "Any worldview which carries with it important implications for our understanding of man and his place in the universe would yield its own distinctive insights into the scope, character and content of morality."[11] The relevance of morality is obvious; societies and individuals need moral values and personal ideals to govern the way in which they act. Anarchism, once eminently fashionable among those pipe-dreaming, cultured, middle-class intellectuals of the 1930s, fortunate enough never to have experienced the results of anarchy, holds no hope for anyone. Christianity offers a worldview, which it declares to be true on the best of authorities, and which in turn leads to the generation of moral values and ideals that are able to give moral meaning and dignity to our existence.

b. *The need to have a framework for making sense of experience.* For example, is suffering something arbitrary, or does it serve a deeper purpose? Psychologists have stressed that there seems to be an inbuilt human need to make sense of things—a phenomenon known as "attributional processes."[12] If there is this basic need to attribute meaning to human events and experiences, it is clearly important to base these interpretations of the world of experience upon as reliable cognitive foundations as possible. The *science* of apologetics stresses the trustworthiness of the cognitive foundations of Christianity, while the *art* of apologetics seeks to show how this framework may make sense of experience. Reliability and relevance thus go hand in hand within effective Christian apologetics.

c. *The need for a vision to guide and inspire.* The utter dreariness of a world without ideals points to our need for inspiration. Yet the vision of a classless society certainly proved capable of inspiring commitment and purpose among those who believed in it; sadly, it has proved to be a mirage. Yet nobody can deny its power to inspire, guide, and encourage those who once took it seriously.

Christianity offers a vision—a vision of God's gracious intervention in our sinful lives, of his forgiveness of our sins through the death of Christ, of the continued presence and power of God in our lives, and of our final entry into the glory of the kingdom, where we share in the resurrection of Christ. That vision keeps us going and keeps us hoping—yet it is a vision grounded in the hard-headed realism of the gospel. The science of apologetics stresses that this vision is no mirage but can be embraced with seriousness and confidence; the art of apologetics is concerned to show how this vision can transform the drabness of our world. "Hope springs eternal in the human breast" (Alexander Pope)—but that hope must be for real. The gospel offers a hope that is anchored in the rock of a trustworthy God, who has moved heaven and earth in order to persuade us that he is indeed worthy of our trust, and whose son Jesus Christ died in order that we might be worthy to stand in his sight.

So is there really a problem about the relevance of the gospel? Christianity can be profoundly relevant. But a *relevant* worldview, as we stressed, must be a *real* worldview! Christianity has a relevance that far transcends that of an inherently interesting set of ideas. People get bored with ideas. Ideas age rapidly and lose the novelty value that once proved their chief attraction. But Christianity is not simply offering new ideas, though new ideas abound within it. It offers to renew us, to captivate us by transforming us, to make available to us the riches of the power and presence of God, and the dynamic vitality of the risen life of Christ, which can even now break into and revolutionize the dullness of humdrum human life. Here is no mere textbook packed with ideas; here is a love affair, a relationship, something that will last and that will go on renewing itself until the day when the limitations of life on this earth are finally abolished. And, as experience shows, it has a remarkably high coefficient of relevance to real life—if rightly understood.

D. MISUNDERSTANDINGS OF THE NATURE OF CHRISTIANITY

But Christianity is, as a matter of fact, rarely understood by those outside its bounds. In fact, this is probably one of the greatest tasks confronting the apologist—to rescue Christianity from misunderstand-ings. Just as the second-century apologists (for example, Justin Martyr) had to persuade their readers that Christians did not eat each other or indulge in sexual orgies at their meetings, so their modern successors must identify and neutralize the prevailing distortions of the gospel. We shall explore this further in what follows.

There is every possibility that a rejection of Christianity— whether a deliberate decision to have nothing to do with it or a vague or unconscious hostility toward it—is actually the rejection of a caricature or distortion of Christianity that has been rejected, while the real thing has escaped unnoticed.

History provides numerous examples of individuals whose misconceptions of Christianity posed a barrier to their coming to faith. An excellent example is Augustine of Hippo.[13] Augustine was a talented young orator from North Africa who was trying to make his mark in the political hothouse of Rome in the late fourth century. He seemed to have some success. Soon after his arrival at Rome he was offered the job of public orator in the major northern Italian city of Milan. Aware that this could be the beginning of a significant career in the Roman civil service, Augustine accepted with alacrity.

As a young man, Augustine had become involved with Mani-chaeism, a cult that aimed to make sense of the riddles of life and the hopes and fears of human beings. Although its precise details need not detain us here, it is important to note that, although similar to Christianity at points, it was radically different at others. For example, it taught that the God of the Old Testament was malicious and evil, having nothing to do with the God of the New Testament. It was the God of the Old Testament who was responsible for all the evil and suffering of the world. The Old Testament, therefore, was irrelevant to Christians, as it concerned a God inferior to that of the New.

Manichaeism was highly critical of Christianity and frequently misrepresented it. Augustine's understanding of Christianity was highly colored by Manichaean polemic. His youthful rejection of Christianity was actually the rejection of a stereotype, a misrepresenta-tion. But he did not know that.

On his arrival at Milan, Augustine discovered that the local Christian bishop, Ambrose, had a reputation as a splendid orator. He decided to find out whether the reputation was merited. Each Sunday, he slipped into the cathedral and listened to the bishop preach. Initially he took a purely professional interest in the sermons as pieces of splendid oratory. What orator can resist picking up tips, unacknowledged, from another? But gradually their content began to take hold of him.

> I used enthusiastically to listen to him preaching to the people, not with the intention which I ought to have had, but as if testing out his oratorical skill to see whether his fluency was better or inferior than it was reported to be. . . . I was not interested in learning what he was talking about. My ears were only for his rhetorical technique. . . . Nevertheless together with the words which I was enjoying, the subject matter, in which I was unconcerned, came to make an entry into my mind. I could not separate them. While I opened my heart in noting the eloquence with which he spoke, there also entered no less the truth which he affirmed.[14]

As the story of Augustine's long journey to faith makes clear, Ambrose removed a major barrier to faith. He dismantled the Manichaean stereotype of Christianity. Yet, interestingly, all that Ambrose did was to preach the gospel regularly. He seems to have known nothing of the spiritual situation of Augustine, even if he had been aware of his presence in the congregation. Regular preaching of the gospel can undoubtedly pay unexpected dividends.

Among the individuals whom we encounter in our apologetic ministry there will certainly be some who have the most astonishingly misguided and muddled ideas about what Christianity is all about. These misunderstandings—some of which will have been picked up unconsciously, others deliberately propagated—need to be identified and firmly yet tactfully disarmed. How?

Let us imagine that as you are talking to someone about Christianity, you become aware that he or she is resistant to it. Invite the person to tell you what he or she thinks Christianity is all about. And *listen carefully*. This conversation could provide the basis for important discussions for a long time to come as it allows the person involved to speak about what he or she thinks Christianity is all about and why he or she finds it unacceptable.

Be prepared to ask the person where his or her ideas came from. Also be prepared to present alternatives—alternatives that are more *reliable*, just as they are more *attractive*.

E. THE HUNGER FOR ABSOLUTE CERTAINTY

"Unless you can prove that to me, I won't accept it!" Many conversations on the claims and relevance of the Christian faith often come to a dead end with statements like this. The demand for proof, for demonstration beyond conceivable doubt, is unquestionably one of the most problematical (and often one of the most common) predicaments the apologist is confronted with. But these conversations need not—in fact, they *should* not—end here. The demand for absolute certainty opens the way to what could be a most fruitful exploration of the limitations placed on any kind of human knowledge—knowledge about God included.[15]

What sort of things can we know with absolute certainty?[16] Vast tracts of human knowledge would have to be set to one side as lacking this characteristic of certainty. Among them, we would have to include historical and scientific knowledge.

a. Historical knowledge. I may believe, firmly, that the Battle of Hastings took place in 1066, or that the Declaration of Independence is to be dated from 1776. But I could be completely wrong. My belief rests on eyewitness reports, which may rest on confusion or misunderstandings, or even represent deliberate fabrications. I was not present at either event, and therefore I lack the ability to verify their accuracy. I have to rely on the accounts of other people—accounts that may be flawed. Of course, I might try to persuade myself that these reports are entirely to be trusted. But I cannot say *with absolute certainty* when these events took place. At best, I could say that they *almost certainly* took place then.

It is surprising how few people have actually thought about this point. The apologist could do far worse than ask a question such as "When did Julius Caesar die?" and immediately follow this up with, "And how do you know this? Are you *sure?*" An important point is being made, even if in a trivial way.

b. Scientific knowledge. The laws of physics would initially seem an excellent example of things we know with absolute certainty. The situation is far from simple, however, as Nancy Cartwright points out in her provocatively titled book, *How the Laws of Physics Lie.*[17] We shall explore some of the issues further (pp. 160–66). But let us explore one problem here, to illustrate how misleading this simplistic approach to scientific theory actually is.

First, we need to recognize that those laws are not prescriptive; they are descriptive. They do not prescribe what nature must be like; they describe what nature seems to be like. They attempt to summarize past observation and predict the future. This prediction is based on the assumption that the future will continue to be like the past, and that what happened in one situation will happen again (or in a recognizable variation) in a different situation. But this raises the problem of induction, probably one of the most difficult areas of the philosophy of science.

Scientific inductivism rests on three principles:[18]

a. The principle of *accumulation,* which lays down that knowledge grows by accumulation of well-attested facts.

b. The principle of *induction,* which asserts that it is possible to infer laws of nature from observations and the results of experiments.

c. The principle of *instance confirmation,* which declares that our belief in the plausibility of a scientific law is directly proportional to the number of instances of observation of the phenomenon to which the law refers.

These might seem superficially credible. But as Rom Harré points out in his magisterial survey of philosophies of science, "inductivism will hardly stand a moment's serious criticism."[19] In particular, the idea that the laws of nature describe a situation with absolute certainty is absurd. One can certainly talk about varying degrees of *probability* in the natural sciences, but any claim to certainty is laughable. For example, an entire series of quite different "laws of nature" can be inferred from any set of facts. Inductivists, aware of this problem, appeal to the "principle of parsimony"—in other words, to the belief that the simplest theory has to be right. But sadly, the history of science shows that it is often the more complex laws that are to be preferred, leaving theory at odds with experience.

All these points are familiar to anyone versed in the philosophy of science. Yet most people have a popular and mythical conception of science that bears little relation to the reality. For them, science is capable of uncovering the mysteries of the world, laying bare its laws and principles with absolute certainty—and thus totally overshadowing Christianity's claims to truth. In reality the situation is rather different and much more exciting. But we shall return to this in a later chapter (pp. 160-66).

So neither the historian nor the natural scientist can demonstrate things with the total certainty that our critic demanded at the opening of this section. Does that mean that historians and scientists are skeptics, wallowing around in a quagmire of uncertainty and confusion? Certainly not. All those whose task it is to make sense of experience use broadly the same principle: You find what seems to be the best explanation of things, knowing that you are unlikely ever to be able to prove that it *is* the best explanation, and continue to work with it until something happens to make you change your mind. Probability, not certainty, is the law of the life of experience.

I cannot prove that the sun is going to rise tomorrow. I cannot prove that all the oxygen molecules in my study will not suddenly migrate somewhere else, causing me to drop dead from asphyxiation. I would even have difficulty in proving, to the satisfaction of philosophers such as David Hume, that other people actually exist. Nor can I prove that God exists. But I can quite happily live my life on the basis of these assumptions without letting this lack of absolute certainty cause me any real difficulty. All of us, Christian and non-Christian, have to make assumptions about life. But they are hardly ever grounded in the hard-nosed certainty that critics of Christianity seem to want and expect. Christians are in the same boat as everyone else— and that boat shows no signs of sinking.

It might be objected that these examples are drawn from the world of experience. Both history and the natural sciences draw on the data of sense experience. And experience is notoriously difficult to interpret, as the recent debate over interpretation-free immediate sense experience has demonstrated.[20] But why not appeal to reason instead of experience? This would result in a type of knowledge in which total certainty is possible. Here are three examples:

a. The whole is greater than the part.
b. It is impossible for a man to marry his widow's sister.
c. 5 + 5 = 10.

All of these are true, although the second might take a moment's thought to register. The first two are true because of the definitions of their terms. By definition, a whole is greater than its part. By definition, a man cannot marry his widow's sister because he must have died before his wife acquires that status. The third is a comforting and familiar illustration drawn from the world of mathematics.

Could we not have certain knowledge about other things, by an extension of this method? Why should we not have a knowledge of everything that matters by using our reason and establishing a series of self-evident truths upon which we could build? This approach has been tried and has failed miserably. The dream of finding self-evident truths, known with total certainty, and on which an entire system of beliefs could be erected, is now seen as a delusion. (We shall explore this further on pp. 147–155.) But the following point can be made at this stage. All our knowledge about anything that really matters is a matter of probability. The things that we can be really sure about seem rather trivial and petty. Is knowing that the whole is greater than the part going to change your life? Is knowing that five and five make ten going to bestow upon you the secret of eternal life—or will it just help you chronicle the ticking away of your years, leading to an inevitable death?

Boris Pasternak, the author of *Dr. Zhivago,* once wrote: "I am an atheist who has lost his faith." There is no paradox here, no contradiction. Atheism, like all other worldviews, is a matter of faith.

It rests on the belief (not the proven certainty) that there is no God. There is no proof—philosophical or experimental—that there is no God. The atheist's decision is a matter of faith, even if that atheist fails to realize that this is the case. The Christian faith is thus in excellent company. When it comes to the big things of life—like believing in the Christian faith or believing in democracy—we live on the basis of probability, not certainty. Anyone who disagrees probably has not given it very much thought. Christian faith is a risk because it cannot be proven. It is not a state of calm and easy security, but is more like an adventure, a ceaseless battling with troubles. The "tranquility of faith" (Luther) is set in the midst of conflict and turmoil, not apart from them. But Christian faith rests on history, reason, experience, and revelation, a formidable quartet that, like the four legs of a well-balanced table, gives security and stability to the life of faith.

F. PRIOR COMMITMENT TO ANOTHER BELIEF SYSTEM

Some people are searching for the meaning of life, for personal fulfillment, and for a belief system that will make sense of the world and their place within it. Others believe that they have found them and need search no longer. The outcome of their quest is often Christianity—often, but not always. So how does the apologist cope with a situation in which there is already commitment to a rival belief system?

At first, it might seem that all is lost. Yet, curiously, it is perhaps easier to enter into a creative dialogue with, for example, an atheist or a Marxist than with an agnostic, because at least the former believe something, whereas the latter sits permanently on the fence of ideas, taking refuge in the ambiguities of life to justify a perpetual stance of indifference and noncommitment. The atheist is prepared to concede—no, that is too negative a word, to *celebrate*—the need for commitment and the existence of evidence to move one in the direction of that commitment. In other words, the atheist recognizes the need to come off the fence and the fact that there are factors in the world of human experience and thought that suggest which side of the fence that ought to be. At present, the atheist happens to sit on the godless side of that fence. That, however, is not a permanent state of affairs. Dialogue is possible.

It must be recognized from the outset, however, that this dialogue may be long and difficult, involving patience as much as intelligence, and loving care as much as argument. The difficulties are well illustrated by considering the way in which belief systems relate to experience. At first sight, it might seem that anything in the world of experience that contradicts a worldview or belief system instantly negates it. The belief system collapses when confronted with a single event in the world of experience that is at odds with the theory. But in practice it just is not that simple.

The Harvard philosopher Willard van Orman Quine has provided us with what is undoubtedly one of the finest accounts of the way belief systems or worldviews relate to experience:

> The totality of our so-called knowledge or beliefs, from the most casual matters of geography and history to the profoundest laws of atomic physics . . . is a man-made fabric which impinges on experience only along the edges. . . . A conflict with experience at the periphery occasions adjustments in the interior of the field. . . . But the total field is so underdetermined by its boundary conditions, experience, that there is much latitude of choice as to what statements to reevaluate in the light of any single contrary experience.[21]

In other words, experience often has relatively little impact on worldviews. Where experience seems to contradict a worldview or system of beliefs, the most likely outcome is an internal readjustment of the system rather than its rejection. In fact, it might even be suggested that some worldviews are so constructed that they are incapable of being falsified on the basis of experience. Quine notes this point with characteristic clarity:

> Our system of statements has such a thick cushion of indeterminacy, in relation to experience, that vast domains of law can easily be held immune to revision on principle. We can always turn to other quarters of the system when revisions are called for by unexpected experiences.[22]

Quine's analysis is important in relation to Christian apologetics. It casts light on the difficulties likely to be faced by the apologist who is dealing with people with prior commitments. A worldview is not simply a collection of beliefs, the disproving of any of which automatically and necessarily leads to the worldview instantly becoming incredible. Rather, it consists of a cluster of ideas, a network of interacting beliefs, often with a considerable degree of flexibility and lack of precision. An argument that appears to dent the system badly is absorbed through the considerable "cushion of indeterminacy." Events from the world of experience that seem to show up fatal weaknesses in the system do not lead to the rejection of that system but to "adjustments in the interior of the field." Disconfirming experiences or negative arguments call into question the internal elements of the system, not the system itself.

Freudianism and Marxism are excellent examples of theories that can account for just about everything that happens, without the need for modification. The situation is neatly illustrated by the often-told story of the man who visited his Freudian analyst. If he was early, the analyst concluded that he was anxious; if he was on time, he was compulsive; if he was late, he was resentful. The theory accounted for everything. It was precisely this inability to be refuted by experience that prompted Karl Popper to develop his celebrated theory of falsification. Irrefutability might seem to be a virtue; in reality, it is a vice.

How then can one refute a worldview? How can one begin to penetrate the "cushion of indeterminacy" that protects vulnerable ideas from exposure and contradiction? The following suggestions may prove helpful.

1. Explore the Issue of Historical Erosion

What seems permanent often proves to be temporary. This is one of the great insights of the Old Testament prophets. Surveying the great empires of the ancient world, each of which seemed so permanent a feature of the political landscape, the prophets stress their utter transitoriness. Thus Isaiah proclaimed the future collapse of Babylon (Isa. 47:1–7). What was here today could be gone tomorrow.

This sense of shattered permanence is evoked to near-perfection by Percy Bysshe Shelley in his poem *Ozymandias*. Shelley tells of a monument in an ancient land:

> I met a traveller from an antique land
> Who said: Two vast and trunkless legs of stone
> Stand in the desert.

This ruined monument turns out to be all that remains of a tribute to the power of a long-dead king:

> "My name is Ozymandias, king of kings:
> Look on my works, ye Mighty, and despair!"

Yet nothing remains of these works. The words ring empty. The monument is a sad testimony to past glory and present ruin, decay and insignificance:

> Nothing beside remains. Round the decay
> Of that colossal wreck, boundless and bare
> The lone and level sands stretch far away.

This same historical perspective needs to be applied to worldviews. In their heyday, they seemed permanent, destined to abide forever and remain a serious threat to Christianity until the end of time. With hindsight, they are shown up for what they really are: systems confined to a narrow band of history.

The words of Tennyson in *In Memoriam* are an eloquent summary of the situation in the eyes of the Christian apologist:

> Our little systems have their day;
> They have their day, and cease to be:
> They are but broken lights of thee.
> And thou, O Lord, art more than they.

If you read the writings of the second-century apologists, such as Justin Martyr, you soon begin to realize that the worldviews they regarded as a serious challenge to faith just are not around any more. The threat of yesterday is often deposited in the trash can of history today.

Christianity has been around for two thousand years. Its main rivals in the Western marketplace of ideas today are recent inventions. For how long will they remain a serious threat? In the 1960s we were told that Marxism was here to stay. If Christianity was going to survive, it would have to adjust to this situation and get used to the idea. Christianity would have to be permanently on the defensive against this greater, more resilient, and more intellectually respectable belief system.

The dramatic destruction of the Berlin Wall in 1989 and the remarkable disintegration of the Communist Party in Moscow in the summer of 1991 showed up the superficiality of this judgment. Marxism collapsed, the myth of its permanence and superiority exposed. Although Marxism will probably remain significant in universities for some time, given the social role of those institutions as homes for lost causes, it has lost its popular appeal. What one generation invented, another discards. What proved liberating to one generation proves oppressive to another. Intellectual fashions change.

The point of this approach is clear. In dealing with a rival belief system, it is perfectly proper to inquire about its historical pedigree. How long has it been around? What reasons are there for suspecting it will continue to be around in a hundred years' time? Christians are notoriously bad about asking awkward questions like this, probably because their faith makes them such nice people. But these questions need to be asked—persistently. The dreadful thought that today's present certainties might be tomorrow's past curiosities undermines the credibility of worldviews with remarkable speed.

2. Examine the Evidence for the Belief System

In theory, people ought to hold to a particular worldview because of the force of the evidence offered in favor of that worldview; in practice, it tends to be nothing of the sort. Often, individuals adopt a belief system because it happens to be fashionable among their peer group or because it annoys their parents. The age-old theme of son revolting against father (Luke 15) often finds its expression at a deeper level—the children's rejection of the belief system of their parents. Thus, to give one example, German literature around the time of the French Revolution is dominated by the theme of young men totally rejecting the old outlook of their parents and embracing the secular worldview of the French Revolution with enormous enthusiasm.

But a day of reckoning awaits, with its hard questions. Why *this* belief system? Sure, it is fashionable—but is it credible? Sure, it makes a statement about your independence from your parents—but is it right? Will your children end up rejecting your belief system, simply to make a statement about their independence? And what does that say about the merits of what you believe? Questions like this have to be asked at some point. You can begin that process of questioning.

To illustrate the questions that need to be asked, we may look at the classic criticism of Marxism made by Karl Popper in *The Poverty of Historicism*,[23] provocatively dedicated to "the countless men and women of all creeds or nations or races who fell victim to the fascist and communist belief in Inexorable Laws of Historical Destiny." Popper's point is this: Marxism claims to rest on a scientific analysis of history that shows that it is inevitably moving toward socialism. And given the historical inevitability of socialism, one can speed things up by working toward socialism, thus making the inevitable happen sooner. As Marx puts it in his preface to *Das Kapital*, one "can shorten and lessen the birthpangs" on the road to socialism. But, Popper points out, the evidence for this "historical inevitability" is specious. It cannot be taken seriously. History shows nothing like the patterns that Marx detected and on which his theory ultimately rested. The entire edifice of Marxism may therefore be said to rest, not merely on a mistake, but on something that is *obviously* a mistake.

This is illustrative of a general approach. Belief systems ultimately rest on something. Your task is to find out what and to begin to challenge those foundations. One of the most interesting features of intellectual history is that worldviews very often linger on long after their theoretical foundations have been demolished and discredited. The base has collapsed. The superstructure remains, at least for a while. You "can shorten and lessen the birthpangs" (Marx) of the process of breaking with that worldview by helping people see that they are presently committed to a dying and decaying philosophy. Christianity offers ideas with a distinguished past—and an assured future. Perhaps they might like to reconsider?

3. Examine the Presuppositions of the Belief System

All belief systems rest on presuppositions. In *The God Who Is There* Francis Schaeffer develops this point as follows:

> Let us remember that every person we speak to . . . has a set of presuppositions, whether he or she has analyzed them or not. . . . It is impossible for any non-Christian individual or group to be consistent to their system in logic or in practice. . . . A man may try to bury the tension and you may have to help him find it, but somewhere there is a point of inconsistency. He stands in a position which he cannot pursue to the end; and this is not just an intellectual concept of tension, it is what is wrapped up in what he is as a man.[24]

The basic point Schaeffer makes is of considerable importance to a person-centered apologetics. It is quite possible that a person's life is actually based on a whole set of unrecognized presuppositions, which your gentle and patient inquiry can bring to light. Experience suggests that such gentle explorations can sometimes be devastating in that they expose the inner contradictions and confusions within someone's outlook on life. A crisis may result in which faith can be born.

Schaeffer provides a number of examples of cases in which exposure of contradictions and tensions within worldviews has important (and negative) implications for their credibility. We may note two. The first relates to a discussion group Schaeffer was leading at Cambridge University, attended by a young Sikh.

> He started to speak strongly against Christianity, but did not really understand the problems of his own beliefs. So I said, "Am I not correct in saying that on the basis of your system, cruelty and noncruelty are ultimately equal, that there is no intrinsic difference between them?" He agreed. . . . The student in whose room we met, who had clearly understood the implications of what the Sikh had admitted, picked up his kettle of boiling water with which he was about to make tea, and stood with it steaming over the Indian's head. The man looked up and asked him what he was doing, and he said with a cold yet gentle finality, "There is

no difference between cruelty and noncruelty." Thereupon the Hindu walked out into the night.[25]

The essential point here is that persistent questioning exposed the inner contradiction within an alternative belief system. The same point emerges in a more celebrated example, which Schaeffer skillfully deploys against the ethical nihilism of Jean-Paul Sartre. Sartre's fundamental point was that ethics is an irrelevance. If there is any ethical component to an action, it lays in the exercise of choice, not the moral decision reached. This famous attitude attracted considerable attention. Then Sartre signed the Algerian Manifesto—a protest against the continuing French occupation of Algeria. Events in the real world called into question his ethical views.

> [Sartre] took up a deliberately moral attitude and said it was an unjust and dirty war. His left-wing political position which he took up is another illustration of the same inconsistency. As far as many secular existentialists have been concerned, from the moment Sartre signed the Algerian Manifesto he was regarded as an apostate from his own position, and toppled from his place of leadership of the avant-garde.[26]

This illustrates Schaeffer's point that Sartre and other nihilists "could not live with the conclusions of their system"—and so points to the need for the apologist to explore what the logical conclusions of a given system might be. "The more logical a man who holds a non-Christian position is to his own presuppositions, the further he is from the real world; and the nearer he is to the real world, the more illogical he is to his own presuppositions."[27]

Schaeffer develops this insight further by analyzing the way in which worldviews construct shields to protect themselves against the real world. The apologist must remove that shield and allow the harsh realities of the real world to raise questions about the credibility of that system.

> It is like the great shelters built upon some mountain passes to protect vehicles from the avalanches of rock and stone which periodically tumble down the mountain. The avalanche, in the case of the non-Christian, is the real and the abnormal fallen world which surrounds him. The Christian, lovingly, must remove the shelter and allow the truth of the external world and of what man is to beat upon him.[28]

Just as Sartre's views proved untenable when confronted with the crises and situations of the political world, so other worldviews, according to Schaeffer, can be discredited in similar ways. Discovering the implications of an outlook is of major apologetic importance, as is a willingness to explore them, gently and lovingly, with those who cling to them.

These, then, are some suggestions for engaging in critical yet creative dialogue with those already committed to worldviews. Accounts of, and responses to, six major worldviews, each a powerful rival to, or a potential critic of, Christianity, are provided in a later chapter as follows:

a. Enlightenment rationalism (pp. 147–55)
b. Marxism (pp. 156–60)
c. Scientific materialism (pp. 160–66)
d. Feminism (pp. 166–75)
e. Postmodernism (pp. 175–81)
f. The neopaganism of the New Age movement (pp. 181-86).

G. THE PROBLEM OF PERSONAL INTEGRITY

Getting people to change their minds might seem a simple matter. All it involves is giving up one set of opinions and adopting another in their place. The main task of the Christian apologist then is to persuade people that Christian ideas are right—or at least *better*—than non-Christian alternatives. And the rest will follow as a matter of course.

Sadly, reality is rather different. Apologetics deals with real people—with human beings who often have deeply held views, a fierce sense of loyalty, and an enormous reluctance to admit that they are wrong about anything.

Suppose you are talking to a lifelong atheist about his ideas. The superficial agenda may be about whether or not God exists. But beneath the surface, there may be a conflict going on within this person, unnoticed. Thoughts like this might be flashing through his mind: "I've been an atheist for twenty-five years now. That's a long time. And everyone knows that I'm an atheist. If I change my mind now, people will laugh at me. I'll lose face. My personal reputation is tied up with my atheistic views. I'm locked into this situation. Somehow, my atheism and my personal identity have become mixed up with each other. If I change my mind on this one, I'll somehow be condemning my whole past." The apologist can very easily reinforce such prejudices through a tactless and insensitive approach to the matter.

A major contribution to the resolution of this problem has been provided by the Harvard Negotiation Project. Based at Harvard University by leading academics such as Roger Fisher, Willison

Professor of Law, this project has concentrated on ways of resolving difficulties without losing face or compromising personal integrity.[29] The same principles that are used in international peace negotiations or for the resolution of conflicts within or between major business corporations can be adapted for use in Christian apologetics. I have conducted a small pilot project among Oxford University students over the last few years and have been greatly encouraged by the results. What follows is the Harvard Negotiation Project, as adapted at Oxford for the purposes of Christian apologetics. It rests on two simple principles:

1. Separate the problem from the people.
2. Make it easy for them to change their minds.

We shall explore these points briefly, with illustrations.

1. Separate the Problem from the People

Someone—let's call her Elizabeth—outlines a position. It happens to be vulnerable at a particular point; there is a defect that has been overlooked. Someone else—let's call her Laura—then launches into an attack on this position, exposing its weakness. Elizabeth has now been put in a difficult position, feeling that her personal standing will suffer if she concedes the point. She digs her heels in and defends her position. But in reality it is no longer the *position* that she is defending; it is her *personal integrity*. Laura has attacked Elizabeth as much as Elizabeth's ideas. The person and the ideas have become so closely linked that they are now inseparable. A similar problem can easily arise in apologetics, especially when the person you are talking to has a well-established reputation as a non-Christian.

A person-centered apologetics can cope with this difficulty precisely because it recognizes individual needs and problems. The basic strategy is as simple as it is effective: separate the person from the idea. Help the other person see that there is no *necessary* connection between their personal identity and the ideas they hold at the moment. Let's look at two different approaches. The first is likely to reinforce the unhelpful link between people and their ideas; the second will weaken that link. Suppose the discussion has been about the Resurrection, which your friend declares himself to have difficulties with. Consider these two responses, and try to imagine how your friend would feel in each case.

   a. Well, I'm sorry, but you're wrong. These objections just aren't important. I can't take them seriously, and I don't think you've even bothered to think about them. I'm sure that if you were to think about them longer, you'd see that. Let's go through these so-called objections that you've just made, and I'll show you how unimportant they really are.

b. I can understand how you must feel about this. In fact, I once felt much the same way myself and can really sympathize with you. And it is a difficult thing to sort out, isn't it? Actually, I've changed my mind since then and see it in a different way now. Let me try and explain the way I see it.

Both these responses are stereotypes. The first is abruptly rude and the second nauseatingly sweet. But the contrast makes the point. The first approach links person and ideas; the second seeks to drive a wedge between them by making it clear that a person's ideas are detachable from their personal integrity. We shall explore this point further in what follows.

2. Make It Easy for Them to Change Their Minds

People find it difficult to change their minds if they are made to feel it is a win-or-lose situation. Bad apologetics creates the impression that changing your mind is equivalent to losing an argument. And nobody likes losing arguments—especially in public. Roger Fisher and William Ury, explaining how the principles of the Harvard Negotiation Project may be applied, make this point as follows:

> Often in a negotiation people will continue to hold out not because the proposal on the table is inherently unacceptable, but simply because they want to avoid the feeling or the appearance of backing down to the other side. If the substance can be phrased or conceptualized differently so that it seems a fair outcome, they will then accept it. . . . Face-saving involves reconciling an agreement with principle and with the self-image of the negotiators. Its importance should not be underestimated.[30]

How can this basic principle be applied? Two major strategies have proved to be useful in apologetic contexts.

1. Do Not Present Christianity as a Confrontational Option

To put this in plain English, do not force your conversation partner to enter into a win-or-lose situation. That is, do not present Christianity as being *right* (which immediately implies that your conversation partner is *wrong,* and thus provokes a confrontation). Instead, present Christianity as being *attractive,* explaining why. Christianity gives you hope in the face of death, a sense of peace in the presence of God, a new perception of personal dignity, and a revitalized sense of purpose (to name but a few of the many attractions of the gospel).

What perception does this create on the part of your dialogue partner? That you are concerned to offer him something which you have found valuable and exciting. You are not telling him that he is wrong; you are offering him something of value. Just as one beggar might tell another where to find bread, so you are offering to make available something you have found to be relevant and helpful. The negative impression you avoid creating is that of defeating your colleague in an argument. The positive impression you succeed in creating is that of caring for your colleague. And is this not one of the fundamental impulses underlying all good apologetics—a sense of love and compassion for our friends?

This does not mean that we avoid Christian claims to truth. Part of the attraction of Christianity is that it is both exciting and true. But it means being aware that truth-claims can, through human weakness and fallibility, very easily be presented or perceived in seriously confrontational terms. You can talk about the truth of the gospel when this seems appropriate; by this stage, your dialogue partner may not find this a problem anymore.

Earlier we noted the wisdom of Francis Schaeffer's strategy of confronting rival worldviews—for example, by pointing out their internal inconsistencies. Yet even this process of creating a climate of uncertainty need not be dangerously confrontational. It is important to confront and challenge ideas rather than the person who holds them. For example, suppose you are speaking to someone who is committed to Marxism (see pp. 156-60). Compare the following approaches.

• Marxism is wrong, and I don't see how anyone could take it seriously anymore. Only someone who is dangerously out of touch with things would find it credible.

• I've always had some problems with Marxism, I'm afraid. Maybe you could help me here. For example, why is it that Marx argued that the coming of the revolution would make religion disappear, yet the coming of Marxism to certain countries during the twentieth century seems to have led, if anything, to a revival of religion? I'd like to know.

The first is likely to be counter-productive, implying that your friend is a fool. The second is much more positive and affirming of your friend, who is presented as someone who can help you think through a difficulty you have had. But it has a potentially lethal sting in its tail in that it raises certain serious inconsistencies between theory and experience, which have led many former Marxists to abandon their political faith. You could begin that process of erosion of confidence with your friends—while you *affirm*, rather than *devalue*, their personal worth.

2. Use Yourself as an Example of Someone Who Changed His or Her Mind

Clearly, this approach depends on your having once been a non-Christian and having subsequently changed your mind. If this is the case, you can help your dialogue partner to see that personal identity and ideas are separable. Furthermore, you can help the other person to explicitly acknowledge the problem and to clear the way for its resolution. Take the simple series of statements: "I used to think that Christianity was something of an irrelevance. But I had the courage to change my mind. And I'm glad I did." You acknowledge the problem, indicate that facing and resolving it is a matter of courage, and bring home that the outcome of that decision was positive. The instinct to "save face" is thus outweighed by the greater human instinct—to do something courageous, and which is *seen* to be courageous. Little things often matter a lot in apologetics; too often they get overlooked.

This also applies to the final barrier to faith we shall consider in this chapter.

H. A SENSE OF GUILT OR INADEQUACY

Perhaps surprisingly, a genuine obstacle to faith on the part of many people is an awareness of sin, or a sense of deep and irredeemable personal inadequacy. For people in this position, it is of relatively little comfort to know that Christianity is true and that it is relevant to their situation. Their problem is that they are convinced that they are simply not capable of relating to God. "If God knew what I was really like," they often argue, "he wouldn't want anything to do with me. How can a holy God want to have anything to do with a sinner like me?" Others are convinced that their total insignificance places them outside the sphere of the gospel of grace. It applies to someone else but not to them.

This problem is not often addressed by textbooks on apologetics, perhaps because it seems out of place in a discussion of the rationality of the Christian faith. But our person-centered approach demands that it should be considered. It really is a barrier to faith for some; therefore it must be addressed by the responsible apologist. Happily, experience suggests that it is an obstacle that is relatively easily removed. We shall deal with these matters briefly, as they represent well-worn paths in Christian evangelism. The basic points you need to stress are the following:

    a. God already knows exactly what you are like (Ps. 139:1–6). There is no question of deceiving God, as if he somehow thinks you are a thoroughly respectable and righteous person, when in reality you are nothing of the sort. The entire gospel rests on the supposition that God knows *exactly* what we are like—and loves us nonetheless.

    b. The gospel is meant for sinners (Mark 2:17). Realizing that you are a sinner is thus the precondition for forgiveness, not a reason for excluding you from faith. The Scottish pastor and writer John Duncan was conducting a communion service one Sunday. When he came to administer the wine to the congregation, a sixteen-year-old girl hesitated, then refused to accept it. She motioned with her hand, indicating that she did not feel able to share in the cup. Realizing that the girl felt unworthy to receive it, Duncan reached out, laid his arm on her shoulder, and said: "Take it, lassie. It's meant for us sinners." The wine is a symbol of God's forgiveness of sins through the death of Christ—*real* forgiveness of *real* sins. Recognizing the full extent of your sinfulness does not disqualify you from the grace of God—it indicates how much you need it.

    c. Sin is a barrier to God—but a barrier that has been broken down by God. The penalty of sin has been cancelled, its power has been broken, and its continuing presence is being diminished, through the cross of Christ. You have been saved from the penalty of sin, you are being saved from the power of sin—all because of what Christ achieved on the cross. It remains for us to accept and appropriate all that he did, through faith in him.

In this chapter we have begun to explore some of the obstacles to faith and have made some suggestions about how these barriers can be rendered less effective. The two chapters that follow deal with certain more specific areas of difficulty. We begin by dealing with a series of individual difficulties that often cause people to hesitate to accept the Christian gospel.

CHAPTER FIVE

Intellectual Barriers to Faith

A central task of apologetics is to create a situation in which it is possible to come to faith. Part of this responsibility involves the neutralization of a number of potential obstacles to faith. These difficulties are often freestanding, so that the resolution of a single issue can often clear the road to faith. The present chapter is concerned with exploring and countering some major difficulties that prevent many individuals from taking Christianity seriously.

A. GOD AS WISH FULFILLMENT?

Is God really there? Or is our sense of his existence nothing more than a secret hope that our greatest longings might be fulfilled? Is God for real—or is he just an illusion, like a dream in the night? These questions have long been debated in Western civilization. In recent years, however, the idea that God is simply some kind of human wish fulfillment has gained credibility and is increasingly used in anti-Christian propaganda.

The two writers who are especially associated with this development are Ludwig Feuerbach (1804–72) and Sigmund Freud (1856–1939).

1. Feuerbach

Feuerbach's chief work is *The Essence of Christianity* (1841), in which he argues that the idea of God arises understandably, but mistakenly, from human experience.[1] Religion in general is simply the projection of human nature onto an illusory transcendent plane.[2] Human beings mistakenly objectify their own feeling. They interpret their experience as an awareness of God, whereas it is in fact nothing other than an experience of themselves. God is the longing of the human soul personified.

We yearn for a being that will satisfy all our desires and dreams—and, by doing so, invent such a being. For Feuerbach, the doctrine of the resurrection of Christ is nothing more than an echo of the deep human longing for immediate certainty of personal immortality. Scripture tells us that God created human beings in his image; Feuerbach declares that we have made God in our image. "Man is the beginning, the center and the end of religion." God is a human wish fulfilled and sustained by an illusion. Christianity is a fantasy world inhabited by people who have failed to realize that when they think they are talking about God, they are simply disclosing their own innermost hopes and fears. What are we to make of this approach, which is developed in so significant a direction in the writings of Karl Marx?[3]

First, the context in which Feuerbach developed his ideas needs to be examined. Feuerbach was writing in the heyday of the great German liberal theologian Friedrich Schleiermacher (1736–1834). Schleiermacher's theological system rests on an analysis of human experience, supremely the experience of being dependent.[4] Whatever the undoubted merits of this approach might be, it has the effect of making the reality of God dependent on the religious experiences of the pious believer. Theology becomes anthropology as an understanding of God is reduced to an understanding of human nature.

Feuerbach's analysis represents a brilliant critique of this approach, which continues to be influential in Western liberal Christianity. The existence of God is held to be grounded in human experience. But, as Feuerbach emphasizes, human experience might be nothing other than experience of *ourselves*, rather than of God. We might simply be projecting our own experiences and calling the result "God." Feuerbach's approach represents a devastating critique of humanity-centered ideas of Christianity. But what of those more reliable versions of the gospel that insist that faith is a response, not to human experience, but to an encounter with the Word of God? Schleiermacher's approach may be faithful to the biblical insight that Christianity affects our experience. But it seems to have lost sight of an entire dimension of biblical Christianity: that God confronts us in saving judgment through his Word.

The recovery of an emphasis on the Word of God outside us,

rather than on our internal religious experience, has been one of the more welcome developments in the twentieth century. For example, consider the writings of Karl Barth, perhaps the sternest critic of Schleiermacher in the Western theological tradition.[5] For Barth, the reality of God is prior to and independent of any human experience of that reality. Neither Christian faith nor theology is a response solely to some subjective human experience. They arise from an encounter with God through Christ, mediated through Scripture.

Feuerbach, interestingly, has not the slightest interest in the identity or history of Jesus Christ. For him, the character portrayed in the New Testament is simply a fantasy figure who endorses human hopes and aspirations. But traditional Christian theology portrays Christ as challenging our hopes and aspirations, bringing home the reality of sin (an idea which Feuerbach conveniently overlooks) before the joy of redemption can be fully appreciated.

Second, Feuerbach generalizes hopelessly about religions. He assumes (without any cogent argument or careful scholarship) that all the world religions have the same basic core components, which can all be explained on the basis of his atheistic projection theory. All gods, and hence all religions, are simply projections of human desires. But what of the nontheistic religions—those world religions, such as Theravada Buddhism, which explicitly deny the existence of a god?

Third, Feuerbach's hypothesis is nothing more than a hypothesis. It does not rest on a rigorous experimental foundation but represents a series of dogmatic assertions about how we come to believe in God. His theory has not been proven and cannot be stated in a form that can either be verified or falsified. For example, he argues that the wish is father of the thought. Human beings wish for God, and their longing is satisfied by their invention of that God by a process of projection. But do all human beings long for the existence of God? Take, for example, an extermination camp commandant during the Second World War. Would there not be excellent reasons for supposing that he might hope that God does *not* exist, given what might await him on the Day of Judgment? And might not his atheism itself be a wish fulfillment? On the basis of Feuerbach's analysis, it is not only Christianity, but atheism itself, that can be regarded as a projection of human hopes.

But perhaps the most serious objection relates to the logic of Feuerbach's analysis. At the heart of Feuerbach's atheism is his belief that God is only a projected longing. Now it is certainly true that things do not exist because we desire them. But it does not follow from this that, because we desire something, it does not exist. Yet this is the logical structure of Feuerbach's analysis. Eduard von Hartmann pointed this out nearly a century ago when he wrote: "It is perfectly true that nothing exists merely because we wish it, but it is not true that something cannot exist if we wish it. Feuerbach's entire critique of religion and the proof of his atheism, however, rest upon this single argument—a logical fallacy."[6]

Furthermore, the Christian doctrine of creation, studiously ignored by Feuerbach, has an important contribution to make here. If we are indeed created in the image and likeness of God (Gen. 1:26–27), is it surprising that we should wish to relate to him? Might not a human desire for God be grounded in the fact that he brought us into being, with an inbuilt capacity to relate to him?[7]

2. Freud

Feuerbach's basic ideas found new life in the writings of the psychoanalyst Sigmund Freud.[8] In fact, it is probably fair to say that the "projection" or "wish-fulfillment" theory is best known today in its Freudian variant, rather than in Feuerbach's original version. The most powerful statement of Freud's approach may be found in *The Future of an Illusion* (1927), which develops a strongly reductionist approach to religion.[9] For Freud, religious ideas are "illusions, fulfillments of the oldest, strongest, and most urgent wishes of mankind."[10]

To understand Freud at this point, we need to examine his theory of repression. These views were first made public in *The Interpretation of Dreams* (1900), a book that was initially largely ignored by the critics and the general reading public. Freud's thesis here is that dreams are disguised fulfillments of wishes that are repressed by the consciousness (the ego) and are thus displaced into the subconscious. In *The Psychopathology of Everyday Life* (1904), Freud argued that these repressed wishes intrude into everyday life at a number of points. Certain neurotic symptoms, dreams, or even small slips of the tongue or pen—so-called "Freudian slips"—reveal unconscious processes.

The task of the psychotherapist is to expose the repressions that have such a negative effect on life. Psychoanalysis (a term coined by Freud) aims to lay bare the unconscious and untreated traumatic experiences, by assisting the patient to raise them up into consciousness. Through persistent questioning, the analyst can identify repressed traumas that are having a negative effect on the patient and thus enable the patient to deal with them by bringing them into the open.

By the time Freud had finished, however, psychoanalysis was no longer primarily a form of therapy, designed to liberate people from the hidden tyranny of repressed traumas. In the spirit of the Enlightenment, it had virtually become a global hypothesis, capable of explaining just about anything.[11] A substantial doctrinal system evolved, centering on such issues as the Oedipal complex, the theory of instincts, and narcissism. It was hardly surprising that Freud declared that religion could also be explained on the basis of this new system.[12]

The first major statement of Freud's views on the origin of religion—which he increasingly came to refer to as "the psychogenesis of religion"—may be found in *Totem and Taboo* (1913). Developing his earlier observation that religious rites are similar to the obsessive actions of his neurotic patients, Freud declared that religion was basically a distorted form of an obsessional neurosis.

Freud's views on the origin of religion need to be considered in two stages: first, its origins in the development of human history in general, and second, its origins in the case of the individual person. We may begin by dealing with his account of the psychogenesis of religion in the human species in general, as it is presented in *Totem and Taboo*.

Freud believes that the key elements in all religions are the veneration of a father figure (such as God or Jesus Christ), faith in the power of spirits, and a concern for proper rituals. Freud traces the origins of religion to the Oedipal complex. At some point in the history of the human race, Freud argues, the father figure had exclusive sexual rights over females in his tribe. The sons, unhappy at this state of affairs, overthrow the father figure and kill him. Thereafter, they are haunted by this secret and its guilt. Religion has its origins in this prehistorical event, has guilt as its major motivating force, and attempts to expiate this guilt through various rituals.

This explanation will strike most readers as unconvincing. Perhaps for this reason, most atheistic appeals to Freud concentrate on his account of the origins of religion in the individual. In an essay on a childhood memory of Leonardo da Vinci (1910), Freud sets out his explanation of individual religion.

> Psychoanalysis has made us familiar with the intimate connection between the father-complex and belief in God; it has shown us that a personal God is, psychologically, nothing other than an exalted father, and it brings us evidence every day of how young people lose their religious beliefs as soon as their father's authority breaks down. Thus we recognize that the roots of the need for religion are in the parental complex.[13]

The veneration of the father figure has its origins in childhood. When going through the Oedipal phase, Freud argues, the child has to deal with anxiety over the possibility of being punished by the father. The child's response to this threat is to venerate the father, identify with him, and project what he or she knows of the father's will in the form of the superego.

Freud explored the origins of this projection of an ideal father figure in *The Future of an Illusion*. Religion represents the perpetuation of a piece of infantile behavior in adult life. Religion is simply an immature response to the awareness of helplessness by going back to one's childhood experiences of paternal care: "My father will protect me; he is in control." Belief in a personal God is thus little more than an infantile delusion. Religion is wishful thinking.

How are we to respond to this approach to religion? We may begin by noting that Freud has unquestionably been influenced here by writings such as W. Robertson Smith's *Lectures on the Religion of the Semites* (1898), which argued that the essence of religion was not so much a set of beliefs or doctrines but sacred actions, rites, or cults. It must be remembered that Freud was writing at a time when the ethnographical explanation of religion was taken very seriously and seemed to possess impeccable scientific credentials. That situation, however, has radically changed since then, and such simplistic and reductionist theories have generally been abandoned as unworkable. But in Freud's day they seemed to point the way ahead. In effect, Freud aligned himself with a scholarly theory that, though significant in its own time, is no longer taken with any great seriousness.

Second, Freud's theory of the psychogenesis of religion predates his study of religions; it does not arise out of that study. He had, in effect, already decided on his theory before beginning to interact with the literature relating to the field. Ernest Jones, one of Freud's most distinguished and perceptive biographers, draws attention to a letter in which Freud grumbles about having to read his way through a great many tedious tomes relating to religion. It is rather pointless, he comments, since he already instinctively knows the answer to his question about the origin of religion. "I am reading books without being really interested in them, since I already know the results; my instinct tells me that."[14]

Third, Freud's theory concerning the origins of religion in the individual is, like that of Feuerbach, generally incapable of being tested. It is a hypothesis, not a fact. Freud could be said to lend psychoanalytical support to Feuerbach, but not to provide the crucial experimental data that would convert a hypothesis into a fact. On the relatively few points at which Freud's hypothesis is capable of being tested experimentally, it is generally accepted to be wrong. For example, overlap between people's notions of "God" and "father" seems to occur only where the father is the preferred parent, while most people tend to model God on their mother.[15] Like Feuerbach's projection theory, Freud's psychoanalytical atheism must now be regarded as a hypothesis that has not been, and indeed cannot be, proved. The apologist has excellent reasons for challenging naive appeals to the Freudian explanation of faith, which rests upon distinctly shaky foundations.

So be confident on this point. Press home those hard questions. Where do Freud's ideas come from—hard experimental evidence, or his own atheist prejudices? Where is the historical evidence that Christianity owes its origins to a father complex? Can we accept such a deeply sexist approach to religion? And why should Christians be expected to abandon their faith because of Feuerbach's projection theory, a hypothesis that in the end, rests upon a logical error?

B. SUFFERING

Suffering poses many problems for faith. At one level, it poses a knotty riddle for the theologian, who has to explain why its existence does not compromise Christian faith. It may reasonably be argued that to treat suffering as a logical, philosophical or theological difficulty is to miss the real point—the emotional and pastoral issues raised for those who are suffering and for those who care for them. This is a fair point, but its importance must not be overstated. Suffering is a problem for Christian apologetics primarily because it appears to demonstrate the logical incoherence of Christianity. The shape of our discussion of the problem of suffering is thus a response to this agenda, set by critics of the Christian faith.

The problem raised for the apologist by the existence of evil or suffering is usually stated in terms of three propositions:

a. God is omnipotent and omniscient.

b. God is completely good.

c. There is suffering and evil in the world.

It is often suggested that these three statements are inconsistent: The omnipotence and goodness of God are not consistent with the existence of suffering or evil in the world. All three statements cannot be true at one and the same time. The reality of suffering and evil cannot be denied. It is an experiential reality. Therefore, either God is not all-powerful or he is not good. And so the logical coherence of the

Christian faith seems to unravel. A fatal logical flaw has been exposed. Or has it?

Let us begin by considering the history of this question. From the time of Plato onward, the existence of pain, suffering, and evil in the world has been recognized and acknowledged. Christian theology has long learned to live with the reality of pain and evil. It is not as if suffering was a well-kept secret, whose existence has suddenly been sprung on a world that fervently believed that it did not exist. But Christian writers prior to the seventeenth century did not believe that suffering posed any serious threat to Christian belief. Indeed, if I may be allowed a personal reflection, I spent many years working through most of the major works on Christian theology written between the twelfth and sixteenth centuries, and I cannot recall any of them treating the reality of suffering as a serious obstacle to Christian faith.

Why has the situation changed? The answer lies in a dramatic development that took place during the seventeenth century and that may be argued to lie at the root of modern atheism.[16] A number of writers on Christian apologetics, such as Leonard Lessius and Marin Mersenne, argued that the best defense of Christianity was to be provided by philosophy. Instead of concentrating on the significance of Jesus Christ for the question of whether God existed and what he was like, an appeal should be made directly and exclusively to reason. Instead of an appeal to the Christian experience of the Holy Spirit, an appeal was to be made to nature. Reason and nature were thus the criteria for the credibility of Christianity. The end result was inevitable. "Christianity entered into the defense of the existence of the Christian God without appeal to anything Christian."[17]

Under the influence of Descartes, this approach to apologetics would prove to have devastating results. The enormous emphasis that came to be placed on the perfection of God by Descartes was compromised by the undeniable fact of the existence of evil and suffering. How could a perfect being allow such imperfection to exist? Yet the "god" of Descartes is not the God of Christianity—it is simply a philosophical idea. "The god of the philosophers" is basically little more than a perfect, ideal, and abstract being, constructed out of the distilled elements of human benevolence. The characteristics of this god are primarily its omnipotence, omniscience, and goodness. Its credibility—but *not* that of the "God and Father of our Lord Jesus Christ" (1 Peter 1:3)—is instantly compromised by suffering.

As Alasdair MacIntyre remarks, "the God in whom the nineteenth and twentieth centuries came to disbelieve had been invented only in the seventeenth century."[18] The god of philosophical theology is a human invention, a product of our reason; the God to whom Christian faith and theology respond is a living and loving being, who makes himself known to us through Christ, Scripture, and personal experience—including, as we shall see, suffering.

Why this digression into history? Because it demonstrates that suffering has only recently been seen as "a final and sufficient ground for skepticism and for the abandonment of Christianity," whereas in the past it was viewed as no more than a difficulty, "an incentive to inquiry but not a ground for disbelief."[19] It is only since the Enlightenment, with its emphasis on universal and rational concepts of divinity and justification of beliefs, that the problem of suffering has come to be seen as grounds for disbelief. But Enlightenment rationalism is in retreat.[20] Perhaps we shall see a return to the older approach to suffering in its wake.

Second, let us consider the logic of the problem posed by suffering. Let us return to the three propositions noted earlier.

    a. God is omnipotent and omniscient.

    b. God is completely good.

    c. There is suffering and evil in the world.

At least one further premise must be added to this list if a logical inconsistency is to result. As things stand, there is no inconsistency. There would, however, be a contradiction if either of the following were to be added to the list:[21]

    d. A good and omnipotent God could eliminate suffering entirely.

    e. There could not be morally sufficient reasons for God permitting suffering.

If either of these propositions could be shown to be correct, a major and potentially fatal flaw in the Christian conception of God would have been exposed. But they have not. And the apologist, having been asked some hard questions by the critics of Christianity, has a right to ask some in reply. How do the critics know that there cannot be morally sufficient reasons for God permitting suffering? Are they not putting themselves in the position so devastatingly criticized by David Hume—that of declaring that a better world than that which we know is possible?[22]

We may explore the issue of suffering further by considering some arguments developed by C. S. Lewis in his celebrated book *The Problem of Pain.* Lewis begins by stating the problem as follows:

    "If God were good, he would wish to make his creatures perfectly happy, and if God were almighty he would be able to do what he wished. But the creatures are not happy. Therefore God lacks either the goodness, or power, or both." This is the problem of pain in its simplest form.[23]

But Lewis is not content to leave the critic of Christianity holding the moral high ground. He demands that this critic clarify what is meant by those terms "omnipotence" and "goodness." Too often, Lewis argues, such critics bandy these terms about without really thinking them through.

What does it mean to say that God is omnipotent? Lewis argues, with considerable skill, that it does not mean that God can do anything he likes. Once God has opted to do certain things, or to behave in a certain manner, then other possibilities are excluded.

> If you choose to say "God can give a creature free-will and at the same time withhold free-will from it," you have not succeeded in saying *anything* about God: meaningless combinations of words do not suddenly acquire a meaning because we prefix to them the two other words: "God can." It remains true that all *things* are possible with God: the intrinsic impossibilities are not things but nonentities. It is no more possible for God than for the weakest of his creatures to carry out both of two mutually exclusive alternatives, not because his power meets an obstacle, but because nonsense remains nonsense, even when we talk it about God.[24]

Lewis then argues that suffering cannot be regarded as arising from a lack of divine omnipotence. Far from it. If God creates a material universe and gives creatures freedom of action, suffering follows on as a matter of course. Having exercised his omnipotence in creating the universe and endowing his creatures with freedom, he cannot block the outcome of that free universe—suffering. "Try to exclude the possibility of suffering which the order of nature and the existence of free-wills involve, and you will find that you have excluded life itself."[25]

Lewis then moves on to consider the implications of that deceptively simple word *goodness*. Too often, Lewis insists, the meaning of that word is assumed to be self-evident, when in fact it requires considerable thought. For Lewis, goodness is the natural outcome and expression of the love of God. Is suffering inconsistent with a loving God? Lewis insists that we pay attention to the term *love* and avoid reading into it trivial and sentimental human parodies of the divine reality. We must learn to discover and appreciate divine love as it really is, instead of confusing or identifying it with our own ideas on the matter. God tells us what his love is like. There is no need for us to guess about it. The love of God, Lewis thus argues, is not a senile benevolence that drowsily wishes you to be happy in your own way, not the cold philanthropy of a conscientious magistrate, nor the care of a host who feels himself responsible for the comfort of his guest, but the consuming fire itself, the love that made the worlds, persistent as the artist's love for his work and despotic as a man's love for a dog, provident and venerable as a father's love for a child, jealous, inexorable, exacting as love between the sexes.[26]

The love of God, then, is not some happy-go-lucky outlook on life that makes hedonism its goal. It is a divine love that proceeds from God and leads back to God, that embraces suffering as a consequence of the greater gifts of life and freedom. Real life implies suffering. Were God to take suffering away from us, he would take away that precious gift of life itself. "The problem of reconciling human suffering with the existence of a God who loves is insoluble only so long as we attach a trivial meaning to the word 'love,' and look on things as if man was the centre of them."[27]

So what purpose might suffering serve? There are several echoes of Luther's ideas of the "strange work of God (*opus alienum Dei*)"—an idea we explored earlier[28]—in Lewis's discussion of the mysterious yet creative role of suffering within the providence of God. Suffering brings home to us the distressing fact of our mortality, too easily ignored. It reminds us of our frailty and hints of the coming of death. "It removes the veil; it plants the flag of truth within the fortress of a rebel soul."[29] In short, it creates a climate in which our thoughts are gently directed toward God, whom we might otherwise ignore. "God whispers to us in our pleasure, speaks to us in our conscience, but shouts to us in our pains; it is his megaphone to rouse a deaf world."[30] Painful though Lewis's point may be, there is enough truth in it to make us take it seriously. All must die, and any worldview that cannot cope with death is fatally deficient. Suffering gently prods our consciousness and forces us to contemplate the unpalatable but real fact of our future death and how our outlook on life relates to this sobering thought. It can sow the seeds of doubt about existing outlooks and lay the foundation for a new way of thinking, living, and hoping.

But the apologist cannot be content to remain on the defensive forever. At some point, the full relevance of the crucifixion and resurrection of Christ must be brought home to the more philosophically minded critics of Christianity.[31] To discuss suffering without reference to the suffering of Christ is a theological and spiritual absurdity. God suffered in Christ. He *knows* what it is like to experience pain. He has traveled down the road of pain, abandonment, suffering, and death—a road they called Calvary. God is not like some alleged hero with feet of clay, who demands that others suffer while he himself remains aloof from the world of pain. He has passed through the shadow of suffering himself. The God in whom Christians believe and hope is a God who himself suffered and who, by having done so, transfigures the sufferings of his people.

Some say that nothing could ever be adequate recompense for suffering in this world. But how do they know? Have they spoken to anyone who has suffered and subsequently been raised to glory? Have they been through this experience themselves? One of the greatest tragedies of much writing about human suffering this century has been its crude use of rhetoric. "Nothing can ever compensate for suffering!" rolls off the tongue with the greatest of ease. It has a certain oratorical force, especially when delivered by a skilled speaker. It discourages argument. But again, how do those who make that claim know that? Paul believed passionately that the sufferings of the present life—and he endured many—would be outweighed by the glory that is to come (Rom. 8:18). How do they know that he is wrong and that they are right?

The situation would be rather different if we could listen to someone who suffers a pitiful and painful death and then returns to us from the dead. He would speak with authority and insight on this matter. Or if God himself were to declare that the memory of suffering and pain were to be wiped out. And the wonder of the gospel is that Christ has died and risen again. God has indeed spoken on such matters.

It is here that the resurrection of Christ becomes of central importance. The Resurrection allows the suffering of Christ to be seen in the perspective of eternity. Suffering is not pointless but leads to glory. Those who share in the sufferings of Christ may, through the resurrection of Christ, know what awaits them at the end of history. It is for this reason that Paul is able to declare with such confidence that "our present sufferings are not worth comparing with the glory that will be revealed in us" (Rom. 8:18). This is no groundless hope, no arbitrary aspiration. It is a hardheaded realism, grounded in the reality of the suffering and resurrection of Christ and in the knowledge that faith binds believers to Christ and guarantees that we shall share in his heritage.

Christianity has been unequivocal on this point, and its voice must be heard. The sufferings of this earth are for real. They are painful. God is deeply pained by our suffering, just as we are shocked, grieved, and mystified by the suffering of our family and friends. But that is only half of the story. The other half must be told. It is natural that our attention should be fixed on what we experience and feel here and now. But faith demands that we raise our sights and look ahead to what lies ahead. We may suffer as we journey—but where are we going? What lies ahead?

The word *heaven* seems inadequate to describe the final goal of faith. Perhaps we should speak more expansively of the hope of eternal life, of the renewing of our frail and mortal bodies in the likeness of Christ's glorious resurrection body, and of standing, redeemed, in the presence of God. But however we choose to describe it, the promise and hope of our transformation and renewal, and of the glorious transfiguration of suffering, are an integral part of the Christian faith. This glorious thread is woven so deeply into the fabric of our faith that it cannot possibly be removed.

The language of "prizes" and "rewards" is helpful in many ways. It reminds us of the need to complete the race in order that we may receive the athlete's crown as a prize (2 Tim. 4:7–8). It reminds us of the need for training and discipline in the Christian life in order that we may have the stamina we need to persevere. But this way of thinking about the relation between suffering and heaven can also be misleading. It suggests that heaven is thrown in as some kind of consolation in order to keep us going here below. This danger is avoided if we pay more attention to the intimacy of the connection between suffering and glory.

When a seed is planted in the ground, it begins to grow and will eventually bear fruit. Can we say that its bearing fruit is a reward for its growth? No. We would say that there is an organic and natural connection between one and the other. One flows naturally into the other. It is not a question of declaring, in some arbitrary way, that a seed that grows will be rewarded with fruit, or that the prize for growth is fruit. Rather, germination, growth, and the bearing of fruit are all part of the same overall process. They are all stages in the natural cycle of growth and development. One follows naturally from the other.

The New Testament is unequivocal. Suffering and glorification are part of, but represent different stages in, the same process of growth in the Christian life. We are adopted into the family of God, we suffer, and we are glorified (Rom. 8:14–18). This is not an accidental relationship. They are all intimately connected within the overall pattern of Christian growth and progress toward the ultimate goal of the Christian life—being finally united with God and remaining with him forever.

We are thus presented with a glorious vision of a new realm of existence. It is a realm in which suffering has been defeated. It is a realm pervaded by the refreshing presence of God, from which the presence and power of sin have finally been excluded. It lies ahead, and though we have yet to enter into it, we can catch a hint of its fragrance and hear its music in the distance. It is this hope that keeps us going in this life of sadness, which must end in death.

But is it for real? Is this hope anything more than wishful thinking, a pitiful aspiration on the part of human beings who long for a better world than that which they now know and inhabit? We are all familiar with the tedious taunt of believing in "pie in the sky when you die." The implication would seem to be that Christians are so unrealistic about life that they need such fictional morsels to keep them going, where others can cope with the grim realities of life unaided.

Karl Marx regarded this outlook on life as little more than nauseating sentimentality.[32] The promise of the final removal of suffering and pain in the kingdom of God distracted us from working for their elimination here and now. To use Marx's famous phrase, Christianity is "an opiate for the masses," a kind of anesthetic or narcotic that dulls our senses and prevents us from changing the world for the better.

Marx has a point. So great is the attractiveness of the Christian hope that it is natural to become fascinated by it and to want to focus our thoughts on it. It is all too easy to become so heavenly minded as to be of no earthly use. If Marx's criticism serves any useful purpose, it is to remind us that we have a Christian duty to work for the transformation of the world as we know it, removing unnecessary causes of suffering. The vision that is held before us is that of trying to bring the peace of heaven to the turmoil of the earth. The Christian hope ought to be a stimulus rather than a sedative. It should spur us to action within the world, rather than encourage us to neglect it.

But when all is said and done, Marx's comment merely reinforces the power and importance of the Christian hope. It *does* enable us to cope with suffering in the present life. Just as a soldier fights on toward the end of a long war, sustained by the knowledge that peace will one day come and he will be reunited with his family and friends, so the Christian continues his pilgrimage, sustained by the knowledge of the joys that await him. Marx is a reluctant, yet eloquent, witness to the power of the Christian hope to enable us to cope with the dark side of life.

Furthermore, Marx evades the vital question concerning the Christian hope: Is it true? If it is, Christians can hardly be criticized for believing in it. Either it is true, or it is not. Which is it? Let us be absolutely clear on this. If the Christian hope of heaven is an illusion, based on lies, then it must be abandoned as misleading and deceitful. But if it is true, it must be embraced and allowed to transfigure our entire understanding of the place of suffering in life.

Just as suffering is real, so are the promises of God and the hope of eternal life. This is no spiritual anesthetic, designed merely to enable us to cope with life's sorrows while they last. The death and resurrection of Christ, linked with the giving of the Holy Spirit, are pledges, sureties, and guarantees that what has been promised will one day be brought to glorious realization. For the moment we struggle and suffer in sadness mingled with bewilderment. But one day all that will be changed for the people of God:

> God himself will be with them; he will wipe away every tear from their eyes, and death shall be no more, neither shall there be mourning nor crying nor pain any more, for the former things have passed away (Rev. 21:3–4 RSV).

In that hope, we go forward into life in faith. We may not know exactly where that faith will lead us. But we *do* know that, wherever we go, the God of all compassion goes ahead of us and journeys with us, consoling and reassuring us, until that day when we shall see him face to face, and know him just as he knows us.

C. RELIGIOUS PLURALISM

One of the most perceptive analysts of the consequences of pluralism for the Christian churches is Lesslie Newbigin, who is able to draw on his substantial firsthand experience of Christian life in India as he reflects on what pluralism means—and does not mean!—for contemporary Christianity. In his book *The Gospel in a Pluralist Society,* Newbigin remarks:

> It has become a commonplace to say that we live in a pluralist society—not merely a society which is in fact plural in the variety of cultures, religions and lifestyles which it embraces, but pluralist in the sense that this plurality is celebrated as things to be approved and cherished.[33]

Newbigin here makes a distinction between pluralism as a fact of life and pluralism as an ideology—that is, the belief that pluralism is to be encouraged and desired, and that normative claims to truth are to be censured as imperialist and divisive. With the former, there can be no arguing. The Christian proclamation has always taken place in a pluralist world, in competition with rival religious and intellectual convictions.

Ancient Israel was acutely aware that its faith was not shared by its neighbors. The existence of other religions was simply a fact of life for the Israelites. It caused them no great difficulties, in that they believed that theirs happened to be right, whereas others were wrong. The same pattern emerges in the New Testament. From the first days of its existence, Christianity has recognized the existence of other religions and the challenge they posed. Initially, Christianity faced a challenge from Judaism, which was rapidly replaced by the challenge of Roman civil religion, various forms of Greek religion of late antiquity, gnosticism, and various pagan mystery cults.

Christianity was born amid religious pluralism; that pluralism has now reemerged, both as a social reality and a theological issue, in the West. In recent decades, widespread immigration from the Indian subcontinent to the United Kingdom, from former French colonies in Africa to France, and from the nations of the Asian Pacific Rim to Australia and the eastern seaboard of the United States and Canada, has brought the issue home to Western society, which had hitherto been shielded from it. The issues raised by the existence of other religions are considerable and would merit books in themselves. This section will identify and discuss only some of the more significant ones.

The rise of religious pluralism can directly be related to the collapse of the Enlightenment idea of universal knowledge. Often there is a crude attempt to divert attention from the collapse of the Enlightenment vision by implying that religious pluralism represents a new and unanswerable challenge to Christianity itself. The Princeton philosopher Diogenes Allen rightly dismisses this as a spurious claim:

> Many have been driven to relativism by the collapse of the Enlightenment's confidence in the power of reason to provide foundations for our truth-claims and to achieve finality in our search for truth in the various disciplines. Much of the distress concerning pluralism and relativism which is voiced today springs from a crisis in the secular mentality of modern western culture, not from a crisis in Christianity itself.[34]

Yet these relativistic preconceptions have become deeply ingrained in secular society, often with the assumption that they are to the detriment of Christian faith. For the apologist, the central issue is, Given that there are so many religions in the marketplace, how can Christianity claim to be true?

Let us note a difficulty here. The word *religion* needs further examination. In his classic but highly problematic work, *The Golden*

Bough (1890), Sir James Frazer made the fundamental point that "there is probably no subject in the world about which opinions differ so much as the nature of religion, and to frame a definition of it which would satisfy everyone must obviously be impossible." Yet largely because of the homogenizing tendencies of modern liberalism, there has recently been a determined effort to reduce all religions to the same basic phenomenon.

But who makes the rules that determine what is religion? The rules of this game determine the outcome—so who decides on them? Underlying much recent Western liberal discussion of "the religions" is a naive assumption that "religion" is a genus, an agreed-upon category. In fact, it is nothing of the sort. John Milbank, in an important study, makes the point that the "assumption about a religious genus" is central to

> . . . the more recent mode of encounter as dialogue, but it would be a mistake to imagine that it arose simultaneously among all the participants as the recognition of an evident truth. On the contrary, it is clear that the other religions were taken by Christian thinkers to be species of the genus "religion," because these thinkers systematically subsumed alien cultural phenomena under categories which comprise western notions of what constitutes religious thought and practice. These false categorizations have often been accepted by western-educated representatives of the other religions themselves, who are unable to resist the politically imbued rhetorical force of western discourse.[35]

We must therefore be suspicious of the naive assumption that "religion" is a well-defined category that can be surgically distinguished from "culture" as a whole.

It is important to see that a cultural issue is often brought into this debate: It is implied that to defend Christianity is to belittle non-Christian religions, which is unacceptable in a multicultural society. Especially to those of liberal political convictions, the multicultural agenda demands that religions, in order to avoid the dangers of imperialism and triumphalism, should not be permitted to make truth-claims. Indeed, there seems to be a widespread perception that the rejection of religious pluralism entails intolerance or unacceptable claims to exclusivity. In effect, the liberal political agenda dictates that all religions should be treated on an equal footing. It is but a small step from this *political* judgment to the *theological* declaration that all religions are the same. But is there any reason for progressing from the entirely laudable and acceptable demand that we should respect religions other than our own to the more radical demand that we regard them all as equally valid manifestations of some eternal or "spiritual" dimension to life?

In its most extreme form, this view results in the claim that all religions lead to God. But this cannot be taken seriously when some world religions are avowedly nontheistic. A religion can hardly lead to God if it explicitly denies the existence of a god or any gods. We therefore need to restate the question in terms of "ultimate reality" or "truth." Thus refined, this position might be stated as follows. Religion is often determined by the circumstances of one's birth. An Indian is likely to be a Hindu; an Arab is likely to be a Muslim. Therefore, it is argued, all religions must be equal paths to the truth.

This makes truth a function of birth. If I were to be born into Nazi Germany, I would likely be a Nazi—and this makes Nazism *true?* If I had been born in ancient Rome, I probably would have shared its polytheism; if I had been born in modern Arabia, I would be a monotheist. So are both polytheism and monotheism true? No other intellectual discipline would accept such a superficial approach to truth. Why accept it here? It seems to rest on an entirely laudable wish to allow that everyone is right, which ends up destroying the notion of truth itself. Consider the two propositions:

a. Different people have different religious views.

b. Therefore all religious views are equally valid.

Is proposition *b* in any way implied by proposition *a?* For the form of liberalism committed to this approach, mere existence of a religious idea appears to be a guarantor of its truth! Yet no one seems prepared to fight for the truth content of defunct religions, such as classical polytheism—perhaps because there is no one alive who is committed to them, whose views need to be respected in a multicultural situation.

The fatal weakness of this approach usually leads to a modified version, which can be stated thus: "Any view that is held with sincerity may be regarded as true." I might thus be a Nazi, a Satanist, or a passionate believer in the flatness of the earth. My sincerity is a guarantee of the truth. It would follow that if someone sincerely believes that modern Europe would be a better place if six million Jews were to be placed in gas chambers, the sincerity of those convictions allow that view to be accepted as true. British philosopher of religion John Hick summarizes the absurdity of this view: "To say that whatever is sincerely believed and practised is, by definition true, would be the end of all critical discrimination, both intellectual and moral."[36]

It is therefore more than a little ironic that the most significant advocate of the pluralist "truth-in-all-religions" approach is this same

John Hick, who argues that the same basic infinite divine reality lies at the experiential roots of all religions—but that this reality is experienced and expressed in different ways in the various religions. "Their differing experiences of that reality, interacting over the centuries with the different thought-forms of different cultures, have led to an increasing differentiation and contrasting elaboration."[37] (A similar outlook is associated with English Deism in the late seventeenth century, which held that there was originally one universal rational religion, which gradually became corrupted and evolved into the various religions of the world. There is no historical evidence for this dogmatic assumption.)

This approach thus suggests that the various religions may be understood to complement one another. In other words, truth does not lie in an "either-or" but in a "both-and" approach: All differences within religions are "differences in perception, not reality." This naturally leads to the idea that dialogue between religions can lead to an enhancement of truth, in that the limited perspective of one religion can be complemented by the differing perspectives of another. Since all religions are held to relate to the same reality, "dialogue" thus constitutes a privileged mode of access to truth.

On the basis of Hick's homogenizing approach, no genuinely conflicting truth-claims can occur. They are ruled out of order on *a priori* grounds. By definition, religions can only complement, not contradict, each other. In practice, Hick appears to contradict himself here, frequently declaring that "exclusive" approaches to religions are *wrong*. For example, he styles the traditional "salvation through Christ alone" statements of the 1960 Congress on World Mission as "ridiculous"—where, by his own criteria, the most stinging criticism that could be directed at them is that they represent a "difference in perception." The inherent absurdity of Hick's refusal to take an evaluative position in relation to other religions is compromised by his eagerness to adopt such a position in relation to versions of Christianity that threaten his outlook, both on account of their numerical strength and their noninclusive theologies.

When all is said and done, and when all differences in expression arising from cultural and intellectual development are taken into account, Hick must be challenged forcefully concerning his crudely homogenizing approach to the world religions. It is absurd to say that a religion that says that there *is* a God complements a religion that declares, with equal vigor, that there is *not* a God (and both types of religion exist).[38] If the religious believer actually believes *something*, then disagreement is inevitable—and proper. As the distinguished

American philosopher Richard Rorty remarked, nobody "except the occasional cooperative freshman" really believes that "two incompatible opinions on an important topic are equally good."[39] Hick has predetermined that there shall not be differences among the religions, and there the matter rests—for him. Where contradiction arises, we are confronted with cases of special pleading, or death by a thousand qualifications, as Hick argues, by introducing increasingly implausible subsidiary hypotheses that so qualify his original views as to render them virtually devoid of meaning. Having dogmatically determined that all religions possess the same core structure, Hick ruthlessly forces them into the same mold—a mold that owes nothing to the outlooks of the world's religions and everything to the liberal cultural agenda that so obviously inspires Hick's theories.

Hick's defense of the homogeneity of all religions often seems to rest on a refusal to allow that there are decisive differences between religions, even where these obviously exist. For instance, the Hindu practice of *bhakti* cannot be described as (and thus assimilated to) "worship" when it so clearly relates to a network of ideas centering on the systematic appeasement of potentially vengeful deities or seeking favors from them.

Furthermore, the notion of "truth through dialogue" has merit if, and only if, the dialogue is between parties who are describing the same thing. Dialogue, from its Socratic form onward, rests on the assumption that participants share a common subject matter and that certain truths can be agreed concerning this subject. Through the process of dialogue, each participant comes to share an increasingly sympathetic understanding of the viewpoint of others—and by doing so, comes to a deeper understanding of the central subject area itself. But it has never been shown that the different world religions share a common subject matter. It has often been asserted that they do, but there is a world of difference between the assertions of those with vested liberal cultural precommitments and the disinterested comparison of religions.

One of the most serious difficulties that arises here relates to the fact that, on the basis of Hick's model, it is not individual religions that have access to truth; it is the Western liberal pluralist, who insists that each religion must be seen in the context of others before it can be evaluated. As many have pointed out, this means that the Western liberal doctrine of religious pluralism is defined as the only valid standpoint for evaluating individual religions. Hick has set at the center of his system of religions a vague and undefined idea of "the Eternal One," which seems to be little more than a vague liberal idea of divinity, carefully defined (or, more accurately, deliberately *not* defined, to avoid the damage that precision entails) to include at least something from all of the major world religions Hick feels is worth including.

To develop this important point, let us consider a well-worn analogy concerning the relationship between the religions. Lesslie Newbigin describes it and makes a vitally important observation:

> In the famous story of the blind men and the elephant . . . the real point of the story is constantly overlooked. The story is told from the point of view of the king and his courtiers, who are not blind but can see that the blind men are unable to grasp the full reality of the elephant and are only able to get hold of part of it. The story is constantly told in order to neutralize the affirmations of the great religions, to suggest that they learn humility and recognize that none of them can have more than one aspect of the truth. But, of course, the real point of the story is exactly the opposite. If the king were also blind, there would be no story. The story is told by the king, and it is the immensely arrogant claim of one who sees the full truth, which all the world's religions are only groping after. It embodies the claim to know the full reality that relativizes all the claims of the religions.[40]

Newbigin brings out with clarity the arrogance of the liberal claim to be able to see all the religions from the standpoint of one who sees the full truth. The liberal pluralist is the king; the unfortunate evangelical is the blindfolded beggar. Or so the pluralist would have us believe. Perhaps a more responsible—and considerably less arrogant—approach would be to suggest that we are all, pluralists included, blind beggars, to whom God graciously makes himself known.

But what framework is to be used for understanding the religions? Elephants have limited potential in this respect. John Hick and Wilfrid Cantwell Smith object to interpreting both the place and the contents of other religious traditions from a Christian point of view. But they seem to miss the point that they have to be interpreted from some interpretative standpoint—and if they have excluded, as a matter of principle, a specifically Christian viewpoint, they are obliged to adopt one which, by definition, is non-Christian. Furthermore, Hick appears to labor under the misunderstanding that where Christian frameworks are biased, those of liberalism are neutral and disinterested. Yet one of the more significant developments in the recent sociology of knowledge has been the realization that there is no neutral point from which a religion or culture may be evaluated; all vantage points imply a valuation. Hick and Cantwell Smith naively assume that their liberal pluralist approach is "detached" or "objective," whereas it is actually nothing of the sort.

To give his case more academic credibility, Hick argues that there is a common core structure to all religions. The various religions represent equally "valid" and "real" experiences and apprehensions of the one divine reality. (Note that the fact that there is only one divine reality is assumed to require no proof—but polytheism cannot be dismissed as easily as this.) On the basis of this assumption he declares that all religions "are fundamentally alike in exhibiting a soteriological structure. That is to say, they are all concerned with salvation/ liberation/enlightenment/fulfillment."[41] It may reasonably be observed, however, that these concepts of salvation are conceived in such radically different ways that only someone who was doggedly determined, as a matter of principle, to treat them as aspects of the same greater whole would have sufficient intellectual flexibility to do so. Do Christianity and Satanism really have the same understandings of salvation? Hick would probably reply that Satanism does not count as a religion, thus neatly illustrating that his theory works for those religions he has preselected on the basis of their ability to fit his pluralist mold. A more neutral observer, relieved of the necessity of insisting that all religions of the world are basically the same, might reasonably suggest that these religions do not merely offer different ways of achieving salvation—they offer different understandings of salvation altogether. The Rastafarian vision of a paradise in which blacks are served by whites; the old Norse concept of Valhalla; the Buddhist vision of *nirvana;* the Christian hope of resurrection to eternal life—all are so obviously different. How can all the routes to salvation be equally "valid" (a favorite liberal *Modewort*) when the goals to be reached in such different ways are so obviously unrelated?

The idea that all religions are the same, or that they all lead to the same God, is thus little more than an unsubstantiated assertion that requires a refusal to acknowledge that there are genuine and significant differences among the religions. It is a kind of fundamentalism in its own right. Only in Western liberal circles would such an idea be taken seriously. (It is not accepted by any Muslim writer I have spoken to.) But what would the Christian apologist wish to say in response about the place of Christianity among the religions?

Michael Green, drawing on his considerable experience as an evangelist and the resources of much recent writing on the relation between Christianity and other religions, perhaps says all that needs to be said:

No faith would enjoy wide currency if it did not contain much that was true. Other faiths therefore constitute a preparation for the gospel, and Christ comes not so much to destroy as to fulfill. The convert will not feel that he has lost his background, but that he has discovered that to which, at its best, it pointed. That is certainly the attitude I have found among friends converted to Christ from Hinduism, Islam and Buddhism. They are profoundly grateful for what they have learned in those cultures, but are thrilled beyond words to have discovered a God who has stooped to their condition in coming as the man of Nazareth, and who has rescued them from guilt and alienation by his cross and resurrection.[42]

The Christian attitude to other religions rests firmly on the doctrines of creation and redemption. Because God created the world, we expect to find traces of him throughout his creation; because God redeemed the world through Christ, we expect to look to Christ for the salvation that the Christian gospel promises. The Lausanne Covenant (1974) states this foundational belief in the uniqueness of Christ by rejecting

as derogatory to Christ and the Gospel every kind of syncretism and dialogue which implies that Christ speaks equally through all religions and theologies. Jesus Christ, being himself the only God-man, who gave himself as the only ransom for sinners, is the only mediator between God and man. There is no other name by which we must be saved.

John Calvin made a forceful distinction between the *knowledge of God the creator* (a universal knowledge, available to all peoples, including Christians), and *knowledge of God the redeemer* (a specifically Christian knowledge of God). The Lausanne Covenant states this: "We recognize that all men have some knowledge of God through his general revelation in nature. But we deny that this can save."

The question therefore becomes: How can we be saved? Who is our savior? And it is here that the doctrine of the divinity of Christ, grounded in his resurrection, becomes of central importance. No other person has ever risen from the dead and conquered death. In no other person does God become incarnate. So important are these issues that we shall consider them and their implications in the two sections that follow.

Yet a point must be noted before proceeding. The pluralist agenda has certain important theological and apologetic consequences. It is a simple matter of fact that traditional Christian theology does not lend itself particularly well to the homogenizing agenda of religious pluralists. The suggestion that all religions are more or less talking about vaguely the same thing finds itself in difficulty when it comes to certain essentially Christian ideas—most notably, the doctrines of the Incarnation and the Trinity. These distinctive doctrines are embarrassing to those who wish to debunk what they term the "myth of Christian uniqueness." We are invited, on the weak and lazy grounds of pragmatism, to abandon those doctrines in order that the pluralist agenda might be advanced.

In response to this pressure, two major Christological and theological developments may be noted. First, doctrines such as the Incarnation, which imply a high profile of identification between Jesus Christ and God, are discarded in favor of various degree Christologies, which are more amenable to the reductionist program of liberalism. Second, the idea that God is in any sense disclosed or defined Christologically is set aside because of its theologically momentous implications for the identity and significance of Jesus Christ—which liberal pluralism finds an embarrassment. Let us consider these two points in more detail.

First, the idea of the Incarnation is rejected, often dismissively, as a myth. Thus John Hick and his collaborators reject the Incarnation on various logical and common-sense counts—yet they fail to deal with the question of why Christians should have developed this doctrine in the first place. There is an underlying agenda to this dismissal of the Incarnation, and a central part of that agenda is the elimination of the sheer *distinctiveness* of Christianity. A sharp distinction is thus drawn between the historical person of Jesus Christ and the principles he is alleged to represent. Paul Knitter is but one of a small galaxy of pluralist writers concerned to drive a wedge between the "Jesus-event" (unique to Christianity) and the "Christ-principle" (accessible to all religious traditions and expressed in their own distinctive but equally valid ways).

It is significant that the pluralist agenda forces its advocates to adopt heretical views of Christ in order to meet its needs. In an effort to fit Jesus into the mold of the "great religious teachers of humanity" category, the Ebionite heresy has been revived and made politically correct. Jesus is one of the religious options available; he is one of the great human teachers of religion.

Second, the idea that God is in some manner made known through Christ has been dismissed. Captivated by the image of a "Copernican Revolution" (probably one of the most overworked and misleading phrases in recent writings in this field), pluralists demand that Christians move away from a discussion of Christ to a discussion of God—yet they fail to recognize that the "God of the Christians" (Tertullian) might be rather different from other divinities and that the doctrine of the Trinity spells out the nature of that distinction. The loose and vague talk about "God" or "Reality" found in much pluralist writing is not a result of theological sloppiness or confusion. It is a considered response to the recognition that for Christians to talk about the Trinity is to speak about a specific God (not just "deity" in general), who has chosen to make himself known in and through Jesus Christ. It is a deliberate rejection of authentically and distinctively Christian insights into God, in order to suggest that Christianity, to rework a phrase of John Toland, is simply the republication of the religion of nature.

Yet human religious history shows that natural human ideas of the number, nature, and character of the gods are notoriously vague and muddled. The Christian emphasis is not on the need to worship gods in general (Israel's strictures against Canaanite religion being especially important here), but on the need to worship a God who has chosen to make himself known. The doctrine of the Trinity defines and defends the distinctiveness—no, more than that: the *uniqueness*—of the "God of the Christians." The New Testament gives a further twist to this development through its language about "the God and Father of our Lord Jesus Christ," locating the identity of God in the actions and passion of Jesus Christ. To put it bluntly: God is Christologically disclosed.

This point is important given the obvious confusion within the pages of *The Myth of Christian Uniqueness* concerning the nature and identity of the god(s) or goddess(es) of the pluralists. Pluralism, it seems to be, possesses a certain tendency toward self-destruction in that there is, if I can put it like this, "a plurality of pluralisms." For example, a vigorously polemical defense of "pluralism" (a word used frequently throughout its pages) may be found in *The Myth of Christian Uniqueness*. According to the authors, Christianity has to be seen in a "pluralistic context as one of the great world faiths, one of the streams of religious life through which human beings can be savingly related to that ultimate Reality Christians know as the heavenly Father." Yet having agreed that Christianity does not provide absolute or superior knowledge of God, the contributors proceed to display such divergence over the nature of God that it becomes far from clear that they are talking about the same thing.

But there is a more important point here. Pluralism is fatally vulnerable to the charge that it reaches an accommodation between Christianity and other religious traditions by willfully discarding every distinctive Christian doctrine traditionally regarded as identity-giving and identity-preserving (to say nothing of the reductionist liberties taken with the other religious traditions). The "Christianity" that is declared to be homogeneous with all other "higher religions" would not be recognizable as such to most of its adherents. It would be a theologically, Christologically, and soteriologically reduced version of the real thing.

It is thus not Christianity that is being related to other world faiths. It is little more than a parody and caricature of this living faith, grounded in the presuppositions and agendas of Western liberalism rather than in the self-revelation of God. And it is related to theologically reduced and homogenized versions of other living religions. Dialogue turns out to involve the sacrifice of integrity. The identity of Christianity is inextricably linked with the uniqueness of Christ, which is in turn grounded in the Resurrection and Incarnation. We may now turn to consider these.

D. THE RESURRECTION

If Jesus Christ was raised from the dead, never to die again, he would instantly stand out as being distinct from every other person in history. There would be something dramatically different about him. He would be unique. The only question remaining would relate to the nature of his uniqueness—a question that Christian theology has answered in the doctrine of the Incarnation. Yet the apologist will be aware that the resurrection of Christ proves a major stumbling block to many people.[43] The reasons for this center on three issues: the improbability of the event, the unreliability of the New Testament witnesses to the event, and its irrelevance to life.

The New Testament is permeated by the resurrection of Jesus of Nazareth. The consequences of this event, both for the personal experience of the first Christians and for their understanding of the identity and significance of Jesus himself, dominate the horizons of the New Testament writers. The astonishing developments in the perceived status and identity of Jesus took place on the basis of their firm belief that the one who was crucified had been raised by God from the dead. The cross was interpreted from the standpoint of the Resurrection, and Jesus' teaching was accorded reverence because of who the Resurrection disclosed him to be. Jesus was worshiped and adored as the living Lord who would come again—and not merely revered as a dead super-rabbi. The tendency to "think of Jesus Christ as of God" (2 Clement 1:1) is already evident in the New Testament. It cannot be emphasized too strongly that the most important developments in the Christian understanding of the identity and significance of Jesus Christ took place, not during the patristic period as a result of the questionable influence of Greek metaphysics, but within twenty years of the Crucifixion itself.

Of course, modern critics of the Resurrection argue, it was easy for the first Christians to believe in the resurrection of Jesus. After all, belief in resurrections was a commonplace at the time. The first Christians may have jumped to the conclusion that Jesus was raised from the dead when something rather different actually happened. Although the crude charges of yesteryear (for example, that the disciples stole the corpse of Jesus from its tomb, or that they were the victims of mass hysteria) are still occasionally encountered, they have generally been superseded by more subtle theories. Thus, to note the most important, the Resurrection was really a *symbolic* event, which the first Christians confused with a *historical* event due to their uncritical presuppositions.

In response to this, however, it may be pointed out that neither of the two general beliefs of the time bear any resemblance to the resurrection of Jesus. The Sadducees denied the idea of a resurrection altogether (a fact Paul was able to exploit at an awkward moment: Acts 23:6–8) while the majority expectation was of a general resurrection on the last day, at the end of history itself. The sheer oddness of the Christian proclamation of the resurrection of Jesus in human history, at a definite time and place, is all too easily overlooked by modern critics, even though it was obvious at the time. The unthinkable appeared to have happened and, for that very reason, demanded careful attention. Far from merely fitting into the popular expectation of the pattern of resurrection, what happened to Jesus actually contradicted it. The sheer novelty of the Christian position at the time has been obscured by two thousand years' experience of the Christian understanding of the Resurrection—yet at the time it was wildly unorthodox and radical.

To dismiss the Christian understanding of the resurrection of Jesus because it allegedly conformed to contemporary expectations is clearly unacceptable. The idea that the resurrection of Jesus can be explained as some sort of wish fulfillment on the part of the disciples also strains the imagination somewhat. Why should the disciples have responded to the catastrophe of Jesus' death by making the hitherto unprecedented suggestion that he had been raised from the dead? The history of Israel is littered with the corpses of pious Jewish martyrs, none of whom were ever thought of as having been raised from the dead in such a manner.

The second attack on the historicity of the resurrection of Jesus mounted in recent years is based on the parallels between pagan myths of dying and rising gods and the resurrection of Jesus. In the first part of the present century, a substantial number of scholarly works drew attention to these pagan and gnostic myths. Perhaps J. G. Frazer's *Adonis, Attis, Isiris* is the most famous of these in the English-speaking world. It was argued that the New Testament writers were simply reproducing this myth, which was part of the intellectual furniture of the ancient world. Rudolf Bultmann was among many scholars of the period who argued for such influence on the resurrection accounts and beliefs of the New Testament, and who then proceeded to take the logically questionable step of arguing that such parallels discredited the historicity of the resurrection of Jesus.

Since then, however, scholarship has moved on considerably. The parallels between the pagan myths of dying and rising gods and the New Testament accounts of the resurrection of Jesus are now regarded as remote, to say the least.[44] For instance, the New Testament documents take care to give the place and the date of both the death and the resurrection of Jesus and identify the witnesses to both. The contrast with the ahistorical narrative form of mythology is striking.

Furthermore, there are no known instances of this myth being applied to any *specific historical figure* in pagan literature, so that the New Testament writers would have given a stunningly original twist to this mythology. It is at this point that the wisdom of C. S. Lewis— who actually knew something about myths—must be acknowledged. Lewis realized that the New Testament accounts of the resurrection of Jesus bore no relation to real mythology, despite the claims of some theologians who had dabbled in the field. Perhaps most important, however, was his realization that the gnostic redeemer myths—which the New Testament writers allegedly took over and applied to Jesus— were to be dated from later than the New Testament itself. If anyone borrowed any ideas from anyone, it seems it was the gnostics who took up Christian ideas.

The challenge posed to the historicity of the Resurrection by these theories has thus passed into textbooks of the history of ideas, but an important point remains to be made. We have seen how allegedly responsible academic scholarship, regarded as competent in its own day, was seen to pose a serious challenge to a central aspect of the Christian faith. It was taken seriously by theologians and popular religious writers. Yet the sheer *provisionality* of scholarship seems to have been ignored. Scholarship proceeds by evaluation of evidence and hypotheses, a process that takes decades; and what one generation took as self-evident is often later demonstrated to be wrong. The fate of the Resurrection myth is a case in point: in 1920 it was treated virtually as an established fact of serious and responsible scholarship; three-quarters of a century later it is regarded as an interesting, if now discredited, idea.

How many more such theories, which now seem persuasive and a genuine challenge to the Christian faith, will be treated as obsolete in fifty years' time? Christianity can hardly be expected to abandon its proclamation of the risen Christ as Savior and Lord on such flimsy grounds. Furthermore, as anyone who works in the field of the history of ideas knows, it is remarkable how rapidly the assured presuppositions of one generation are abandoned by another! Christianity has a duty to speak for two thousand years of history, as well as for the future; it cannot allow the short-term preoccupations of modernity to dictate its character for posterity.

A third line of criticism of the historicity of the Resurrection comes from the German sociologist Ernst Troeltsch, who argued that, since dead men do not rise, Jesus could not have risen. The basic principle underlying this objection goes back to David Hume and concerns the need for present-day analogues for historical events. Before accepting that an event took place in the past, we need to be persuaded that it still takes place in the present. Troeltsch asserted that since we have no contemporary experience of the resurrection of a dead human being, we have reason for supposing that no dead man has ever been raised.

Of course, since Christianity insists that the resurrection of Jesus was a unique historical event, the absence of present-day analogues is only to be expected. If people were raised from the dead on a regular basis, there would be no difficulty in accepting that Jesus Christ had been raised. But it would not stand out. It would not *say* anything, either about the identity of Jesus himself or about the God who chose to raise him in this way. The Resurrection was taken so seriously because it was realized that it was totally out of the ordinary—unique in the proper sense of the word.

Nevertheless, a more sophisticated reply to this line of criticism is needed. The most vigorous response to Troeltsch's criticism has been made by Wolfhart Pannenberg, who points out that Troeltsch adopted a remarkably dogmatic view of reality, based on questionable metaphysical presuppositions, a view that effectively dictated what could and could not have happened in history on the basis of his preconceived views. Troeltsch, Pannenberg argued, had already laid down in advance that the Resurrection could not happen. The argument seemed to move as follows:

    a. Dead people do not rise from the dead.

    b. Therefore Jesus Christ did not rise from the dead.

    c. End of discussion.

But this is unacceptably superficial. The philosophical question of induction, noted earlier, does not allow the conclusion to be drawn from the premise. Observation does not determine fixed laws that may be used to determine whether something did or did not happen in the past. It merely establishes the probability of events of a certain type.

For Pannenberg, the decisive factor in determining what happened on the first Easter Day is the evidence contained in the New Testament and not dogmatic and provisional scholarly theories about the nature of reality. How, asks Pannenberg, are we to account for the New Testament evidence? What is its most probable explanation? The historical evidence liberates us from the dogmatic metaphysical presuppositions about what can and cannot have happened in history that underlie Troeltsch's critique of the Resurrection, and it allows us to return to the Jesus of history. For Pannenberg, the resurrection of Jesus is the most probable and plausible explanation of the historical evidence. Perhaps it lacks the absolute certainty the more fundamentalist of metaphysicians seem to demand—but, as Bishop Butler so carefully demonstrated in his *Analogy of Religion,* probability is the law of religious life, whether orthodox or deist.

E. THE DIVINITY OF CHRIST

Modernism has laid down two fundamental challenges to the doctrine of the divinity of Christ, especially as it is expressed in the doctrine of the Incarnation. First, it is *wrong.* Our growing understanding of the background to the New Testament, the way in which Christian doctrine has developed, the rise of the scientific worldview, and so on, force us to abandon the idea that Jesus was God in any meaningful sense of the word. Second, it is *unnecessary.* Christianity can exist without the need for such obsolete and cumbersome ideas as God becoming man, traditionally grounded in the resurrection of Jesus Christ and expressed in the doctrine of the Incarnation. In a world come of age, Christianity, if it is to survive, must learn to abandon these ideas as archaic and irrelevant.

It is significant that most recent criticisms of the Incarnation, such as those expressed in *The Myth of God Incarnate* (1977), demonstrate a tendency to concentrate on objections to the *idea* of incarnation, rather than on objections to the *basis* of the idea. After all, the idea of God incarnate in a specific historical human being was quite startling in its first-century Jewish context, whatever may have been made of it in the later patristic period, and the question of what caused this belief to arise requires careful examination. Of central importance to this question is the Resurrection itself, a subject studiously ignored (along with the major contributions to the incarnational discussion by Wolfhart Pannenberg, Jürgen Moltmann, Walter Kasper, and others) by most of the contributors to *The Myth of God Incarnate.*

The idea of incarnation is easy to criticize: it is paradoxical, enigmatic, and so on. But everyone already knows this, including the most fervent advocates of the idea. And it is absurd, even offensive, to suggest that those who regard a belief in the Incarnation as legitimate are intellectually hidebound or trapped in their traditions, unable to think for themselves. The question remains, and always has been: Is the Incarnation a proper and legitimate interpretation of the history of Jesus of Nazareth?

The fact that something is paradoxical and even self-contradictory does not invalidate it. Those who have worked in the scientific field are only too aware of the sheer complexity and mysteriousness of reality. The events behind the rise of quantum theory, the difficulties of using models in scientific explanation—to name but two factors that I can remember particularly clearly from my own period as a natural scientist—point to the inevitability of paradox and contradiction in any except the most superficial engagement with reality.[45] Our apprehension of reality is partial and fragmentary, whether we are dealing with our knowledge of the natural world or of God. The Enlightenment worldview tended to suppose that reality could be totally apprehended in rational terms, an assumption that still persists in some theological circles, even though it has been abandoned as unrealistic elsewhere. All too many modern theologians cry "Contradiction!" and expect us all to abandon there and then whatever it is that is supposed to be contradictory. But reality just is not like that.

An example of this approach deployed against the principle of the Incarnation is provided by John Hick, who asserts ("argues" is not the *mot juste*) that the idea of Jesus being both God and man is logically contradictory.[46] Quoting Spinoza, Hick asserts that talk of one who is both God and man is like talking about a square circle. Hick's consistency at this point is difficult to trace since he is already committed to the belief that all the concepts of God to be found in the world religions—personal and impersonal, immanent and transcendent—are compatible with each other. Indeed, such is the variety of the concepts of divinity currently in circulation in the world religions that Hick is obliged to turn a blind eye to the resulting logical inconsistency between them—only to seize upon and censure this alleged "inconsistency" in the case of the Incarnation.

But Hick cannot be allowed to make this robust assertion concerning the logical incompatibility of God and man unchallenged, and his less than adequate knowledge of the development of Christology in the medieval period is clearly demonstrated in this matter. The fact that there is no *logical* incompatibility between God and man in the Incarnation is demonstrated, and then theologically exploited, by that most brilliant of all English theologians, William of Ockham.[47] Ockham's discussion of this point is exhaustive and highly influential, and it has yet to be discredited. Indeed, it is confirmed by the superb recent study of Thomas V. Morris, *The Logic of God Incarnate*,[48] which has received considerable critical acclaim within philosophical circles.

Let us look briefly at some of the points that might be raised here. Under what circumstances might the idea of Jesus Christ being both God and man, divine and human, be considered a logical absurdity? We can bring out the point at issue by considering Spinoza's example of the square circle, made to bear such theological weight by Hick. Why is the idea of a square circle an absurdity? Because "square" and "circle" both occupy the same space on a logical map. They are both examples of shapes. A single shape cannot conform to two irreconcilable forms. It is one (a square), the other (a circle), or neither (perhaps a triangle, or some ill-defined shape). "Circle" and "square" thus define mutually exclusive categories of shape: a shape cannot be both of them at one and the same time.

But now consider Jesus Christ as God and man. What common logical area is occupied by "God" and "man"? Of what species are they both examples? In fact, they occupy no common ground; God is creator, man is a creature. As Thomas Aquinas stressed, divinity and humanity occupy no common logical—or even, as his famous distinction between *essentia* and *existentia* makes clear, *ontological*— territory. They are totally distinct. The parallel between the square circle and the Incarnation is thus devoid of any serious logical basis.

Again, at the purely logical level, it is interesting to challenge Hick as to why "divinity" and "humanity" should be treated as irreconcilable.[49] They are different—but why should they not coexist? Square circles do not exist, for the simple reason that they are mutually exclusive categories of shape. But why should not divinity and humanity be complementary? On the basis of what logical rule can such a possibility be excluded? A trivial example is suggested by a colleague of mine who has both British and Swiss citizenship. Dual nationality is a common enough occurrence to make its theological potential worth exploring. Hick's crude analysis of the logic of the Incarnation suggests that the following are logically incompatible:

    a. Jesus is divine.

    b. Jesus is human.

But consider my friend Francis, who is fortunate enough to have dual nationality.

    a. Francis is British.

    b. Francis is Swiss.

A logical contradiction exists if, and only if, being British excludes being Swiss. But it does not. And why, at the logical level, should being human exclude Jesus from being divine? Might he not be a citizen of heaven as well as of earth?

The charge of logical incoherence thus remains unpersuasive, except to those precommitted, for whatever reason, to anti-incarnational viewpoints. At times Hick seems to reject incarnationalism because of the difficulties it raises for his theory of religions, which is more than a little disrupted by the traditional doctrine of the Incarnation. Hick's interest in challenging the doctrine seems to be motivated by a quite different agenda, concerned with the homogenization of religions—a process to which the doctrine of the divinity of Christ is a serious stumbling block.

More seriously, Hick seems to work on the basis of the assumption that he already knows exactly what God is like, and that on the basis of this knowledge he is in a position to pass judgment on the logical niceties of the Incarnation. But this is obviously not the case. (None of us has privileged access to God in this way; we are all limited in our knowledge of God, which is why the news that God has revealed himself is such good news. We need to be told what God is like; left to our own devices, we would wallow about in confusion and chaos.) Hick may be saying that there is a logical problem involved with classical theism (a philosophical system) in relation to the Incarnation—but this merely suggests that classical theism is not necessarily compatible with Christianity. (This point has been made in recent years with increasing force by theologians such as Jürgen Moltmann and Eberhard Jüngel.) It is not to discredit the Incarnation. Hick may be in a position to say that God is totally unable to come among us as a human being and that the Incarnation is impossible on account of who and what God is—but if he can do so, he would seem to have access to a private and infallible knowledge of God denied to the rest of us. And do we really fully understand what is meant by that deceptively familiar word *human?* Many of us would prefer to say that the Incarnation discloses the true nature of divinity and humanity, rather than approaching the Incarnation on the basis of preconceived ideas of divinity and humanity.

Critics of the Incarnation appear to envisage their criticisms as establishing a new, more relevant and universal version of Christianity. But what might this new version of Christianity be like? The inclusion of the word "new" is deliberate: historically, Christianity has regarded both the Resurrection and the Incarnation as essential to its historical self-understanding, and any attempt to eliminate or radically modify them would seem to lead to a version of Christianity that is not continuous with the historical forms it has taken in the course of its development. In the following section, we shall look at the consequence of the elimination or radical modification of these two traditional ideas.

Let us suppose that Jesus was not God in any meaningful sense of the term. Let us suppose that he was a man, like the present writer in every way (although hopefully a nicer person), but far superior religiously and morally, and that everything Christianity has wanted to say about the significance of Jesus can be said, and said well, without the belief that he was God as well as man. Let us see if this can actually be done.

First, let me explore a comment made by Paul Elmer Moore, the American Platonist who became a Christian late in life. He wrote powerfully of the "loneliness of an Ideal world without a Lord" (see pp. 30-31). He longed for Platonic forms to turn into a face—into something personal. Without the Incarnation we are left in the realm of ideas, unable to put a human face to God. We are left in a world of ideas and ideals—a chilly world, in which no words are spoken and the tenderness of love is unknown. The Incarnation allows us to speak with authority of God being personal. It speaks of God entering into our history, and allows us to abandon the cold and unfeeling world of ideals in favor of a world charged with the thrilling personal presence of God. That difference matters profoundly.

Let us develop this point in a slightly different direction. On the basis of a number of important works reflecting the spirit of Enlightenment modernism, it is clear that a central idea congenial to the modern spirit is that Jesus reveals to us the love of God. It is frequently pointed out that the modern age is able to dispense with superstitious ideas about the death of Jesus (for example, that it represented a victory over Satan or the payment of a legal penalty of some sort), and that instead we can get to the real meat of both the New Testament, so movingly expressed in the parable of the prodigal son, and modern Christianity—the love of God for humanity. In what follows, I propose to suggest that abandoning the ideas of resurrection and the Incarnation means abandoning even this tender insight.

This may seem an outrageous suggestion to make, but I cannot see how this conclusion can be avoided. How may the death of Jesus Christ on a cross at Calvary be interpreted as a demonstration of the love of God for humanity? Once modernism dispenses with the idea of incarnation—that Jesus is God—a number of possible alternative explanations of the cross remain open.

a. It represents the devastating and unexpected end to the career of Jesus, forcing his disciples to invent the idea of the Resurrection to cover up the totality of this catastrophe.

b. It represents God's judgment on the career of Jesus, demonstrating that he was cursed by the Law of Moses and thus disqualified from any would-be messianic status.

c. It represents the inevitable fate of anyone who attempts to lead a life of obedience to God.

d. It represents the greatest love one human being can show for another (cf. John 15:13), inspiring Jesus' followers to demonstrate an equal love for others.

e. The cross demonstrates that God is a sadistic tyrant.

f. The cross is meaningless.

All of these are plausible within the framework of modernism. The idea that the cross demonstrates the love of God for humanity cannot, however, be included among this list. It is not *God* who is dying on the cross, who gives himself for his people. It is a man—an especially splendid man, who may be ranked with others in history who have made equally great sacrifices for those they loved. The death of an innocent person at the hands of corrupt judges is all too common, even today, and Jesus cannot be singled out for special discussion unless he *is* something or someone qualitatively different from us.

Someone might, of course, immediately reply that Jesus is a higher example of the kind of inspiration or illumination to be found in all human beings, so that he must be regarded as the outstanding human being—and that for that reason, his death assumes special significance. But his is a remarkably dogmatic assumption—that Jesus is unique among human beings in this respect. One of the puzzles about *The Myth of God Incarnate* is that its contributors seem content to dismantle what they term the "myth" that God became incarnate in a human being—only to make extravagant claims about the religious superiority of Jesus, which cannot be justified by their basic assumptions. Commenting on these trends, a perceptive American theologian notes:

> Extravagant claims are . . . made about the supreme religious worth, the sublime teaching, the transforming power, the overwhelming and vibrant God-consciousness, the tremendous ability to challenge and change people, and the contagious spirituality of Jesus. . . . After reading such romantic pap, one wonders why anyone would have bothered to crucify Jesus. Such Christologies try to explain the existence of Christianity apart from the discontinuity and shock of cross and resurrection, and so end by making highly inflated claims about the "human" Jesus.[50]

The uniqueness of Jesus was established by the New Testament writers through the Resurrection and the subsequent recognition that Jesus was none other than the living God dwelling among us. But this insight is given and guaranteed by two doctrines modernism cannot allow. It would seem that modernists are prepared to retain insights gained through the traditional framework of resurrection and incarnation—and then declare that this framework may be dispensed with.

But this is clearly questionable, to say the least. If the traditional framework is declared to be wrong, the consequences of this declaration for each and every aspect of Christian theology must be ascertained. Discard or radically modify the doctrines of resurrection and incarnation, and the idea of the "uniqueness" or the "superiority" of Jesus becomes a dogmatic assertion without foundation, an assertion that many with more humanist inclinations would find offensive. We would be equally justified in appealing to other historical figures— such as Socrates or Gandhi—as embodying the best of Christian moral behavior.

This point becomes more important when we return to the question of how the death of Jesus can be interpreted as a self-giving divine act, demonstrating the love of God for humanity. It is not God who is on the cross—it is a human being. That point must be conceded by those who reject the Incarnation. It may then be the case that God makes his love known indirectly (and, it must be said, in a remarkably ambiguous manner) through the death of Jesus Christ, but we have lost forever the insight that it is God himself who shows his love for us on the cross.

What the cross might conceivably demonstrate, among a number of other, more probable, possibilities, is the full extent of the love of one human being for others. And as the love of human beings can be thought of as mirroring the love of God, it would therefore be taken as an indirect demonstration of what the love of God is like, in much the same way that countless other individuals have given up their lives to save their friends or families throughout history. But whom did Jesus die to save? None, save possibly Barabbas, can be said to have benefited directly from his death, yet it would seem that modernism would like us to understand Jesus' death as making some sort of religious point that will enrich our spiritual lives. But this is not how the New Testament writers understood his death (not least because they insisted on interpreting that death in the light of the Resurrection, a procedure regarded as illegitimate by modernists), and it is certainly difficult to see how it would have cut much ice in the hostile environment in which Christianity had to survive and expand in the first period of its existence.

Had Jesus died in western Europe in the modern period, such an interpretation of his death might have had a certain degree of plausibility—but the historical significance of Jesus' death was determined by its historical context, and we are committing historical errors that parallel those of the ill-fated nineteenth-century "quest of the historical Jesus" if we project modern cultural preoccupations onto the event of the death of Christ. The interpretation modernism wishes to place on the death of Christ is culturally conditioned by the social and personal values of Western society and is imposed on (rather than discerned within) the history of Jesus.

The traditional framework for discussion of the manifestation of the love of God in the death of Christ is that of God humbling himself and coming among us as one of us, taking on himself the frailty and morality of our human nature in order to redeem it. To deny that the lonely dying figure on the cross is God is to lose this point of contact and to return to the view that Christianity overturned in its own day and age—that "God is with us only in his transcendence" (Don Cupitt). A divine representative—not God himself—engages with the pain and suffering of this world. It is his love, not God's, which is shown. And to those who might think that this difficulty may be eliminated by developing the idea of God allowing himself to be identified with the dying Christ, it may be pointed out that the exploration of this idea by Moltmann and Jüngel leads not merely to an incarnational, but to a *Trinitarian*, theology. In order to do justice to the Christian experience of God through Jesus Christ, we cannot view Jesus Christ merely in terms of his function—we are dealing with an identity of being, rather than just an identification of function. Jesus acts as and for God precisely because he *is* God.

A similar point may be made in relation to suffering. As we noticed earlier, twentieth-century apologetics has recognized that any theology that is unable to implicate God in some manner in the sufferings and pain of the world condemns itself as inadequate and deficient. The twentieth century has witnessed previously unimagined horrors of human suffering in the trenches of the First World War, in the extermination camps of Nazi Germany, and in the programs of genocide established by Nazi Germany and Marxist Cambodia. The rise of "protest atheism"—perhaps one of the most powerful sentiments modern theology must address—reflects human moral revulsion at these acts. Protest atheism has a tendency to select soft targets, and there are few targets softer in this respect than a nonincarnational theology.

An incarnational theology speaks of God subjecting himself to the evil and pain of the world at its worst, in the grim scene at Calvary. God suffered in Christ, taking upon himself the agony of the world which he created. A nonincarnational theology is forced, perhaps against its intuition, to speak of a God who may send his condolences through a representative but who does not (or cannot, for fear of being accused of logical contradiction?) enter into and share his people's suffering at firsthand. And for a modernist who rejects substitutionary theories of the Atonement, God can hardly be allowed to take on himself his own punishment for the sins of humanity through a human representative who suffers instead of and on behalf of man.

In 1963, the English Sunday newspaper *The Observer* publicized John Robinson's book *Honest to God* with the headline "Our image of God must go." The image that Robinson had in mind was that of an old man in the sky. But the "image of God that must go" in the face of the intense and deadly serious moral criticisms of protest atheism is that of a God who does not experience human suffering and pain at firsthand—in short, a nonincarnational image of God. Many of those who criticize the Incarnation seem to realize the force of this point and attempt to retain it despite their intellectual misgivings. A nonincarnational theology is fatally flawed. Perhaps in the end it will not be the protests of orthodoxy that destroy nonincarnational theologies, but protest atheism, which rightly detects the fundamental weakness of such a theology.

A final point concerns the permanent significance of Jesus Christ. Why is he of such importance to the Christian faith here and now, some twenty centuries after his death? The traditional answer is that his significance lay in his being God incarnate—that in his specific historical existence, God assumed human nature. All else is secondary to this central insight, derived from reflection upon the significance of his resurrection. The fact that Jesus was male; the fact that he was a Jew; the precise nature of his teaching—all these are secondary to the fact that God took upon himself human nature, thereby lending it new dignity and meaning.

But if Jesus is not God incarnate, his significance must be evaluated in terms of those parameters which traditional Christianity has treated as secondary or accidental (in the Aristotelian sense of the term). Immediately, we are confronted with the problem of historical conditioning. What conceivable relevance may the teachings and lifestyle of a first-century male Jew have for us today, in a totally different cultural situation? The maleness of Christ has caused offense in radical feminist circles: Why should women be forced to relate to a male religious teacher, whose teaching may be compromised by his very masculinity, as well as by the patriarchal values of his cultural situation? And why should modern Western humanity pay any attention to the culturally conditioned teaching of such an individual, given the seemingly insuperable cultural chasm dividing first-century Palestine and the twentieth-century West? And even the concept of the "religious personality" of Jesus has been seriously eroded, as much by New Testament scholarship as by shifts in cultural perceptions.

For reasons such as these, a nonincarnational Christianity is unable to convincingly anchor the person of Jesus Christ as the center of the Christian faith. He may be the historical point of departure for that faith, but its subsequent development involves the leaving behind of the historical particularity of his existence in order to confront the expectations of each social milieu in which Christianity may subsequently find itself. Jesus says *this*—but we say *that*. *This* may be acceptable in a first-century Palestinian context—but *that* is acceptable in a modern Western culture in which we live and move and have our being. Jesus is thus both relativized and marginalized. Many nonincarnational versions of Christianity accept and welcome such insights— but others find them disturbing and perhaps unconsciously articulate an incarnational Christianity in order to preserve insights which they intuitively recognize as central.

Critics of doctrines such as the divinity of Christ tend to work on the basis of two presuppositions. First, that there exists a theological equivalent of precision surgery, which allows certain elements of the Christian faith to be excised without having any detrimental effect whatsoever upon what remains. Second, that by eliminating logical and metaphysical difficulties a more plausible and hence more acceptable version of Christianity will result. Both these assumptions are clearly questionable and must be challenged.

To return to our surgical analogy, we are not talking about removal of an appendix (a vestigial organ serving no useful purpose), but about the heart, the life-pump of the Christian faith. As C. S. Lewis so perceptively noted: "The doctrine of Christ's divinity seems to me not something stuck on which you can unstick but something that peeps out at every point so that you'd have to unravel the whole web to get rid of it."[51] Far from being an optional extra, the divinity of Christ, given expression in the doctrine of the Incarnation, is an essential and integral part of the authentically Christian understanding of reality.

Faith in the Resurrection and Incarnation is what kept and keeps Christianity growing and spreading. The sheer vitality, profundity, and excitement of the Christian faith ultimately depends on these. In a day and age when Christianity has to fight for its existence, winning converts rather than relying on a favorable cultural milieu, a nonincarnational theology despoiled of the Resurrection has little to commend it. It is perhaps significant that many critics of the Resurrection and Incarnation were themselves originally attracted to Christianity through precisely the theology they are now criticizing. What, it must be asked in all seriousness, is the *converting power* of an incarnationless Christianity?

The history of the church suggests that such a version of Christianity is a spiritual dead end. To recall the words of Thomas Carlyle: "If Arianism had won, Christianity would have dwindled to a legend." To its critics, incarnationless Christianity seems to be scholarly, bookish, and devoid of passion, without the inner dynamism to challenge and conquer unbelief in a world in which this is essential for its survival. But this is where history will pass its own judgment. Only a form of Christianity that is convinced that it has something distinctive, true, exciting, and relevant to communicate to the world in order to transform it will survive.

F. SIN AND SALVATION

The ideas of sin and salvation, together or in isolation, are often seized upon by opponents of Christianity as classic examples of outdated and pessimistic relics of a bygone age. A world come of age can well do without such vestiges of the religious dark ages, we are told. This criticism stings because of a recent failure to preach about sin or to even allow it to remain a serious theological option within mainstream Christianity. In the headlong rush to develop a doctrine of cheap grace acceptable in the liberal cultural marketplace, the idea of sin has been conveniently omitted from the mainstream Christian agenda. Thomas C. Oden summarizes this modern trend:

> We have learned in modernity to keep fashionably silent about the incarnation, atonement and resurrection and to develop theological positions less controversial and more agreeable with the assumptions of modernity—that Jesus is a good teacher (with minimum "mythological" additions), that God is good, but would not dare to judge our iniquities, and so on. In only one century of focussing on the ethical relevance of Jesus' teaching, we have almost forgotten how to speak of and pray to Jesus Christ, the Son of God and Savior of the world. In the well-intentioned attempt to deliver the Christian message in a language acceptable to moderns, we have peeled the onion almost down to nothing. We have cheated our young people out of the hard but necessary Christian word about human sin and divine redemption.[52]

Sin needs to be put back on the theological agenda—fast. The ideas of sin and salvation need to be explained, and some of the misunderstandings associated with them eliminated.

1. What Is Sin?

"Sin" is a complex idea. It is too easy to focus attention on individual aspects of sin, and neglect as a result the fundamental idea underlying them all. In its proper sense, sin does not refer to individual acts of sin, whether omission (failing to do something we know we should have) or commission (doing things which we know we ought not to have done). It is a state, an underlying condition. And just as an illness has visible symptoms, so *sin* (the state) produces visible *acts of sin*. Sin causes sins. And just as a competent physician knows that there is little point in treating symptoms while failing to deal with their root cause, so the Christian proclamation declares the need to deal with our *state* of sin, rather than merely with individual acts of sin. A worldview that deals only with individual sins is little more than a puritanical moralism such as Pelagianism. That is most emphatically what Christianity is *not*.

Sin is an underlying state of alienation from God. It is like a flaw in human nature—not a flaw created by God, but a crisis resulting from the fallenness of humanity. It expresses itself at every level of human existence—personal, social, and structural. At the personal level it is experienced in many different ways:

—in existential anxiety about death;[53]

—in a sense of unfulfilled yearning for something undefinable, which no created object can ever satisfy;[54]

—in a sense of moral guilt;

—in a sense of frustration, in that our highest ideals seem permanently beyond us.

—in a desire to be totally independent of God, ignoring both his existence and his demands on us.

At the social and structural levels, sin expresses itself in the radical selfishness that characterizes humanity. Philanthropic philosophies founder on the rock of human nature. It is as if there is something flawed about human nature that proves incapable of achieving the high ideals laid down by these well-meaning, yet totally unrealistic, philosophies. The great liberal dream was that education would change this situation radically and produce a generation of morally enlightened and responsible people, dedicated to the construction of a better world. Sadly, the history of the world lends little support to such a utopian dream. All too often, education seems to turn out people who are merely *informed* and self-centered.

These sorts of reflections could be extended, but there is little reason for doing so. The basic point the apologist needs to stress is this: There is something seriously and radically wrong with human beings. It is pointless to blame human ills on society—what is society, if it is not other human beings? To talk about people "being corrupted by society" is merely to evade the fact that we are corrupted by other people. This basic flaw in human nature—rather than any one of its many consequences—constitutes the essence of the Christian idea of sin. But the Christian will insist that sin is not primarily a moral concept. It is theological. At the root of our predicament lies a flawed relationship with God. The heart of sin is alienation from God. That state of alienation is the root of the human dilemma and must be addressed if our situation is to be transformed.

Thus far we have talked about sin in rather abstract and general terms. The time has come to be a little more precise and to appeal to well-established models of sin that have a distinguished history in Christian theology.[55] Four such models are especially helpful in apologetic contexts because they have considerable potential to illuminate the themes of both sin and salvation.

a. Sin is like an illness. Chronic physical illness provides one of the most powerful models of sin. It implies loss of a state of health and a present state of debilitation and weakness in which the way we are is considerably less than the way we could be. The Greek verb *sozein*, "to save," has the root sense of "to make whole" or "to heal," indicating the very close association between the concept of salvation and healing. Augustine of Hippo declared that the church is like a hospital—full of people who know that they are ill and need help, and who are prepared to entrust themselves to the care of the healing Christ. Sin is like a genetically inherited disorder—something we are born with ("original sin," a concept further below). The model is also important in helping us understand how sin persists in believers, a theme which we will explore presently.[56]

b. Sin is like moral guilt. Sin puts us in a wrong relationship with God. He is holy; we fall far short of him. He is righteous; we fall far short of his righteousness. One of the basic ideas here is that of falling short of a mark, failing to hit a target. There is a moral component to sin: knowing what God expects of us, we fail to meet it. Salvation includes as one of its vital components the idea of the cancellation of moral guilt and the forgiveness of sins. The death of Christ leads to the removal of our guilt:

> Surely he has borne our griefs
> and carried our sorrows;
> yet we esteemed him stricken,
> smitten by God and afflicted.
> But he was wounded for our transgressions,
> he was bruised for our iniquities;
> upon him was the chastisement that
> made us whole,
> and with his stripes we are healed (Isa. 53:4–5 RSV).

c. Sin is like an enslaving force. Sin entangles us. It is like a muddy swamp; once we are trapped, we are unable to break free. Someone has to pull us out. It is like an electromagnet, holding us as if we were iron filings. Someone has to turn the current off if we are to break free. It is like gravity, which drags everything to the ground. An apple suspended on its own in mid-air will fall to earth, just as a human being will fall into sin. It is like being addicted to a narcotic. We find that we cannot break the habit. One of the finest expositions of the way in which sin traps us is provided by Paul (Rom. 7:13–23). All Paul's good intentions are frustrated by a power (sin) which he finds at work within him and which he knows he cannot control. His concluding comments are vitally important: "Wretched man that I am! Who will deliver me from this body of death? Thanks be to God, through Jesus Christ our Lord!" (Rom. 7:24–25). The power of sin can be broken through the death and resurrection of Jesus Christ, which liberate us from the stranglehold of sin.

d. Sin is like existential alienation. Existential analysis is the new kid on the apologetic block.[57] Although it could be argued that its roots go back at least as far as Martin Luther (1483–1546), its modern use dates from the 1930s.[58] In his penetrating analysis of the structures of human existence, the existential philosopher Martin Heidegger distinguishes between two different ways of existing: *inauthentic existence* and *authentic existence.* The former is a fallen way of existence that ignores the harsh realities of life, a way of existence in which human beings lose their distinctiveness by "falling into the world" and by failing to achieve their full potential. The latter is a fulfilling way of existence, in which we achieve our full stature of life, fulfilling our human potential. Although God does not come into Heidegger's thinking in a big way, the Christian apologist can easily remedy this deficiency by recasting his analysis of existence within a Christian framework.

We see the same dichotomy in the New Testament, with its brilliant imagery of death and life (Rom. 6:3–8), darkness and light (John 1:5; 1 Peter 2:9), sin and grace (Rom. 5:20–6:1), lostness and "being found" (note the three parables of Luke 15). Two ways of existence are mapped out and described. One is the way of darkness, lostness, sin, and death—unredeemed life, in all its bleakness and self-centeredness. The other is the way of life made possible through the death and resurrection of Jesus Christ, which is offered to us as a gift.

Often, these models of sin are merged in Christian thinking, preaching, and praise. For example, these two extracts from well-known hymns combine elements of the model of sin as a power and of sin as guilt. In *Rock of Ages*, Augustus M. Toplady writes:

> Let the water and the blood,
> From thy riven side which flowed,
> Be of sin the double cure,
> Cleanse me from its guilt and power.

The death of Christ cleanses the sinner from both the moral guilt and the spiritual power of sin. Charles Wesley includes the following lines in *O for a Thousand Tongues to Sing:*

> He breaks the power of cancelled sin,
> He sets the prisoner free.

The power of sin is broken, and its moral guilt canceled, through the saving death of Christ. These hymns provide a useful model for the apologist in that they show the considerable potential for building up an overall comprehensive picture of sin—before going on to explore the purpose and power of God in dealing with it through Christ.

2. What Is Original Sin?

The term *original sin* probably owes its origin to Augustine of Hippo. The idea, however, is thoroughly biblical and is deeply embedded in the Christian proclamation. The basic idea is this: we do not become sinners by committing acts of sin—we demonstrate that we already are sinners by those acts. In other words, sin is something that is there from our birth, from our *origin* (hence the phrase *original sin*). The flaw in human nature is not acquired; it is "built in."

Infants are not free of sin until they are contaminated by the sins of a fallen world. They are born into that fallen world and share its fallenness from the moment of their birth. Christians have always insisted that Christ is the Savior of all people. And that implies that everyone has something he or she must be saved from—in other words, sin. And as Christ is the Savior of infants, as much as of anyone else, it follows that even infants have something from which they need to be saved.

Another way of putting this may be more helpful apologetically. Sin is the antithesis of salvation. It is the "before" to which salvation is the "after." We are not born believing Christians; we have to become believers. Original sin is that state into which we are born—the state of unbelief or lack of faith. This is expressed by the idea of "being born again" (John 3:3, 7: there are strong semantic links here between being "born again" and being "born from above"). The doctrine of original sin basically affirms that we are born with a *need* to be born again. It points to our natural state being that of alienation from God. God has to enter into our lives in a salvific manner; he is not naturally there in this way. We are born in darkness; we need to respond to God's call to enter into his marvelous light (1 Peter 2:9).

Apologetically, the idea of original sin allows us to break free from the moralist shackles that so often confuse people's thinking about sin. Original sin is obviously not a moral idea—how can one talk about infants doing immoral things? It is a theological idea, concerned to point out that our natural state, from birth, is that of estrangement from God. But the gospel proclamation is that of reconciliation to that same God through Jesus Christ. Original sin thus does not present formidable difficulties. It needs to be explained as the negative presupposition of redemption. It is an affirmation of the universality of sin that comes prior to the affirmation of the universality of the proclamation of redemption.

3. Why Do Christians Continue to Sin?

The hypocrisy of Christians is a constant source of complaint outside Christian circles and a perennial thorn in the flesh of Christian apologetics. So what can be done about it? Apart from wishing that their fellow Christians would be less prone to public lapses into sin, spectacular or otherwise, apologists need to explain the manner in which Christians are forgiven sinners. They nevertheless remain sinners (note Karl Barth's famous term *Sündermensch*, which embodied his conviction that the human person *[Mensch]* could never be separated from sin *[Sünde]*—whether Christian or nonbeliever). Christians are those who

a. have been delivered from the *penalty* of sin;
b. are being delivered from the *power* of sin; and
c. will finally be delivered from the *presence* of sin.

There are thus past, present, and future elements to the Christian understanding of the relation between salvation and sin.[59] Sin remains a real presence in the Christian life (1 John 1:8–10).

Christianity proclaims the reality of sin, not the perfectibility of human nature. It is secular ideologies—such as liberalism —which proclaim the latter and find themselves utterly frustrated by its perennial contradiction by the harsh facts of life (a point stressed by Reinhold Niebuhr). This point is made forcefully by the English novelist and apologist G. K. Chesterton, who stresses the reality of sin and its implications for human life. For example, he notes that the Christian church in the United Kingdom was criticized heavily in the aftermath of the First World War (1914–18) for failing to prevent the outbreak of war. Yet this, he argues convincingly, is simply an example of a frustrated secularism trying to transfer its own failings and weaknesses to Christianity:

> It was the anti-clerical and agnostic world that was always prophesying the advent of universal peace; it is that world that was, or should have been, abashed and confounded by the advent of universal war. As for the general view that the church was discredited by the war—they might as well say that the Ark was discredited by the Flood. When the world goes wrong, it proves rather that the church is right. The church is justified, not because her children do not sin, but because they do.[60]

The reality of human sin and our inability to control it or eliminate it—of which the First World War was so telling a symbol—make redemption from outside the human situation a necessity. We are, quite simply, unable to redeem ourselves. As the Roman historian Livy remarked, surveying the moral chaos into which Rome had degenerated in his own day and age, "We have got to the point where we can bear neither our vices nor the measures necessary for their cure."

So how may a theoretical framework be constructed to account for the continuing fact of sin in the lives of those who are being saved? Why does sin persist in the life of the saints? And how can God treat sinners as if they are righteous, without lapsing into immorality? It would be a legal fiction for God to pretend that sinners are not sinners.

Martin Luther provides us with an answer.[61] Luther's emphasis falls upon the promise of God to forgive sinners. Our justification rests in the grace and mercy of the God who promises. We remain sinners— although *forgiven* sinners—who are assured that we will one day be righteous because of God's faithfulness to his promises. We are thus sinners in fact but righteous in hope. Luther sums up this situation in his famous maxim *simul iustus et peccator* (at one and the same time a righteous person and a sinner). Luther explains this situation by means of a medical analogy:

> It is just like someone who is sick, and who believes the doctor who promises his full recovery. In the meantime, he obeys the doctor's orders in the hope of the promised recovery. And he abstains from those things which he has been told to lay off, so that he may in no way hinder the promised return to health. . . . Now is this sick man well? In fact, he is both sick and well at the same time. He is sick in reality—but he is well on account of the sure promise of the doctor, whom he trusts, and who reckons him as already being cured.

We are both ill (in that we are still not healthy) and healthy (in that we are on the road to recovery). Just as you can think of someone on the mend as being ill and healthy at the same time, so you can think of forgiven believers as simultaneously sinful and righteous. The justified sinner

> is at one and the same time both a sinner and righteous. He is a sinner in reality, but righteous by the sure imputation and promise of God that he will continue to deliver him from sin until he has completely cured him. So he is entirely healthy in hope, but a sinner in reality.

In other words, the justified sinner's righteousness rests on the promise of God, not on his or her present state of righteousness. The promised gift of righteousness is both eschatological (in that it rests in the future) and present (in that the believer, knowing that God is faithful to his promises, may have sure knowledge *now* of his future righteous state).

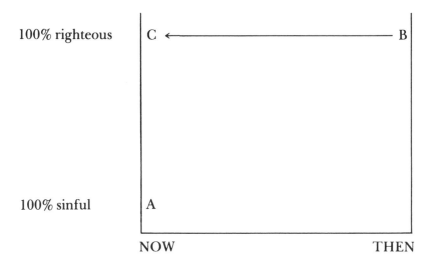

Figure 5.1
The relation of righteousness and sin in justification

God treats the sinner now on the basis of what he knows the final outcome of the process of justification to be.

We can represent this situation diagrammatically (figure 5.1). The present situation of the believer is represented by point *A* on this diagram. The situation on the final day, when the healing and forgiving promise of God finds its final fulfillment, is represented by point *B*. But the believer, even though remaining a sinner, may know of this final outcome of the process of justification *now*—and thus, although continuing to remain at point *A*, knows what that final outcome will be. The believer may thus have knowledge of the future righteousness and final elimination of sin, in effect existing at both points *A* and *C* simultaneously. There is a strongly eschatological element in Luther's thought on justification, salvation, and forgiveness, mingling the "here and now" and the "not yet."

So there is no legal fiction, no deception on the part of God. The verdict of justification—that is, the declaration of righteousness—is based on the final outcome of the action of healing grace. Just as the Old Testament prophets spoke of the future as if it were already present (the so-called "prophetic present"), so God, knowing what the end result of our justification will be, is able to declare that believers now possess the *status* of righteousness on the basis of the fact that we will one day possess the *nature* of righteousness.

4. Will Everyone Be Saved?

The apologist often encounters difficulties arising from the idea of universal salvation. If everyone will be saved, what is the point of listening to the gospel, let alone responding to it? G. K. Chesterton put the situation pithily: "We very much hope that all will be saved—but we must act on the presumption that they will not."

The New Testament proclaims the universal saving will of God. God wishes all to be saved. "Everyone who calls upon the name of the Lord will be saved" (Rom. 10:13). But this is only half the story. It is a very important half of that story, to be sure. But if there is one failing that has crippled Christian theology since its beginning, it is an unwillingness to tell the full story about central Christian beliefs. For example, it is so much easier to speak about Jesus being just a man, or just God, and to ignore the knotty problems that arise from having to speak of him being both God and man.[62] But responsible theology demands that the full story be told, regardless of the intellectual difficulties this raises. The full story is this:

a. God very much wants everyone to be saved;

b. Salvation is conditional upon our response to Christ.

Romans 10:7–17 is an excellent summary of these points.

So how are we to handle this apologetically? By devising analogies and illustrations that illustrate the internal rationality of the Christian approach. The following is offered as an illustration. The cross shows the love of God for us and brings home the full extent of his care and compassion for his world. He very much wants all of us, as his creatures, to respond to his love. But God has created us with freedom to accept him or reject him. Love offered to someone does not imply that that person will love you in return. Every high school student soon discovers that just because you love someone does not mean that he or she will automatically love you in return. It is not something that can be imposed on someone. God may love us, but that does not coerce us to love him in return.

The doctrine of universal salvation initially seems attractive. It seems to be very good news. All will be saved. But on closer inspection, this seems to amount to some kind of spiritual authoritarianism. All *will* be saved, whether they like it or not. Human freedom is compromised. And, as every apologist knows only too well, the idea of spending eternity with God is profoundly unattractive to many people! The idea that this is going to be forced on them will hardly strike them as good news!

Try to imagine the following scene. An individual does not want to be saved. He is very grateful to God for the offer, but with all due respect, he wishes to decline it. Are we to imagine God forcing him to accept it? That is not love—it is dangerously close to rape. No. God respects our God-given freedom. The offer of salvation is real. God's desire that we accept it is real. But the ball is in our court. A response is needed, but that response need not be forthcoming. It is our decision. Jesus asked the ill man by the pool of Bethzatha, "Do you want to be healed?" (John 5:6 RSV). It was up to him to respond to that real offer of healing. And so it is up to us to decide whether to accept the gracious offer of healing that comes to us through the gospel.

The basic logical structure of this approach is the following:

a. God loves us.

b. Love is a free response of one person to another.

c. Therefore God cannot impose his love upon us; he can only offer it.

d. Only those who want to respond to that love will be saved.

e. Those who do not want to be loved by God need not be.

This account obviously glosses over the questions theologians will want to discuss concerning the respective human and divine contributions to salvation, especially the question of the role of grace in prompting our response to God. This is not the place to enter into the complexities of the Arminian-Calvinist debate. Our concern is simply to demonstrate that the idea of universal salvation, which initially seems both attractive and plausible, actually includes a number of less palatable ingredients.

These, then, are some of the individual difficulties with which the apologist must expect to engage in the course of the defense of the faith. They are fairly specific problems that can be laid out on the dissecting table and handled individually. But not all difficulties are of this kind. Often a cluster of hostile ideas are bundled together, building up to give a cumulative case against Christianity. The ideas are seen to be linked together so that to counter one is not necessarily to remove the difficulty. These collections of ideas and attitudes are usually referred to as "worldviews," a rough English translation of the German term *Weltanschauung*. It is the clash of worldviews that often sets the scene for Christian apologetics. The chapter that follows deals with some of the more significant worldviews the apologist is likely to encounter.

CHAPTER SIX

A Clash of Worldviews

"Christianity is passé." Clichés like this have become part of the staple diet of modern thought. For the last three centuries Christianity has been on the defensive. It has been confronted with a series of intensely antireligious worldviews that have constantly sought to discredit Christianity, dismissing it as outdated and premodern. Reason reigns supreme in the modern world because it fails to conform to the intellectual standards laid down as self-evidently correct by modernity. Christianity belongs to the past.

Or does it? One of the most significant developments in the last decade or so has been the increasing realization that modern worldviews rest on distinctly vulnerable foundations. Diogenes Allen perceptively notes the "narrow view of reason and the reliance on natural science that are characteristic of the modern mentality."[1] Yet modernity, he writes, is dead; we live in a postmodern world.

> A massive intellectual revolution is taking place that is perhaps as great as that which marked off the modern world from the Middle Ages. The foundations of the modern world are collapsing, and we are entering a postmodern world. The principles forged during the Enlightenment (c. 1600–1780), which formed the foundations of the modern mentality, are crumbling.

Christian apologetics must address itself to this postmodern situation—a task which we shall undertake in the final section of this chapter.

But a more urgent task awaits the apologist. Apologetics must have the courage to declare that modernity—with all the allegedly fatal challenges that it brought to bear against the Christian faith—is dead. The apologist must be prepared to be like Nietzsche's madman, who ran around shouting "God is dead! We have killed him!" Except that this time it is the modern worldview that is dead, killed off by its failure to live up to its own promises. In this chapter we will explore some of the reasons why the modernist outlook is dead and look at three of its most significant worldviews—or, more accurately, three variations on themes within the modern worldview. In a sense, we are carrying out three autopsies. Although for some these worldviews remain real options in today's world, for most they are intellectual corpses; they once lived and flourished, but they are now laid out, cold and naked, on the dissection tables of intellectual historians.

What are the main features of this massive change in outlook that is now gaining sway in the Western world?[2] Four major developments may be singled out as having precipitated a crisis in confidence within the modern anti-Christian worldview.

1. The search for a universal rationality, so fundamental to the modern outlook, is now generally regarded as a dead end. There is no one single way of thinking that we can identify with reason and that would force us to acknowledge all other ways of thinking as "irrational." Philosophers such as Alasdair MacIntyre have stressed that there are many ways of thinking, each with its own internal standards of rationality and concepts of evidence.[3]

2. The search for a universal morality, based on reason rather than on the Christian revelation, now seems bankrupt and sterile.[4] This conclusion follows logically from the collapse of faith in a universal rationality. The title of Alasdair MacIntyre's devastating critique of such Enlightenment-inspired projects is itself a telling argument against them. *Whose Justice? Which Rationality?* The words immediately alert us to the historically undeniable fact that there is enormous disagreement on notions of rationality and concepts of justice. There is no single universal rule to which all others are subservient. The Christian approach to morality, like the Christian approach to rationality, has every right to be heard and respected in this new climate—not least because of its thoroughly realistic critique of human nature.

3. The touching Enlightenment *belief in the goodness of human nature and the inevitability of human progress* has received a series of rude setbacks. Where once it was believed that liberal education and the application of science would abolish the problems of the world, these beliefs are now treated with open skepticism. Knowledge itself is no longer seen as necessarily being a good thing. The shocking use to which science has been put—whether in the atom bomb dropped on Hiroshima, or the chemical nerve agents developed to eliminate population centers—brings home the fact that knowledge can be used for evil as much as for good.

Human nature is tainted with evil. No worldview that ignores this can hope to be taken seriously anymore. And the atrocities of Nazism (and their parallels in the Soviet Union under Stalin and his successors) raise a difficult question for the modernist. Is this the shape of the rational future? Is this what we can expect when traditional Christian values are abandoned? The moral question raised cannot be evaded.

4. *Belief in God* is no longer to be regarded as outdated or eccentric. The natural sciences, once hailed as the discipline that abolished God, now seem to be allowing him to return by the back door. "The embargo on the possibility of God is lifted" (Diogenes Allen). The new questions raised by the natural sciences about the order and existence of the universe raise the possibility of God. It is up to responsible Christian apologetics to make sure that these new questions receive Christian responses.[5]

This, then, in brief outline, is the new situation in Western culture faced by the Christian apologist. It is, in many ways, an enormously exciting situation. The old certainties are dead and gone. No longer does reason seem capable of delivering the insights we need in order to live, hope, and die. No longer does science by itself seem capable of making sense of the universe. The opportunities are there, and they must be exploited.

But old ideas die hard. Indeed, modernity seemed to believe that it could never become outdated. As Thomas C. Oden put it:

> Modernity pretends that all futures are likely to reflect the assumptions of modernity. That in fact is one of the assumptions of modernity. Its advocates simply cannot imagine their own assumptions ever being transcended. This gives the odd pretense of permanence to the radical relativism and infinite mutability of modernity.[6]

The three sections that follow seek to identify the basic features and the fatal weaknesses of three modern worldviews that still receive a hearing today. A person-centered apologetic must be capable of responding to these outlooks, even if they are being increasingly rarely encountered in the modern world. They are still there, and the challenge they pose must be met with a reasoned and informed response.

But with the death of modernity, new challenges have arisen— challenges to which the Christian apologist must be capable of rising.

Two are of special importance; one—postmodernism—is especially linked with academic institutions such as universities, while the other—neopaganism, often referred to more generally as the New Age movement[7]—has gained a significant, if relatively uncritical, hearing in vast tracts of modern Western society. Scorned by scholars and academics, neopaganism has nevertheless gained a significant committed following in the United States and Australia. To exploit the new opportunities that have arisen for Christianity in the New Age, the apologist needs to be able to handle rival worldviews competing for the same space.

But we begin with three worldviews which, in one sense, are dead, yet, in another sense, continue to live.

A. ENLIGHTENMENT RATIONALISM

A radical statement of the rationalist gospel might take the following form. Reason is capable of telling us everything we need to know about the world, ourselves, and God (if there is one). One of the most graphic portrayals of this enormous confidence in reason is the frontispiece to the eighteenth-century rationalist philosopher Christian Wolff's ambitiously titled book *Reasonable Thoughts About God, the World, the Human Soul, and Just About Everything Else* (1720). The engraving in question portrays a world enveloped in shadows and gloom, representing the old ideas of superstition, tradition, and faith. But on part of the engraving, the sun has broken through, lighting up hills and valleys, and bringing smiles to the faces of what we must assume to have been a hitherto rather gloomy group of peasants. The message is clear: reason enlightens, dispelling the fog and darkness of Christian faith, and ushers in the glorious light of human reason. Divine revelation is an irrelevance, if it exists at all.

At this point, we need to stress the difference between "reason" and "rationalism," which may appear identical to some readers. *Reason* is the basic human faculty of thinking, based on argument and evidence. It is theologically neutral and poses no threat to faith—unless it is regarded as the only source of knowledge about God. It then becomes *rationalism*, which is an exclusive reliance on human reason alone and a refusal to allow any weight to be given to divine revelation.

Classical Christian theology, including all responsible evangelical theology, makes use of reason—for example, in thinking through the implications of certain aspects of God's self-revelation. For example, consider the role of reason in exploring the relation between a functional and ontological Christology: if Jesus is our Savior, yet only God can save, reason suggests that Jesus must (in some sense of the word) be God. Yet here reason is reflecting on revelation, seeking to explore its implications. Rationalism declares that all thinking about God must be based upon human reason, thus immediately locking theology into the fallen human situation, with no possibility of being extricated from our confusion and distortion by God himself.

How did this remarkable—and, it must be said, totally misplaced—confidence in reason in matters of religion develop? Three stages can be identified, each leading naturally into the next one.

1. First, it was argued that the gospel is rational. Since the natural antithesis of rationality is irrationality, it seemed to many writers of the Middle Ages, such as Thomas Aquinas, that it is possible to demonstrate that Christianity makes sense. It rests on thoroughly reasonable foundations. For example, Aquinas argued that Christian belief in God does not involve some kind of intellectual suicide, and he suggested five lines of reasoning that showed that this belief was entirely reasonable. But Aquinas and the Christian tradition he represented did not for one moment believe that Christianity was limited to what could be ascertained by reason. Faith goes beyond reason, having access to truths and insights of revelation that reason cannot hope to fathom or discover unaided.

The noted historian of medieval Christian thought Etienne Gilson made a delightful comparison between the great theological systems of the Middle Ages and the cathedrals that sprang up throughout Christian Europe at this time. They were, he remarked, "cathedrals of the mind." Christianity is like a cathedral that rests on the bedrock of human reason but whose superstructure rises beyond the realms accessible to pure reason. It rests on rational foundations, but the building erected on that foundation goes far beyond what reason can uncover. Thus John Calvin, a distinguished representative of this approach, suggested that reason was perfectly capable of arriving at a knowledge of God the Creator. But real knowledge of God—*saving* knowledge of God—can be had only through revelation. Knowledge of God the Redeemer is a matter of revelation, not reason. This knowledge does not contradict knowledge of God the Creator; it brings it to perfection by showing that the God who created the world now acts to redeem it.

2. By the middle of the seventeenth century, a new attitude began to develop, especially in England and Germany. Christianity, it was argued, was reasonable. But where Thomas Aquinas understood this to mean that faith rested securely on rational foundations, this new school of thought had different ideas. If faith is rational, they argued, it must be capable of being deduced in its entirety by reason. Every aspect of faith, every item of Christian belief, must be shown to derive from human reason.

An excellent example of this approach is found in the writings of Lord Herbert of Cherbury, especially in *De veritatis religionis*, which argued for a rational Christianity based on the innate sense of God and human moral obligation. This had two major consequences. First, Christianity was in effect *reduced* to those ideas that can be proven by reason. If Christianity was rational, then any parts of its system that cannot be proved by reason cannot be counted as "rational." They have to be discarded. And second, reason was understood to take priority over Christianity. Reason comes first, Christianity comes second. Reason is capable of establishing what is right without needing any assistance from revelation. Christianity has to follow. It can be accepted where it endorses what reason has to say and must be disregarded where it goes its own way. So why bother with the idea of revelation when reason can tell us all we could possibly wish to know about God, the world, and ourselves? This absolutely settled conviction of the total competence of human reason underlies the rationalist depreciation of the Christian doctrine of revelation in Jesus Christ and through Scripture.

This approach to Christianity (or, more accurately, this form of Deism tinged with faintly Christian hues) treats God as an idea, a construction of the human mind. God is something that is posited, an idea we generate within our minds and then choose to call "God." We have created this idea. It is the work of our own minds. Traditional Christianity argues that God cannot simply be posited in this crudely rationalist manner. God has to be experienced. He has to be encountered. He is one who engages us, and by engaging us, forces us to reevaluate our ideas concerning him. Yet the God of pure reason is trapped within the limits of human mind. And small minds make for a small God.

3. Finally, this rationalist position was pushed to its logical outcome. As a matter of fact, it was argued, Christianity does include some beliefs that are inconsistent with reason. And since reason reigns supreme, guess which is wrong? God, having been posited by human reason, is now deposed by his own creator. An excellent example of this rational critique of Christianity can be seen in relation to the doctrine of justification. This doctrine declares that we are accepted by God without having done anything to deserve it. Reason declared that we had to *do* something to merit our justification. Otherwise, God was

simply being irrational. Therefore the gospel doctrine of justification by faith was wrong; the gospel was really about being able to merit our justification by our achievements. There is a certain sense in which Pelagianism is the most reasonable (in the sense of "rational") of heresies!

A similar critique was made of an entire series of doctrines that were deemed to be irrational—for example, the divinity of Christ (how could Jesus be both God and man at one and the same time?), and the doctrine of the Trinity (how can one God be three persons simultaneously, without lapsing into crude logical contradiction?) One of the early American presidents, Thomas Jefferson, who was deeply influenced by eighteenth-century French rationalism (and French cooking—but that is another story)—poured reasoned scorn on the doctrine of the Trinity:

> When we shall have done away with the incomprehensible jargon of the Trinitarian arithmetic, that three are one and one is three; when we shall have knocked down the artificial scaffolding, reared to mask from view the very simple structure of Jesus; when, in short, we shall have unlearned everything which has been taught since his day, and got back to the pure and simple doctrines he inculcated, we shall then be truly and worthily his disciples.

Jesus was really a very simple rational teacher who taught a very simple and reasonable gospel about a very simple rational idea of God. And at every point, Christianity chose to make things more complicated than they need be.

A direct consequence of this view was the movement in New Testament studies known as the "Quest of the Historical Jesus." This quest, which dates from the late eighteenth century, was based on the belief that the New Testament got Jesus entirely wrong.[8] The real Jesus—the "Jesus of history"—was a simple Galilean teacher who taught entirely sensible ideas based on reason. The New Testament erroneously presented him as the risen Savior of sinful humanity. Although the intellectual credentials of this movement have long since been discredited, the idea is still occasionally encountered today, as books published with sensational titles like *The Real Truth About Jesus* show.

It soon became increasingly clear that the "quest of the historical Jesus" was based on a naive view of the objectivity of human judgment, not to mention a quite unrealistic approach to history itself. These theologians apparently thought they were rediscovering the real Jesus; in fact, all they were doing was projecting their own ideas about the meaning of life onto Jesus. German theological professors, remarked one observant English critic, made Jesus look and sound just like a German professor of theology. Far from "rediscovering" Jesus, these writers were simply inventing a Jesus of their own making, one who uncritically echoed their own ideas, values, and hopes.

Perhaps the most famous demonstration of this disturbing point came from Albert Schweitzer. In his *Quest of the Historical Jesus* (1906), Schweitzer erected a monument to this movement, which proved to be its gravestone. Like Mark Anthony's funeral speech in *Julius Caesar*, Schweitzer's proved to be a tribute with fatal consequences. With great skill, he showed how the great nineteenth-century attempts to rediscover the real Jesus were misplaced. All they had done was to clothe Jesus in their own ideas.[9] A Kantian made Jesus sound just like a Kantian. A liberal made Jesus sound just like a liberal. And a rationalist made Jesus sound just like a rationalist. It was all rather like Hans Christian Andersen's story of the emperor's new clothes. Once someone had the courage to expose the delusion, everyone rushed in to join in the fun. The idea that the church had got Jesus completely wrong became little more than some kind of theological joke—a joke that is still told occasionally but gets fewer laughs every time.

But there is an important point underlying all this. Reason was held to be able to judge Christ. In his celebrated work *Religion Within the Limits of Reason Alone*, Immanuel Kant argued powerfully for the priority of reason and conscience over the authority of Jesus Christ. Where Jesus endorses what reason has to say, he is to be respected; where he goes against or beyond reason, he is to be rejected.

So what is the outcome of all this? Quite simply that reason can deliver everything humanity needs. There is no need to listen to other voices once we have consulted reason. This is the rational person, so devastatingly parodied by Iris Murdoch, who "confronted even with Christ turns away to consider the judgment of his own conscience and to hear the voice of his own reason."[10] By definition, the Christian cannot have anything to say that is at one and the same time distinctive and right. If it is distinctive, it departs from the path of reason—and thus must be untrue. To be different is, quite simply, to be wrong.

We have now outlined the development of Enlightenment rationalism and indicated its importance for Christianity. But what of the situation now, at the end of the twentieth century? A series of developments, of which we may here note a few, have damaged the credibility of this approach. The Enlightenment approach could be said to rest on the idea of the "immediately given," whether in reason or experience. Knowledge rests on a foundation, whether this is self-evident truths, immediately recognized as such by the human mind, or immediate experience, deriving directly from contact with the outside world. But these foundations do not seem to exist.

We may begin by exploring reason itself. Surely human reason is capable of basing itself on self-evident first principles, and, by following these through logically, deducing a complete system? Just about everyone who favors this approach makes some sort of appeal to Euclid's five principles of geometry. On the basis of his five principles Euclid was able to construct his entire geometrical system. Philosophers such as Spinoza were deeply attracted to this: maybe they could use the same method in philosophy. From a set of certain assumptions, a great secure edifice of philosophy and ethics could be erected. But the dream turned sour. The discovery of non-Euclidian geometry during the nineteenth century destroyed the appeal of this analogy. It turned out that there were other ways of doing geometry, each just as internally consistent as Euclid's. But which is right? The question cannot be answered. They are all different, each with their own special merits and problems.[11]

And the same turns out to be true of rationalism. Where once it was argued that there was one single rational principle, it is now conceded that there are—and always have been—many different "rationalities." Enlightenment thinkers appear to have been shielded from this disconcerting fact by the limitations of their historical scholarship, which remained firmly wedded to the classical Western tradition. But this illusion has now been shattered. At the end of his brilliant analysis of rational approaches to reason, Alasdair MacIntyre concludes:

> Both the thinkers of the Enlightenment and their successors proved unable to agree as to precisely what those principles were which would be found undeniable by all rational persons. One kind of answer was given by the authors of the *Encyclopédie*, a second by Rousseau, a third by Bentham, a fourth by Kant, a fifth by the Scottish philosophers of common sense and their French and American disciples. Nor has subsequent history diminished the extent of such disagreement. Consequently, the legacy of the Enlightenment has been the provision of an ideal of rational justification which it has proved impossible to attain.[12]

Reason promises much yet fails to deliver its much-vaunted benefits. It is for such reasons that Hans-Georg Gadamer wrote scathingly of the "Robinson Crusoe dream of the historical Enlightenment, as artificial as Crusoe himself."[13] The notion of "universal rationality" is a delusion.

But what of experience? Surely the immediate data of sense experience can be the basis of certain universal knowledge? The great Austrian logical positivist Rudolf Carnap stated this classic Enlightenment belief (which he once held himself) with crystal clarity in a late autobiographical reflection:

> We assumed that there was a certain rock bottom knowledge, the knowledge of the immediately given, which was indubitable. Every other kind of knowledge was supposed to be firmly supported by this basis, and therefore likewise decidable with certainty.[14]

But it is now generally agreed that there is no such thing as "knowledge of the immediately given." This has been variously termed "the myth of the given" and "the theory-laden nature of observation." "It is generally agreed that scientific knowledge is not read off nature but is a highly mediated relation to the natural world. Our observations are 'theory laden,' that is, they are made possible and are affected by our instruments and mental constructions" (Diogenes Allen).[15]

We may begin our exploration of this idea in a very elementary way.[16] Consider a statement such as the following. When I see a red circle, I am seeing a red circle—this is a basic fact of experience, quite independent of theories. Observational knowledge, in other words, would appear to be perfectly capable of standing upon its own two feet, if I might use the metaphor. But this allegedly simple fact of observation actually rests upon a system of concepts—concepts such as redness and circularity. The observation thus rests on a conceptual framework.

A more rigorous and informed discussion of the idea, firmly grounded in the world of experimental physics, is found in Norwood Hanson's work, especially in *Perception and Discovery*. Hanson's central idea is that of what he refers to as the "theory-laden nature of observation." He offers us the image of a pair of spectacles, worn behind our eyes, that affect our interpretation of what we see. We do not merely see things; we see them as *something*. Happily, he provides an illustration to make his point effectively. He suggests that we consider two observers, one located in the thirteenth, the other in the twentieth century observing the dawn. Both have the same visual experience. The same set of images impact upon their retinas. Yet, in a sense, they do not see the same thing.

The thirteenth-century observer, who intuitively assumes that the sun moves around the earth, sees the sun rise; the twentieth-century observer sees the horizon turning away. Now the point needs to be tempered with a certain degree of social realism. For example, a survey in *Le Figaro* not that long ago showed that about 30 percent of the French population thought that the sun went round the earth, thus making Hanson's clear distinction between thirteenth- and twentieth-century images of the dawn a little hazardous. But we can see the point he is making: The knower is not passive but interacts with the data, assessing their significance and their rationality on the basis of previous knowledge.[17]

In many ways, Hanson merely echoes what are fairly standard ideas within the scientific community. One might cite Ludwig Boltzmann, whose work on entropy remains significant: "In my opinion, we cannot utter a single statement that would be a pure fact of experience." Or one might turn to Niels Bohr, who wrote: "Any experience . . . makes its appearance within the frame of our customary points of view and forms of perception." Nevertheless, Hanson has made a distinct and original contribution in that he has drawn out the implications of these considerations for what is too easily described as empiricism. Human experience, he argues, is not uninterpreted sense data because we view sense data through irremovable (although not necessarily unalterable) theoretical spectacles.

In effect, Hanson is arguing that any view of the world that regards "facts" as things or situations in the real objective world, while "theories" are logical or systematic compilations or explanations of the facts, is deficient. We do not simply see and then interpret. Interpretation is not "something tacked on to this visual impression. It is not an afterthought."[18] To put this more explicitly: Hanson argues that "nothing can constitute a fact unless understood in terms of some theory."[19]

To illustrate this point, Hanson uses the well-known experimental proof that light has the characteristics of waves. A pebble dropped into water will cause a series of concentric waves that move away from the point of impact. If we drop two pebbles in water, a few inches apart, the two sets of waves will interfere with each other, and there will be a predictable interference pattern. We can do the same thing with light and show that light produces interference patterns.

The observer who, informed by theoretical knowledge, knows what to look for, realizes the significance of the interference patterns. This observer understands the rationality of the experiment and its intended purpose—and is thus able to make sense of its result. He does not merely see a pattern of light; he sees the pattern of light *as* an indication of the wave-nature of light. The untrained observer sees the same result—and yet does not see it. Hanson concludes his analysis as follows:

> Mere looking, unguided by theoretical consideration of any sort, is from most scientific points of view wholly insignificant and without consequence. And this is another reason why the attitude of some philosophers who think that the business of scientists is primarily just to observe the universe at large, collecting a great body of facts before sitting down to think about their relations and interconnections, is so myth-eaten.[20]

What is the relevance of this for our theme? To put it quite simply, it is very bad news indeed for all those who argue that human knowledge derives directly from experience without the interposing of theoretical frameworks. Another pillar of the Enlightenment worldview thus crumbles, incapable of bearing the theoretical weight placed on it by an increasingly tottering structure.

The Enlightenment vision thus fails. It proves impossible to establish a firmly established and indubitable starting point for human knowledge, from which a certain system of knowledge could be constructed. The Enlightenment criticized Christianity for basing itself on the person of Jesus Christ rather than on the permanent, universal, unshakable foundations of reason. Yet it is now generally conceded that no such unshakable and universal foundations actually exist. Just about all human knowledge rests upon a degree of *uncertainty*—which is all excellent news for Christianity.

The fact that we cannot prove that Christianity is true is no longer the crippling disadvantage it was once thought to be (which just goes to show how much intellectual fashions can change over the years). It merely places Christians in the best of intellectual company and marks them off from those who naively think that the really important things in life *can* be proved with certainty. Those who lack psychological maturity may need to cling to the illusions of certainty; the rest of us are content to learn to live in a world in which nothing important is certain and nothing certain is important.

But this critique of rationalism in no way invalidates an appeal to reason in Christian apologetics. It simply negates a hopelessly naive understanding of the potential of reason, in which one reaches inside one's head a total understanding of the world and God. Reason is a starting point—a distinguished, useful, and eminently proper starting point. But it is *only* a starting point. Rationalism fails when it believes that reason can guide us all the way to the city of God—it merely sets us on the right road.

B. MARXISM

Until very recently, Marxism was a major challenge to the Christian faith. It competed for the minds of young men and women on the campuses of universities throughout the world. It seemed to pose an unstoppable threat to Christianity in large parts of the world where Marxist governments attempted to eliminate Christian faith in various ways. That now belongs to the past. The collapse of the Berlin Wall in 1989 marked the end of the popular appeal of the movement, just as the fall of the Bastille in 1789 marked the end of the French *ancien régime* and the dawn of the new revolutionary era (to which Marxism was heir).

But Marxism lives on in the universities, so often the home of lost causes. It continues to have an impact on many people. Its criticisms of Christianity continue to be voiced, even if they are taken with decreasing seriousness. And for that reason it is important for the Christian apologist to be able to respond to that criticism and to make criticisms in return. This section seeks to provide an account of Marxism and indicate both its appeal and its vulnerability.[21]

Before exploring the Marxist critique of Christianity itself, we may consider three basic ideas that are of central importance. Fundamental to Marxism is the notion of *materialism*. This is not some metaphysical or philosophical doctrine that affirms that the world consists only of matter. Rather, it is an assertion that a correct understanding of human beings must begin with material production. The way in which human beings respond to their material needs determines everything else. Ideas, including religious ideas, are responses to material reality.

This first idea flows naturally into the second. A number of factors bring about *alienation* within the material process, of which the two most significant are the division of labor and the existence of private property. The former causes the alienation of the worker from his product, whereas the second brings about a situation in which the interests of the individual no longer coincide with that of society as a whole. As productive forces are owned by a small minority of the population, it follows that societies are divided along class lines, with political and economic power concentrated in the hands of the ruling class.

Marx believed that the third consideration naturally followed from the first two. Capitalism—the economic order just described—is inherently unstable, due to the tensions arising from productive forces. As a result, it will break down. Some versions of Marxism present this breakdown as happening without any need for assistance. Others present it as the result of a social revolution led by the working class. The closing words of the *Communist Manifesto* (1848) seem to suggest this latter: "Workers have nothing to lose but their chains. They have a world to gain. Workers of the world, unite!"

In practice, Marxism had virtually no influence until the period of the First World War. This can be attributed partly to internal party problems and partly to the lack of opportunities for political expansion. The internal problems are especially interesting. The suggestion that the working class could liberate itself from its oppression and bring about a political revolution soon proved to be illusory. It rapidly became clear that Marxists, far from being drawn from the ranks of the politically conscious working class, were actually depressingly middle class (like Marx himself). Aware of this problem, Lenin developed the idea of a "vanguard party." The workers were so politically naive that they needed to be led by professional revolutionaries who alone could provide the overall vision and practical guidance that would be needed to bring about and sustain a world revolution.

The Russian Revolution gave Marxism the break it needed, establishing itself in a modified form (Marxism-Leninism) within the Soviet Union. However, it proved unsuccessful elsewhere. Its establishment in eastern Europe after the Second World War can be attributed mainly to military strength and political destabilization. Its successes in Africa were due largely to the seductive appeal of Lenin's carefully devised concept of "imperialism," which allowed alienated elements within certain African and Asian countries to attribute their economical and social backwardness to the ruthless and systematic exploitation by the external agency of Western capitalism, rather than to any inherent deficiencies. The economic failure and political stagnation that resulted when such countries experimented with Marxism in the 1970s and 1980s soon led to disillusionment with this new philosophy.

In Europe, Marxism found itself locked into a spiral of decline. Its chief advocates increasingly became abstract theoreticians, detached from any working-class roots, with virtually no political experience. The idea of a socialist revolution gradually lost its appeal and its credibility. The publication of Marx's *German Ideology* in 1932 (it had not attracted a publisher until then) revealed Marx's muddled concepts of the future communist society. They proved totally inadequate for the needs of later Marxists, already discouraged by the failure of events to conform to Marxist theories.

As a worldview, Marxism was dead before the fall of the Berlin

Wall provided its obituary. But its failure as a worldview must not lead to the conclusion that it has lost its critical authority. Few take its more pompous claims seriously, but its critical views remain important. Now we shall consider the Marxist critique of Christianity and see what remains of it.

In his later writings, Marx adopted the "progressive" scientific outlook so popular in the early nineteenth century. Religion in general, according to this view, is outmoded superstition. Since Christianity is a religion, it falls into this general category. Worse than that, it is a superstition that dulls the ability of the working class to rise up and overthrow the ruling class. It is the "opium of the people," which enables them to endure their sufferings—when they ought to be throwing off the shackles that had condemned them to such suffering. This simplistic approach was adopted by many of Marx's followers, especially Lenin and the Bolsheviks. Lenin's words on religion leave us in little doubt as to his views on its merits:

> Religion is opium for the people. Religion is a kind of spiritual intoxicant in which the slaves of capital drown their humanity and blunt their desire for a decent human existence. . . . The class-conscious worker of today . . . leaves heaven to the priests and bourgeois hypocrites. He fights for a better life for himself, here on earth.[22]

A more sophisticated (and interesting) approach to religion may be found in earlier works of Marx himself, such as the 1844 political and economic manuscripts. Religion has no real, independent existence. It is a reflection of the material world. "The religious world is but the reflex of the real world."[23] There is an obvious and important allusion here to Feuerbach's critique of religion, which we considered earlier.[24] Thus Marx argues that "religion is just the imaginary sun which seems to man to revolve around him, until he realizes that he himself is the centre of his own revolution."[25] In other words, God is simply a projection of human concerns. Human beings "look for a superhuman being in the fantasy reality of heaven, and find nothing there but their own reflection."[26]

But why should religion exist at all? If Marx is right, why should people continue to believe in an illusion? Marx's answer centers on the notion of alienation.[27] "Humans make religion; religion does not make humans. Religion is the self-consciousness and self-esteem of people who either have not found themselves or who have already lost themselves again."[28] Religion is the product of social and economic alienation. It arises from that alienation and at the same time encourages that alienation by a form of spiritual intoxication that renders the masses incapable of recognizing their situation and doing something about it. Religion is a comfort that enables people to tolerate their economic alienation. If there were no such alienation, there would be no need for religion. The division of labor and the existence of private property introduce alienation and estrangement into the economic and social order.

Materialism affirms that events in the material world bring about corresponding changes in the intellectual world. Religion is thus the result of a certain set of social and economic conditions. Change those conditions so that economic alienation is eliminated, and religion will cease to exist. It will no longer serve any useful function. Unjust social conditions produce religion and are in turn supported by religion. "The struggle against religion is therefore indirectly a struggle against *the world* of which religion is the spiritual fragrance."[29]

Marx thus argues that religion will continue to exist as long as it meets a need in the life of alienated people. "The religious reflex of the real world can . . . only then vanish when the practical relations of everyday life offer to man none but perfectly intelligible and reasonable relations with regard to his fellow men and to nature."[30] In other words, when a nonalienating economic and social environment is brought about through communism, the needs that gave rise to religion will vanish. And with the elimination of those material needs, spiritual hunger will also vanish.

Feuerbach had argued that religion was the projection of human needs, an expression of the "uttered sorrow of the soul." Marx agrees with this interpretation. His point, however, is more radical. It is not enough to explain how religion arises because of sorrow and injustice. We must change that world and thus remove the causes of religion. It is important to note that Marx regards Feuerbach as correct in his analysis of the origins of religion, even if he failed to discern how an understanding of those origins might lead to its eventual elimination. It is this insight that underlies his often quoted eleventh thesis on Feuerbach: "The philosophers have only interpreted the world, in various ways; the point, however, is to change it."[31]

This, then, is the outline of the Marxist critique of religion. But is it right? Can it be justified? Let us present a critique of the Marxist critique. The following basic points, which command general assent outside Marxist circles and increasing acceptance within them, are of fundamental importance.

  a. Marx's atheism is ultimately an unproved hypothesis.[32]
  b. Marx's critique of religion is based virtually entirely on his

views concerning its social function in nineteenth-century Germany and is therefore inadequate.

   c. With the coming of the Communist state in various parts of the world, religion has not merely survived—it has prospered, despite the concerted efforts of the state to eliminate it and make events conform to theory.

   d. Marx assumes that one can speak of "religion" in general and then proceed to criticize specific religions. Marx never shows any real familiarity with the specifics of Christianity, giving instead vague generalities about religion in general.[33]

   Marx's critique of Christianity is actually a criticism of the institution of the established church in nineteenth-century Germany. But to criticize the church or its clergy hardly amounts to a cogent refutation of Christianity when most modern Christians would direct precisely the same criticisms against the German established churches of Marx's period. Marx may even be an ally of the gospel at points by exposing deficient versions of Christianity. But the essential ideas of the Christian gospel remain untouched by Marx's salvoes. What does Marx tell us about Jesus Christ that causes us to have anxiety about the gospel? Nothing. He has missed the mark. Marxism, once seen as the most credible alternative to Christianity in the Western world, is now itself passing into the history books.

C. SCIENTIFIC MATERIALISM

   "I believe in science," wrote A. J. Ayer. "That is, I believe that a theory about the way the world works is not acceptable unless it is confirmed by the facts, and I believe that the only way to discover what the facts are is by empirical observation."[34] Such views are still widely held, usually in tandem with the related notion that science eliminates the need to believe in God. Science, to the popular way of thinking, is capable of giving a completely objective and certain view of the universe, whereas Christianity rests on unproved ideas that cannot be believed with certainty.

   This is not, however, a particularly reliable way of viewing the way in which science and Christianity relate to one another. One way of exploring the complexity of the relationship between Christian thought and the natural sciences is to identify areas in which the methods and presuppositions of the natural sciences illuminate aspects of Christian theology. To many people it seems questionable even to speak of such convergence. Many, still firmly in the grasp of a positivist worldview fostered by the polemical literature of the nineteenth century,[35] tend to regard theology and natural science as unequally-matched sparring partners rather than willing and compatible bed partners.

In fact, however, scholarship has done much to dispel such myths. For example, consider the popular conception of Charles Darwin's theory of evolution as a purely scientific theory concerned with the explanation of the world, which posed a fundamental challenge to Christianity. This conventional and benign view of the author of *The Origins of Species* is belied by a critical study of Darwin's own writings.[36] As is becoming increasingly clear, Darwinism achieved its popular success in England, not because of its scientific credentials, nor because of its potential threat to traditional Christianity, but because Darwin's ideas happened to coincide with advanced Whig social thinking relative to matters of competition, free trade, and the natural superiority of the English middle classes and their social values. Darwin's science thus provided a theoretical foundation for Victorian liberalism by endorsing its values and outlook. Far from being a genius out of time or a scientist concerned only with facts, Darwin emerges as someone deeply tainted by the social prejudices of his period (non-Europeans and women, for example, are both treated as nonentities) and whose scientific theories were closely linked with his social beliefs. A dedicated secular "Darwin industry" has ensured that the received view of Darwin is that of a lonely and heroic figure, struggling to find the truth in the face of religious bigotry. The truth is only now emerging through a vast corpus of letters, diaries, and notebooks recently published.

Although the popular impression of the monolithic hostility of Christianity toward the natural sciences still prevails among what I shall reluctantly—but, I fear, entirely accurately—call the more unreflective members of both communities (and many outside them), it is fair to suggest that there has been a fundamental shift in our understanding of the question at issue over the past thirty years, a shift that makes a real dialogue between the disciplines both possible and potentially fruitful. There has been a realization of the radical difference between "science" and "scientific materialism." The former is a discipline, a way of investigating the structure of the physical world. The latter is a worldview that seeks to reduce everything to the level of observables, which—by definition—excludes God.

A helpful point of entry to this discussion is provided by the question of the evidential foundations of beliefs. The problem is well-known from Christian theology. It is possible to describe Christian theology as having a certain degree of coherence. For example, there is a well-established line of argumentation, going back at least as far as F. D. E. Schleiermacher and probably much further, to the effect that the Christian doctrines of God, the person and work of Christ, and of human nature, interact in such a manner as to give a consistent whole.[37] If "truth" is defined in terms of internal consistency, traditional Christian theology scores highly.[38]

But what of its relation to the world outside? A theory may be internally consistent, but how does it relate to the world it purports to describe or depict? At this point, significant difficulties emerge. How can one have any degree of certainty that there is a God? Or, to take a characteristic question posed on the basis of nineteenth-century historiographical presuppositions, how can one be sure that Jesus, as he can be uncovered by historical research, bears any direct relation to the Christ of faith? To put it bluntly: how can a substantial theology be erected on the basis of unproven—and probably inherently unprovable—assumptions? It might be allowed that theology makes some kind of sense of the world—but its evidential foundations are insecure in that they have not been demonstrated to be beyond doubt.

Let us explore this with the help of a classic discussion of the point: John Henry Newman's early lecture "Christianity and Scientific Investigation."[39] What happens, Newman asks, if faith and experience seem to be in contradiction? Or if something that is known to be true seems to contradict a Christian belief? Newman's response proceeds as follows. It may seem that faith and experience, or two matters of truth (one secular, one religious) seem to be irreconcilable. While truth cannot contradict truth, it may *seem* to contradict truth. Therefore "we must be patient with such appearances and not be hasty to pronounce them to be really of a more formidable character." Why? Because it may turn out that one of the "truths" rests upon an error of reasoning or observation. It may transpire that the truths alleged to be in tension can, in fact, be readily reconciled through means at present unknown. In short, the apparent problem may be resolved through new theoretical or observational developments.

If the last sentence seems to echo the vocabulary of the natural sciences, it is because I have chosen to cast Newman's ideas in terms calculated to heighten the parallel between Christianity and those sciences at this point. It is significant that the natural sciences are confronted with a similar problem, although it is a problem that is rarely discussed with the candor and frankness it deserves. The difficulty has long been recognized. It is discussed, for example, by William of Ockham in the fourteenth century. It is this. What I shall term the "positivist" view of science, which rests securely on nineteenth-century foundations, has as its leading assumption that scientific knowledge relates to the real, objective world—a world that is regular, constant, and uniform. Science is concerned with the uncovering and representation of the forms and patterns that occur in the natural world. Whereas philosophy and theology take recourse to conceptual speculation, the natural sciences engage directly with the natural world and are able to uncover its universal structure and pattern directly and unequivocally.

But how do we *know* that nature possesses regularity? How do we know that there are uniform structures and patterns throughout the totality of the natural order? Is this the conclusion of scientific research—or is it an essential assumption underlying this research? This question has been pursued vigorously by Norwood R. Hanson, especially in his work *Perception and Discovery*.[40] Hanson writes:

> To gain knowledge of these principles by experiment and observation is to presuppose in the search the very existence of that for which we are in search. If the principles are true, we cannot learn of it empirically, for the essence of the principles is that their truth is presupposed in every empirical inquiry.[41]

In other words, having presupposed the uniformity of nature, this uniformity is duly disclosed.

An immediate objection might be raised. If nature were, in actuality, to lack uniformity, this would be disclosed by empirical observation. In other words, the assumption of the uniformity of nature is open to challenge by experimentation. This, it might be argued, is no dogma or axiom but merely a working hypothesis of essentially heuristic value that can be checked out as things go along.

Hanson, however, provides a series of examples, which suggest that this is not actually the case. The basic features of his conclusions can be summarized as follows. If an experimental observation indicates that nature is not uniform, there are several possibilities open to us:

a. The experiment is in error, a fact that will be disclosed by later research.

b. The observation can be explained by a refinement in existing understandings of the way things are.

c. Nature is not uniform.

Hanson's point is that the third option is never taken seriously. There is a total commitment to the dogma of the uniformity of nature, which is not necessarily itself the result of empirical inquiry. It is an assumption that actually lies beyond challenge. Hanson argues that experimental evidence that appears to point to disuniformity is explained away by an appeal to present-day inadequacies in scientific technique and concepts.

The scientific community's tenacious grasp of the principle of the uniformity of nature thus bears an interesting and illuminating relation to the Christian community's belief in God. Both beliefs are regarded as foundational; indeed, for the Christian, they are even related, given the strong emphasis on the ordering of nature that is so characteristic a feature of the Augustinian tradition, especially in its Calvinist modifications. Yet neither, curiously, is entirely harmonious, if I might use the term, with observation.

Furthermore, each community is committed to the belief that it is defects in our existing understandings of reality that give rise to the apparent disharmony between theory and observation—whether it relates to the law of gravity (one of Hanson's examples) or the existence of evil (a traditional bugbear for the theologian). John Wisdom's parable of the garden tended by a mysterious gardener, leading to his dismissal of God through the "death of a thousand qualifications,"[42] is of importance here. The natural scientist is obliged to hedge his or her belief in the uniformity of nature with so many qualifying and modifying statements that, like belief in God or an invisible gardener, it seems to become a remarkably tenuous belief. Is there any way in which this belief could be proven wrong?

This leads us to consider the contribution of Karl R. Popper. In his youth, Popper was actively concerned with the formulation of a criterion that would be seen to set science apart from the confusion and vagueness, not to mention downright polemicizing, of writers such as Marx and Freud. He believed he found the answer in a remark attributed to Albert Einstein. "If," Einstein was reported as saying, "the red shift of spectral lines due to gravitational potential doesn't exist, then the general theory of relativity is untenable." Popper responded as follows:

> Here was an attitude utterly different from the dogmatic attitude of Marx, Adler and Freud, and even more so from that of their followers. Einstein was looking for crucial experiments whose agreement with his predictions would by no means establish his theory; while a disagreement, as he was the first to admit, would show his theory to be untenable. This, I felt, was the true scientific attitude.[43]

In other words, Popper is demanding that a belief should be capable of being stated in a form capable of being falsified. But is belief in the uniformity of nature actually capable of being falsified in the manner

Popper suggests, when it is so clearly inextricably enmeshed in the assumptions underlying its empirical investigation?

Popper himself is sufficiently honest to recognize the point at issue. He writes in *The Logic of Scientific Discovery:*

> In point of fact, no conclusive disproof of a theory can ever be produced, for it is always possible to say that the experimental results are not reliable, or that the discrepancies which are asserted to exist between experimental results and the theory are only apparent, and that they will disappear with the advance of our understanding.[44]

The implications of this are clear. The doctrine of the uniformity of nature is actually treated as being beyond falsification. If the experimental results appear to contradict it, these results are, in practice, not interpreted as implying that nature lacks uniformity. The explanations considered more probable are either that the experiment is flawed or that subsequent experiments or developments in theoretical analysis will explain the result without the need to reject the notion of the uniformity of the natural world.

My purpose here is not to criticize Popper; it is to demonstrate what seem to be insurmountable difficulties in verifying or falsifying the central—indeed, we might say the foundational—assumption of modern natural science, which comes remarkably close to being an article of religious faith. (Martin Heidegger once challenged the German physicist G. F. von Weizsäcker on this point at a meeting of Marburg University alumni in 1959, and received the reply: "Science believes in the regularity of nature and it is rooted in this belief as firmly as a religious belief is rooted in a system of religion.") Wittgenstein showed himself to be familiar with similar paradoxes in the world of philosophy (for example, Russell's paradox) when he wrote: "The same proposition may get treated at one time as something to test by experience, at another as a rule of testing."[45] It is not entirely clear which is the foundation and which is the superstructure, which the support and which the supported.

There are important parallels here with Christianity. Consider, for example, belief in God, which is of foundational importance to Christianity. That belief may reasonably be presented as an attempt to explain the nature of the world, and especially our place within it, consistent with the way the world is. It is not capable of demonstration or falsification in rigorously empirical terms. Yet, like the natural scientist who declines to abandon faith in the uniformity of nature on the basis of an experimental result, since he or she believes that this experiment will eventually be seen in a different light, so the theologian declines to abandon belief in God because of what might seem to be disagreement with experience at points—the problem of suffering being an example. When history is ended, the theologian asserts, and we are able to see things in the context of eternity, that problem will be seen in a totally new light—and be resolved. Is there really an enormous difference between the scientist and theologian at this point?

But what of the idea that science has rendered God unnecessary? As scientific understanding advances, will not God be squeezed out from the gaps in which Christian apologists have tried to lodge him? Curiously, the reverse seems to be taking place, as discussed in the section dealing with the ordering of the world as a point of contact.[46]

D. FEMINISM

Feminism has come to be a significant component of modern Western culture. Although it is possible to argue that it is not so much a comprehensive worldview in itself, but rather a collection of loosely connected critiques of a series of male-dominated worldviews, it is convenient for our purposes to discuss feminism as if it were a coherent worldview in its own right.

At its heart, feminism is a global movement working toward the emancipation of women. The older term for the movement—"women's liberation"—expressed the fact that it is at heart a liberation movement directing its efforts toward achieving equality for women in modern society, especially through the removal of obstacles—whether beliefs, values, or attitudes—that hinder that process.

Feminism has come into conflict with Christianity (as it has with just about every religion) because of the perception that religions treat women as second-rate human beings, in terms of the roles those religions allocate to women, as well as the manner in which they are understood to image God. The writings of Simone de Beauvoir—such as *The Second Sex*—develop such ideas at length. A number of post-Christian feminists—such as Mary Daly and Daphne Hampson—argue that Christianity, with its male symbols for God, its male savior figure, and its long history of male leaders and thinkers, is biased against women and incapable of redemption.[47] Women, they urge, should leave its oppressive environment. Others, such as Carol Christ and Naomi Ruth Goldenberg,[48] argue that women may find religious emancipation by recovering the ancient goddess religions (or by inventing new ones).

Yet the feminist evaluation of Christianity is not as clear-cut or as monolithically hostile toward women as these writers might suggest. Feminist writers have stressed how women have been active in the shaping and development of the Christian tradition from the New Testament onward and how they have exercised significant leadership roles throughout Christian history.[49] Indeed, responsible feminist writers have shown the need to reappraise the Christian past, giving honor and recognition to generations of faithful women whose practice, defense, and proclamation of their faith had hitherto passed unnoticed by much of the Christian church and its (mainly male) historians.

We may begin to explore the feminist critique of Christianity by considering the implications of the Christian doctrines of creation and redemption. Men and women are created in the image of God. Due to the Fall, the relationship between men and women has been disrupted and distorted through sin. The way things are is not the way things are meant to be. Indeed, a fundamental characteristic of responsible Christian theological reflection is a willingness to accept that the empirical situation cannot be allowed to control normative theological statements. As we noted in considering approaches to natural theology, it is necessary to concede that the results of a fallen human nature reflecting on a fallen creation can lead only to unreliable theological results. The oppression and domination of women by men, which has been the subject of so much feminist analysis, is an empirical reality that serves to emphasize the extent to which creation has fallen from its intended goal. In Christ, the process of reversal and renewal has begun.

In the light of this observation, let us turn to the criticism that the church has oppressed women in the course of its long history. Let us begin by noting that sin affects the structures of the church as much as it does the personal lives of individual believers. The Christian church, as human institution, is as prone to all the temptations and weaknesses of fallen nature as any other institution. The perceptive comments of Richard Holloway, writing from deep within the Scottish church establishment, need to be heeded (although the manner in which he expresses them would be found offensive by feminists, who would suggest that they betray a passive acceptance of women as polluting and carnal):

> There's a certain irony in Paul's language about the church as the pure bride of Christ. In spite of the church's white wedding dress, we know that she has been around, we know that she is not quite what she would like us to believe she is. . . . The church is the

bearer of momentous tidings that are confused and muddled by her own reputation and obvious imperfections.[50]

Part of that confusion is a temptation for the Christian church, as an institution, to become corrupted by ideas and values that are part of the furniture of the secular world. For example, its bishops wear gold mitres and purple robes. In the ancient world, both gold and purple were symbolic of wealth and power. The church too easily assimilated such secular symbols to its own use: what, many within the churches asked, has a gold mitre to do with a crown of thorns? Or a purple robe with the blood-spattered loincloth of the dying Christ?

This accommodation to secular values can be seen at work in the way in which the original, and remarkably liberating, attitude of Jesus Christ himself toward women became corrupted and confused because the church adopted attitudes that had more to do with the attitudes of the (male-dominated) secular world around it. We may begin by exploring the attitude of Jesus himself toward women[51]—an attitude that, on the basis of any responsible Christology, ought to be an inalienable part of the heritage of the Christian church.

a. Jesus' commendation of the single state as a legitimate calling for those to whom it was given stands in sharp contrast to traditional Palestinian views of a human duty to marry and procreate. As a result, women who chose to follow Jesus were able to assume roles other than those of wife or mother.

b. Jesus treats women as human subjects, rather than as objects or possessions. Throughout his ministry, Jesus can be seen engaging with and affirming women—often women who were treated as outcasts by contemporary Jewish society because of their origins (e.g., Syro-Phoenicia or Samaria) or their lifestyle (e.g., prostitutes).

c. Jesus refused to make women scapegoats in sexual matters— for example, adultery. The patriarchal assumption that men are corrupted by fallen women is conspicuously absent from his teaching and attitudes, most notably in his attitude toward prostitutes and the woman taken in adultery. The Talmudic recommendation that its readers (assumed to be men) should "not converse much with women, as this will eventually lead you to unchastity" is studiously ignored by Jesus, who made a point of talking to women (John 4 being an especially celebrated instance).

d. The traditional view that a woman was "unclean" during the period of menstruation was dismissed by Jesus, who made it clear that it is only moral impurity that defiles a person (Mark 7:1–23). Women could not be excluded from acts of worship for this traditional reason.

e. Women were an integral part of the group of people who gathered round Jesus, and they were affirmed by him, often to the dismay of the Pharisees and other religious traditionalists. Not only were women witnesses to the Crucifixion; they were also the first witnesses to the Resurrection. The only Easter event to be explicitly related in detail by all four of the gospel writers is the visit of the women to the tomb of Jesus. Yet Judaism dismissed the value of the testimony or witness of women, giving only men significant legal status in this respect. The greatest news that the world has ever known was thus first disclosed to women! Interestingly, Mark tells us the names of these women witnesses—Mary Magdalene, Mary the mother of James, and Salome—*three times* (Mark 15:40, 47; 16:1), but he does not mention the names of any male disciples who were around at the time. (It might also be worth noting that it was *a man* who betrayed Jesus, and a group of *men* who crucified Jesus!)

f. The gospels frequently portray women as being more spiritually perceptive than men. For example, Mark portrays the male disciples as having little faith (Mark 4:40; 6:52), while commending women—a woman is praised for her faith (Mark 5:25–34), a foreign woman is commended for responding to Jesus (Mark 7:24–30), and a widow is singled out as an example to follow (Mark 12:41–44).

g. Christian baptism was for all, male and female. The traditional Judaism of the period ordained that only male children could receive the initiation rite of the people of God—circumcision. But in the church no distinction was to be made between male and female at this level.

It is difficult to appreciate how novel these attitudes were at the time. Jesus' ministry represents an attempt to reform the patriarchalism of his day and to permit women to hold a new kind of authority in religious matters.

> Possibly the most revolutionary aspect of Jesus' approach to women is not that he associated freely with them and treated them as responsible human beings, not that he had women as friends and not that he allowed them to listen to his teaching; but rather that he taught them personally, indulging in theological conversation with them, encouraging and expecting a response.[52]

It is hardly surprising that early Christianity proved to have a deep appeal for women. As one scholar observes:

> It is probable that Jesus' teachings attracted women in part because of the new roles and equal status they were granted in the Christian community. There were many cults in Greece and Rome that were for men only or, at best, allowed women to participate in

very limited ways. Further, it is easy to see why women who were on the fringe of the synagogue community became Christian converts. Judaism offered women proselytes a circumscribed place at best, for they were faced with the Jewish restrictions that limited their participation in religious functions. While women were not allowed to make up the quorum necessary to found a synagogue, nor to receive the Jewish covenant sign (circumcision), these limitations did not exist in the Christian community.[53]

Sadly, this became corrupted as Christianity came under increasing pressure to conform to, rather than to transform, secular stereotypes. But throughout its history, these original attitudes can be seen coming to life again. At the time of the Reformation of the sixteenth century, the doctrine of the priesthood of all believers declared that all believers—whether male or female—were true priests of Christ.[54] Society was not ready for this new development—but its theological foundations had been securely laid.

This new emphasis on the potential roles of women was regarded with horror by many at the time. Cardinal Cajetan, charged with handling the Lutheran crisis in Germany, believed that the inevitable (and shocking) outcome of the new reforming movements was that women would become accepted as theologians. The French reformer Etienne Le Court was burned alive for teaching that women would proclaim the gospel. Jacques Lefèvre d'Etaples pointedly dedicated his French translation of the New Testament "to all Christian men *and women*"; he had no doubts that its readership would—and should—include this hitherto marginalized component of the people of God. In his *Women of the Reformation*, Roland Bainton has given us a fine account of aspects of this important development, viewed through the prism of the lives of leading women of the sixteenth century.[55] In practice, the Reformation tended to adopt socially conservative approaches to the role of women, perhaps because of a reluctant social realism: society was not yet ready for this radical new social development, even if its theological basis had been securely and irreversibly established.

The church, as an institution, has too easily lost sight of these insights. Christianity may have liberated women—but, for many, the institution of the church seems to have ended up oppressing them. As the reformers of the sixteenth century observed, there was a need to demand that the church reform itself by returning to its foundations in the New Testament. The slogan *ecclesia semper reformanda*, "the church must always be reforming itself," is a concise statement of this reforming agenda. The church must always reexamine itself and ensure that its patterns of behavior and belief correspond to its God-given models in Jesus Christ and in Scripture. The oppression of women in the past by the church is a matter of history; it is time that Christianity triumphed over the institution of the church at this point. For, as we have stressed, sin is structural, not just personal. The church itself, as much as individual Christians, is prone to sin. It is a reminder of how the past history of the church can become a present argument against Christianity—as well as an incentive to reform the church of our own day and age so that it can bear a more effective witness to our own generation.

But some feminist critics of Christianity wish to press their case further. Christianity itself—not merely the church—is profoundly oppressive to women because of its male concept of God. A religion committed to a male God will inevitably devalue and degrade women. This criticism seems to rest on a serious misunderstanding of the nature of theological language and Christian symbolism, which we may explore with profit.

There seems to be something about the human mind that makes images more memorable than concepts. The nineteenth-century poet Alfred Lord Tennyson once remarked that most Englishmen pictured God as an enormous clergyman with a long beard. Whether this is a helpful way of thinking about God is open to question, but it does draw attention to the fact that we need to visualize God in some sort of way. How often have we been reminded that a picture is worth a thousand words? The early fathers of the Christian church used to compare understanding God with looking directly into the sun. The human eye is simply not capable of withstanding the intense light of the sun. And just as the human eye cannot cope with the brilliance of the sun, so the human mind cannot cope with the fullness of God.

As every amateur astronomer knows, however, it is possible to look at the sun through dark glass, or in the early morning through a mist, both of which greatly reduce the brilliance of the solar disc to manageable proportions. In these ways, the human eye can cope with an object that is otherwise completely beyond its capacities. In much the same way, it is helpful to think of Scripture making available models of God: scaled-down versions of the real thing, which we are capable of comprehending and visualizing.

The scriptural models or pictures of God reveal God in manageable proportions so that the human mind can cope with him. As Calvin declared, "God accommodates himself to our weakness." The scriptural models of God—for example, God as shepherd, rock, or king—are powerful and profound visual aids to our thinking about God, lending depth to what otherwise might be superficial, and the vividness of life to what otherwise might be dry and dull.[56]

These models of God are firmly located in real life. Just as Jesus used real-life parables to make theological points (see pp. 26–27), so the writers of Scripture use models drawn from the experiential world of ancient Palestine to allow us insights into the nature and purposes of God. In that this society was male-dominated, many of the available models are male. For example, the idea of the authority of God could only be represented using male imagery—such as that of a father, a judge, or a king.

But other models are used. God is often compared to a (genderless) rock, for example, conveying the idea of strength, stability, and permanence. Feminine imagery abounds to describe God's care and compassion for his people, which is often likened to the love of a mother for her children. But it is not the imagery that matters; it is what is being said about God that is of fundamental importance.

We can explore this point further by thinking about a situation familiar to many people who study science at high school. If you take some gas in a container of some sort and compress it, you find that the volume the gas occupies gets smaller as the pressure you apply gets greater. This observation, stated in mathematical form, is known as Boyle's Law. If you think of the molecules of gas as billiard balls continually bumping each other, you find that you can predict this law. The smaller the space in which the billiard balls are forced to move (in other words, the volume), the more they collide with each other and the sides of the container (in other words, they exert more pressure). This model is sometimes known as the *kinetic theory* of gases.

But this does not mean that gas molecules are identical with billiard balls. It means that billiard balls are a good model for gas molecules, for two reasons. First, they allow us to picture what molecules are like. We cannot see the molecules because they are infinitesimally small. But the model allows us to visualize them, to form a mental picture of what they are like. It is not ideal, but it allows us to think of the molecules, to form a picture of them, where otherwise we could not picture them at all.

Second, it allows us to understand and explore at least one aspect of the behavior of those molecules. Obviously, it does not allow us to explain every aspect of their behavior, but it does help us to understand at least part of what is going on and to try to predict some other properties of the system.

It is like an analogy—and analogies are helpful, providing we remember that every analogy breaks down at some point. Models help us think about things we otherwise probably could not visualize at all and allow us to understand at least *part* of what is going on.

But a serious error can easily arise here. We may improperly identify the model with what is being modeled. To go back to the kinetic theory, it might be mistakenly assumed that gas molecules are billiard balls, when in fact gas molecules behave in certain respects as if they were billiard balls. Similarly, when we suggest that a suitable model for God is a father, we are saying that in certain respects God may be thought of as being like a father—for example, in his disciplining of his children. And in certain respects God is like a mother—for example, in his care and compassion for his children. But God is not male. God is not female. We must always remember that a model is both like and unlike what is being modeled—the important thing is to identify what the points of likeness are. To model God on a human father is not to say that God is male or that males are superior to females. The maleness of this language is, to use Calvin's notion, an accommodation to human speech and ways of thinking—not a literal representation of God.

Of course, as some feminist writers point out, many male theologians do indeed think of God as being male. But this represents a criticism of their interpretation of Scripture, not of Scripture itself. As George Caird points out, "It is precisely when theologians have claimed biblical authority for their own beliefs and practices that they have been peculiarly exposed to the universal temptation . . . of jumping to the conclusion that the biblical writer is referring to what they would be referring to, were they speaking the words themselves."[57]

It is only if God is understood to be a projection, a result, of human culture that the objections raised by feminist writers have decisive force. Now it is true that many radical feminist writers subscribe to this theory of the origins of religion (associated with writers as diverse as Feuerbach, Marx, and Freud).[58] But it remains a hypothesis, not a fact. Traditional Christian theology speaks and knows of a God who reveals himself through human culture but is not bound by its categories. God is supracultural, just as he is suprasexual. There is all the difference in the world between saying that God is the product of a culture and that God reveals himself in and through a culture.

The Christian revelation declares that a father in ancient Israel society is a suitable model for God. But this is not equivalent to saying

that God is male or that God is confined to the cultural parameters of
ancient Israel. Mary Hayter, reflecting on such issues, writes:

> It would appear that certain "motherly prerogatives" in ancient
> Hebrew society—such as carrying and comforting small chil-
> dren—became metaphors for Yahweh's activity *vis-à-vis* his
> children Israel. Likewise, various "fatherly prerogatives"— such
> as disciplining a son—became vehicles for divine imagery.
> Different cultures and ages have different ideas about which roles
> are proper to the mother and which to the father.[59]

To speak of God as father is to say that the role of the father in ancient
Israel allows us insights into the nature of God, not that God is a male
human being. Neither male nor female sexuality is to be attributed to
God. Indeed, sexuality is an attribute of the created order that cannot
be assumed to correspond directly to any such polarity within the
creator God himself.

This analysis of the language of theology indicates that there are
no grounds for maintaining that the Christian way of talking about
God authorizes the oppression of women. It merely indicates the need
for people to be informed about the status of theological statements
and language.

> Ultimately, whether theological vocabulary is masculine or femi-
> nine is of little consequence. The masculine terminology does not
> denote a male deity; the female terminology does not denote a
> female deity; nor does the mixture of masculine and feminine
> terminology denote an androgynous God/ess. Rather, the indica-
> tions are that the God of the Bible uniquely incorporates and
> transcends all sexuality.[60]

Indeed, the Old Testament avoids attributing sexual functions to God
because of the strongly pagan overtones of such associations. The
fertility cults of the prevailing Canaanite culture emphasized the sexual
functions of both gods and goddesses. The Old Testament refuses to
endorse the idea that the gender or the sexuality of God is a significant
matter. As Mary Hayter puts it:

> Today a growing number of feminists teach that the God/ess
> combines male and female characteristics. They, like those who
> assume that God is exclusively male, should remember that *any*
> attribution of sexuality to God is a reversion to paganism.[61]

There is no need to revert to pagan ideas of gods and goddesses to
recover the idea that God is neither masculine nor feminine. Those
ideas are already firmly embedded in Scripture and need to be
recovered if Christianity is to address the new apologetic situation in
Western society.

Feminism, then, is a powerful challenge to Christianity. Just as Marxism challenged Christianity to reconsider its attitudes toward the powerless, the poor, and the marginalized, so feminism challenges it to reconsider its attitudes toward women and to recover its original Christ-based attitudes toward them. Just as Marxism failed in its attempt to provide a credible alternative worldview to that of Christianity, so it seems that feminism will fail also. As a critique of Christianity, it has much to offer and much to say and deserves a careful hearing. But where it seeks to replace the gospel with its own secularized worldview, it seems certain to fail, having overstepped its resources and failed to recognize its own limitations. In the postmodern worldview, feminism is one voice among many, not *the* voice that relativizes everything else—an observation that brings us to consideration of that postmodern worldview in more detail.

E. POSTMODERNISM

Postmodernity is a broad concept that describes the general intellectual outlook arising after the collapse of modernity.[62] Although there are those who maintain that modernity is still alive and active, this claim is becoming increasingly rare. Further, we need to note that modernity itself is a broad concept; the very idea of postmodernism might be argued to "presuppose that our age is unified enough that we can speak of its ending."[63] Nevertheless, profound changes have taken place that warrant the concept of postmodernity. The trauma of Auschwitz is a powerful and shocking indictment of the "pretense of new creation, the hatred of tradition, the idolatry of self" characteristic of modernity.[64] It is modernity, especially its compulsive desire to break totally with the past, that gave rise to the Nazi holocaust and the Stalinist purges. There has been a general collapse of confidence in the Enlightenment trust in the power of reason to provide foundations for a universally valid knowledge of the world, including God. Reason fails to deliver a morality suited to the real world in which we live. And with this collapse of confidence in universal and necessary criteria of truth, relativism and pluralism have flourished.

To give a full definition of postmodernism is virtually impossible.[65] Nevertheless, it is possible to identify its leading general features as they are likely to be encountered by the Christian apologist, especially on North American college and university campuses.

One of the main features of postmodernism is the precommitment to relativism or pluralism in relation to questions of truth. To use the jargon of the movement, one could say that postmodernism represents a situation in which the signifier has replaced the signified as the focus of orientation and value. In terms of the structural linguistics developed initially by Ferdinand de Saussure and subsequently by Roman Jakobson and others, the recognition of the arbitrariness of the linguistic sign and its interdependence with other signs marks the end of the possibility of fixed, absolute meanings. Thus writers such as Jacques Derrida, Michel Foucault, and Jean Baudrillard argued that language is whimsical and capricious and does not reflect any overarching absolute linguistic laws. It is arbitrary, incapable of disclosing meaning. Thus Baudrillard argued that modern society is trapped in an endless network of artificial sign systems that *mean* nothing and merely perpetuate the belief systems of those who created them.

One aspect of postmodernism that illustrates this trend (and reflects its obsession with texts and language) is *deconstruction*—the critical method that virtually declares that the identity and intentions of the author of a text are irrelevant to the interpretation of the text, followed by the observation that, in any case, no meaning can be found in it. All interpretations are equally valid, or equally meaningless (depending on your point of view). As Paul de Man, one of the leading American proponents of this approach, declared, the very idea of "meaning" smacks of fascism. This approach blossomed in post-Vietnam America, given intellectual respectability by academics such as de Man, Geoffrey Hartman, Harold Bloom, and J. Hillis Miller.[66]

The lunacy of this position only became publicly apparent with the sensational publication of some articles written by de Man. On December 1, 1989, the *New York Times* reported the discovery of anti-Semitic and pro-Nazi articles, written by de Man for the Belgian Nazi newspaper *Le Soir*. A scandal resulted. Was de Man's deconstructionalism an attempt to deny his own past? Was de Man himself a fascist, trying to escape from his own guilt? Nobody could very well argue that de Man had actually meant something different from the impression created by those articles. After all, the author's views were, according to deconstruction, an irrelevance. No attempt could be made to excuse de Man by an appeal to his historical circumstances, for de Man himself had written that "considerations of the actual and historical existence of writers are a waste of time from a critical viewpoint." Deconstruction thus seemed to sink into the mire of internal inconsistency.

Apologetically, the question that arises is the following. How can Christianity's claims to truth be taken seriously when there are so many rival alternatives? No one can lay claim to possession of the truth. It is all a question of perspective. All claims to truth are equally valid. There is no universal or privileged vantage point that allows anyone to decide what is right and what is wrong.

This situation has both significant advantages and drawbacks for the Christian apologist. On the one hand, apologetics no longer labors under the tedious limitations of the petty and asphyxiating Enlightenment worldview, fettered by the illusions and pretensions of pure reason. Christianity can no longer be dismissed as a degenerate form of rational religion. The severe limitations of the modern mentality are intellectually *passé* and need no longer be a difficulty for the apologist. Princeton philosopher Diogenes Allen summarizes this development well:

> In a postmodern world, Christianity is intellectually relevant. It is relevant to the fundamental questions, Why does the world exist? and Why does it have its present order, rather than another? It is relevant to the discussion of the foundations of morality and society, especially on the significance of human beings. The recognition that Christianity is relevant to our entire society, and relevant not only to the heart but to the mind as well, is a major change in our cultural situation.[67]

While intellectual dinosaurs still stalk our campuses, unaware that the days of a blind secular faith in human reason are behind us, the general atmosphere has changed. Christianity has as much right as any other belief-system to gain a hearing.

But with that advance has come a retreat. All belief-systems are to be regarded as equally plausible. Something is true if it is true for me. Christianity has become acceptable because it is *believed to be* true by some—not because it *is* true. The apologist will wish to stress that Christianity believes itself, on excellent grounds, to possess insights that are both true and relevant. How can Christianity commend itself on campus when the truth question is virtually dismissed in advance?

This is an instance of a situation in which the apologist must adopt a tactical approach in order to gain a strategic advantage. No Christian will wish to abandon a passionate commitment to the truth. Nevertheless, the postmodern situation demands that Christian truth-claims be, for purely tactical reasons, relegated to the background temporarily, in order to commend the claims of Christianity on grounds more acceptable in the postmodern worldview. Once the thin end of this apologetic wedge has penetrated the postmodern citadel, the truth-claims inherent within Christian faith may begin to make their presence felt, and their validity obvious. Let us explore this approach.

Christianity is profoundly attractive. The "God and Father of our Lord Jesus Christ" (1 Peter 1:3) possesses an attraction that exceeds anything the world can offer.[68] This is a celebrated theme of Christian theology from the patristic period onward, perhaps reaching a climax in the writings of Jonathan Edwards, and it should be fundamental to modern apologetics. If the world seems attractive, the Christian must ensure that God, as its creator, is seen to be even more attractive. The world reflects the attractiveness of its creator, as the moon reflects the light of the sun.

Two incidents from classical Greek mythology suggest themselves here. Homer introduces us to the Sirens, a group of women whose singing was so seductive that they caused sailors to crash their vessels through inattention to their duties. When Ulysses was attempting to sail his ship past the Sirens, he prevented the Sirens from causing any difficulties by the simple expedient of blocking his sailors' ears so that they could not hear the captivating Siren song. Orpheus, on the other hand, was a skilled lyre player. His method of dealing with this kind of threat was rather indifferent. He played his lyre, the music of which proved so enchanting and fascinating that its beauty totally outweighed anything else.

The Christian apologist should be able to present God in his full attractiveness so that his rivals in the world are eclipsed. What are the attractions of God? The following would be important elements of this presentation, which the apologist could modify or supplement as seems appropriate:

   a. The ability of God to satisfy the deepest human longings.

   b. The overwhelming love of God, as seen in the death of Christ.

   c. Relativism settles nowhere and nothing; faith in God anchors people, giving them stability and purpose.

To this should be added our analysis of the relevance of Christianity to life, including the arguments that Christianity meets three central needs.[69]

   a. The need to have a basis for morality. Christianity offers a worldview that leads to the generation of moral values and ideals that are able to give moral meaning and dignity to our existence.

   b. The need to have a framework for making sense of experience, which correlates with the inbuilt human need to make sense of things.

   c. The need for a vision to guide and inspire people. Life without a vision, or a reason for keeping going, is dreary, dull, and pointless.

Having thus established the attractiveness and relevance of God, the question of truth may be addressed. Once an attractive belief has been presented and its attractiveness conceded, the key question becomes: Is it right?

This brings us to the real challenge postmodernism poses to the apologist. Postmodernism has an endemic aversion to questions of truth. But the need to have the truth question on the agenda is relatively easily argued. One approach might be the following. To the postmodern suggestion that something can be "true for me" but not "true," the following reply might be made. Is fascism equally as true as democratic libertarianism? Consider the person who believes, passionately and sincerely, that it is an excellent thing to place millions of Jews in gas chambers. That is certainly "true for him." But can it be allowed to pass unchallenged? Is it equally as true as the belief that one ought to live in peace and tolerance with one's neighbors, including Jews?

The moral seriousness of this question often acts as the intellectual equivalent of a battering ram, bringing out the fact that certain views just cannot be allowed to be true. There must be some criteria, some standards of judgment, that allow one to exclude certain viewpoints as unacceptable. Otherwise, postmodernism will be seen to be uncritical and naive, a breeding ground of the political and moral complacency that allowed the rise of the Third Reich back in the 1930s. Even postmodernism has difficulties in allowing that Nazism is a good thing. Yet precisely that danger lies there, as evidenced by the celebrated remark of Sartre: "Tomorrow, after my death, certain people may decide to establish fascism, and the others may be cowardly or miserable enough to let them get away with it. At that moment, fascism will be the truth of man."

This is an important point, perhaps the point at which postmodernism is at its most vulnerable. To lend extra weight to it, we may consider the consequences of the ethical views of Michel Foucault, generally regarded as one of the intellectual pillars of postmodern thought. Foucault argues passionately, in a series of highly original and creative works, that the very idea of "truth" grows out of the interests of the powerful. "Truth" can support systems of repression by identifying standards to which people can be forced to conform.[70] Thus what is "mad" or "criminal" does not depend on some objective criterion, but on the standards and interests of those in authority. Each society has its "general politics of truth," which serves its vested interests. "Truth" thus serves the interests of society by perpetuating its ideology and by providing a rational justification for the imprisonment or elimination of those who happen to contradict its general outlook. And philosophy can too easily become an accomplice in this repression by providing the oppressors with rational arguments to justify their practices. Philosophers have allowed society to believe that it was persecuting its marginal elements on the basis of "truth" or "morality"—universal and objective standards of morality, of what is right and wrong—rather than on the basis of its own vested interests.

For such reasons, Foucault believes that the very idea of objective truth or morality must be challenged. This belief has passed into the structure of much of postmodernism. But is it right? Is not the truth that Foucault's criticism actually rests on a set of quite definite beliefs about what is right and what is wrong? To give an illustration, throughout Foucault's writings, we find a passionate belief that repression is wrong. Foucault is committed to an objective moral value—that freedom is to be preferred to repression. Just as Schaeffer demonstrated the inner contradictions of Sartre's ethical agnosticism,[71] so we have every right to point out that Foucault's critique of morality actually presupposes certain moral values. Foucault's critique of the moral values of society seems to leave him without any moral values of his own—yet his critique of social values rests on his own acceptance of certain moral values, which he clearly expects his readers to share. Why is struggle preferable to submission? Why is freedom to be chosen, rather than repression? These normative questions demand answers if Foucault's position is to be justified, yet Foucault has vigorously rejected an appeal to general normative principles as an integral part of his method. In effect, he makes an appeal to sentimentality rather than reason, to pathos rather than principles.[72] That many shared his intuitive dislike of repression ensured he was well received, but the fundamental question remains unanswered. Why is repression wrong? And that same question remains unanswered within postmodernism, which is vulnerable precisely where Foucault is vulnerable.

As Richard Rorty, perhaps the most distinguished American philosopher to develop Foucault's dislike of general principles and normative standards, remarks, a consequence of this approach must be the recognition that

> there is nothing deep down inside us except what we have put there ourselves, no criterion that we have not created in the course of creating a practice, no standard of rationality that is not an appeal to such a criterion, no rigorous argumentation that is not obedience to our own conventions.[73]

But if this approach is right, what justification could be given for opposing Nazism? Or Stalinism? Rorty cannot give a justification for the moral or political rejection of totalitarianism, as he himself concedes. If he is right, Rorty admits, then he has to acknowledge

> . . . that when the secret police come, when the torturers violate the innocent, there is nothing to be said to them of the form "There is something within you which you are betraying. Though you embody the practices of a totalitarian society, which will endure forever, there is something beyond those practices which condemns you."[74]

It is difficult to avoid the conclusion that, for Rorty, the truth of moral values depends simply upon their existence. And it is at this point that many postmodernists feel deeply uneasy. Something seems to be wrong here.

If the word *truth* continues to cause intractable problems, an alternative approach may be tried. Instead of asking whether Christianity is *true*, the postmodernist might be asked whether it can be regarded as *credible*. This is a direct invitation to discuss the foundations of Christian belief, not least the resurrection of Christ. Why should anyone believe that Christianity is credible? The question of the evidential basis of Christianity can thus be placed directly on the agenda.

Happily, there are indications that postmodernism is unlikely to remain a significant feature of our cultural landscape. But while it is, the apologist must be able to respond to its outlook. Much the same is true of the New Age movement, to which we now turn.

F. THE NEW AGE

One of the most important alternative belief systems in modern Western society is loosely known as the "New Age movement."[75] This media-generated catchall phrase sweeps into its *omnium gatherum* a remarkably diverse number of late twentieth-century American (or perhaps one should say Californian?) spiritual practices and beliefs. In many ways, the New Age movement is a natural reaction to the efforts of a generation of pseudointellectual mainline Protestant writers and preachers who attempted to eradicate the supernatural, mystical, and transcendent element of Christianity in the name of some imaginary "universal rationality" or "global secular culture." America got bored with the resulting liberal religion of platitudes and adopted the New Age instead.[76]

This astonishingly complex movement knits together strands of contemporary concerns with the idea that there is a fundamental identity between the human and the divine self. To use a phrase strongly defended by many New Agers: "Every human being is a god." Shirley MacLaine, publicly defending this key New Age doctrine in New York, was challenged by one of her audience: "With all due respect, I don't think you are a god." Her immediate response? "If you don't see me as God, it's because you don't see yourself as God." [77]

The attraction of this idea is enormous. If you are a god, you can make your own rules, and nobody can argue with you. Laying down the law is, after all, one of the privileges of divinity. Unlike Christianity, there are no Ten Commandments or Sermon on the Mount to provide moral guidance; the New Ager can rely on "the god within" to provide a conveniently undemanding ethic of self-fulfillment. (Interestingly, many New Agers profess to admire the religious teachings of certain Hindu gurus but are less than enthusiastic about the rigorous programs of abstinence and chastity linked with these teachings.) But deep within this approach lurks an obvious—some would say, fatal—contradiction. As G. K. Chesterton pointed out, worshiping the "god within" turns out to be nothing more than self-worship.

These ideas are not new. Indeed, one of the paradoxes of the New Age is that it seems to rest on some very old ideas. The paganism of late antiquity has been revived, merged with ideas drawn from native American religions, and supplemented by pantheistic ideas deriving from Eastern religions.[78] The revival of pagan ideas has reached such proportions that modern Christians can relate with the greatest of ease to New Testament accounts of Christian encounters with classical paganism. As David K. Clark and Norman L. Geisler perceptively remark of Paul's Areopagus (or Mars Hill) sermon:

> Christians today stand again on Mars Hill. In the first century, Saint Paul debated with two groups of Greek philosophers at a place in Athens called Mars Hill. Paul's antagonists were the Epicureans and the Stoics. Like Paul, Christians today are locked in debate with both Epicureans and Stoics. When the American Atheists met in Denver recently, Madalyn Murray O'Hair declared that there is no God. Shirley MacLaine soon came to town to pronounce that she and all her listeners are gods. Shortly thereafter, in a Denver crusade, Billy Graham preached that Jesus alone is God. These well-known champions of three worldviews have rekindled that ancient Mars Hill debate.[79]

So diverse is the New Age movement that it is pointless to speak of it having "doctrines." It does not possess well-defined doctrines of God, generally believing that to define God is to limit him. It is perhaps more appropriate to speak of the movement having themes or attitudes, rather than definitely shaped belief systems. This feature of the New Age movement is perhaps one of its most frustrating features; open to endless variations, the movement cannot be defined with any degree of precision. The apologist is thus often obliged to adopt an ad hoc approach, responding to whatever variation on the movement's themes happens to be encountered. What approaches may be adopted in responding to it?

One approach is to confront the logical and philosophical deficiencies of pantheism and panentheism. There are serious difficulties attending the religious outlooks of the New Age movement, which can easily be identified and addressed.[80] This approach has the advantage of intellectual sophistication and theological integrity. Nevertheless, it suffers from a weakness, characteristic of classical apologetics. *The academic approach adopted often cuts no ice with the intended audience.* The ideas and approaches are excellent, but the situations in which dialogue can and does take place preclude such detailed argumentation. Pantheism has a certain degree of resistance to logic, believing that the mystical nature of reality renders argumentation and logical analysis irrelevant. The approach adopted by the classical apologist is thus likely to be dismissed as inappropriate. The classical approach is, of course, enormously important for Christians wanting to reassure themselves of the coherence and credibility of the Christian faith in the face of the New Age challenge. But it has strictly limited potential in public debate, often casting the Christian apologist as pedantic and petty over against the openness of the New Ager.

The sort of simple and unsophisticated arguments that are likely to get home to New Age devotees are pragmatic and direct. If you are god, why are you so unhappy? What privileges does being a god confer? Does it make them immune from unemployment, from suffering or pain? From death? What hope does it give them in the face of the present reality of suffering and the future event of death?

The argument is not taking place in university seminar rooms but in the public arena. And that public is not interested in conceptual sophistication and finely honed technical arguments; it is interested in quickly grasped and easily understood points. Time is not on the side of the philosophically minded apologist who needs space to develop the concepts he presents—the attention span of skeptical New Age audiences is strictly limited. In the end, the debate with the New Age movement will not be won through philosophy but through the proclamation of Christ. The New Testament offers us invaluable guidance here, which we ought to accept with confidence. It sets before us a crisp, concise, and convincing approach, ideally suited to the New Age challenge—both in terms of the movement's ideas and the opportunities available for confronting it. The resurrection of Christ may hold the key to engagement with the New Age.

I have to confess that I have found the approach adopted by Paul at Mars Hill to be far more effective than detailed philosophical debate. Let's sketch the background before exploring the approach. The key question is this: How do we know anything about God? New Agers are reluctant to put a name to God. To define is to limit, and God is limitless. Your mind gets in the way of knowing God. Stop using it. Don't evaluate. Don't judge. Don't think. Just *experience* God. There is no way of validating this experience. Just let it happen; what happens to you is God. You are God; your experiences are thus divine. Reason—especially someone else's reason—is not competent to judge your firsthand experience.

Such approaches allow us to understand why many sociologists regard the New Age movement as a symbol of the collapse of Enlightenment rationalism. The total irrationality of the movement is one of its most striking features. It is locked into its worldview, allowing no means of entry for criticism or evaluation. But the movement, like classical paganism, is willing to dispute about God. Unlike the cold hostility of Enlightenment rationalism, the New Age is generally very receptive to religious ideas, acknowledging them as a potentially valuable contribution to the spiritual side of human existence. A dialogue is thus genuinely possible.

The apologist can argue along a number of lines. Let's begin with a very simplistic approach. Consider near-death experiences, often exploited by New Agers as evidence both of the reality of the supernatural and of their own interpretation of the realm of "transcendent knowing, a domain not limited to time and space."[81] These accounts are related by those who are thought to have come very close to death yet to have survived to relate what they experienced. But none of these reports concern experiences of death, or of what exists after death. They are simply perceptions of what seems to happen close to death.

But what if someone were to die—really die—and return from the dead to tell us about the experience of death, and what lies beyond? Would not his or her witness be of first-rate importance? Would it not possess an authority totally lacking in any other? Would we not pay attention to such a person? The Christian has immediately gained a hearing for Christ and the message of the gospel in terms that make sense to New Agers. It may lack theological sophistication. It would cut little ice in a philosophy seminar. But the apologist must learn to adapt arguments and imagery to suit the audience. Learn to gain credibility in terms of the worldview of the New Age. Otherwise, you will not get a hearing.

A more sophisticated approach draws on the parallels between classical Athenian paganism and the New Age movement, and uses Paul's Areopagus sermon in Acts 17:16–34 as a model (note how verses 24–28 echo ideas now prevalent within the New Age movement). Let's consider Marilyn Ferguson's words: "You have to be willing to have experiences and not have words for them."[82] But why? Why not be able to put one's experiences of God into words? After all, we have already seen how words do indeed possess the ability to point to and communicate God.[83] Christ puts a name and a face to this God; the Resurrection establishes his credentials in this respect. To lapse into quasi-New Age language, Christ has broken through into the realm of transcendent knowing, making it knowable and available. Such an approach provides a point of contact in that it links into the New Age worldview, without endorsing it, in order to establish the authority of Christ—the Resurrection being of supreme importance. And the authority of Christ having been established, the apologist is in a position to begin introducing other key aspects of the gospel proclamation to his or her audience.

A third approach might be to argue along the following lines. The Resurrection shows that Christ has some superiority over the rest of us when it comes to knowing spiritual reality. So we should listen to him as to one who has penetrated far deeper into the transcendent realm of knowing than anyone else. Again, note the emphasis on the Resurrection. Christ has a spiritual authority which, you would argue, sets him above others, such as Shirley MacLaine. Why listen to Shirley when you can listen to Jesus? Jesus' credentials are more impressive than hers! Shirley hasn't died, let alone been raised from the dead, and thus has not had a firsthand account of transcendent spiritual realities. Thus, by operating tactically within a New Age worldview, you have set the scene for presenting the Christian gospel and eventually allowing your audience to break free from their existing worldview.

It will be clear that, because of its amorphous and irrational structure, the New Age presents the apologist with peculiar difficulties. The approaches outlined above are just some of the many ways into the movement. But the effort, though worth making, has difficulties. The most serious problem arises from the fact that New Age is generally committed to a syncretistic program of claiming Christ as one ascended master among many others. The uniqueness of Christ is denied. The Christian apologist must thus insist on the total qualitative distinction between Christ and any other religious teacher. Christ does not teach us—he transforms us, as no other ever has and no other ever can. The uniqueness of Christ, grounded in the event of the Resurrection and the doctrine of the divinity of Christ, is the most secure foundation of Christian apologetics at this point. It must not be compromised. The New Age is largely a reaction against the spiritual inadequacies of liberal Christianity; this same liberalism must not be allowed to deprive us of our most potent weapons against it. Liberalism got the church into this mess, but it does not possess the resources to get us out of it. Only orthodox Christianity has the apologetic and spiritual means to reclaim the lost ground. This point is a potent reminder that good apologetics rests on responsible and reliable theology.

But the best theological and spiritual arguments and insights can be compromised through lazy presentation and thoughtless application. Our concluding chapter aims to make the vital transition from theory to practice, as we move from textbook to application.

PART 3

Apologetics in Action

CHAPTER SEVEN

From Textbook
to Real Life

Apologetics is not a craft confined to the seminar room—it is a vital resource for all engaged in Christian ministry. It is important as a resource for more effective evangelism; it also enables those who are already Christians to deepen the quality of their faith, reinforcing commitment with understanding and conviction. In this final chapter, we look at some ways of grounding apologetics in situations that really matter by exploring some practical issues that are too often overlooked in textbooks on this theme.

I am not for one moment suggesting that successful evangelism is simply concerned with the development of good technique. Rather, I am concerned to stress that apologetics includes both theoretical and practical components. Sadly, experience suggests that mastery of the former rarely extends to the latter. This final chapter aims to make the vital transition from the textbook to real life by addressing some of the difficulties and obstacles faced by many who have wrestled with unbelief at the level of ideas and who now want to engage with unbelief as it is found in real life. We begin by stressing the need for careful listening as a first step in effective apologetics.

A. APOLOGETICS AS DIALOGUE

Traditionally, apologetics textbooks have concentrated on more academic issues than some of those discussed in this work. They often have focused on familiarizing their readers with the history and theory of Christian apologetics. But that is only part of the story. Explaining the theory of an internal combustion engine does not enable someone to drive a car, any more than explaining the percussion mechanism of a piano turns someone into Arthur Rubinstein. The science must be supplemented by the art, in apologetics as elsewhere. Creative apologetics means a passionate and caring commitment to the people who have yet to discover the gospel of Christ, and a willingness to take the trouble to relate the gospel to their needs. If God went to all the trouble of becoming like us in Christ in order to redeem us, it seems perfectly reasonable to expect apologists to imitate this excellent example set for them in Christ.

Consider the consulting room of a medical practitioner. The doctor in question has been trained in the science of medicine and has a fund of knowledge without which she would be powerless to deal with the situations she encounters.

But there is more to medicine than knowledge. Many of my medical friends complain that their patients often seem reluctant to tell them what the real problems are. Perhaps they are embarrassed by their symptoms. Perhaps they are afraid of what the implications of those symptoms might be. But the doctor has to be able to relate to the patient and discover what the problem really is. There is an art of cultivating a good bedside manner, being a good and attentive listener, gaining the patient's confidence, and enabling the patient to disclose his or her anxieties.

Only once the problem has been fully exposed can the science of medicine be fully applied. The art and the science go hand in hand, the former enabling the latter to be brought into play to maximum effect. The apologist is like a sensitive doctor, prepared to talk to individuals and listen to them, in order to establish what the real problems are, so that the appropriate aspects of his fund of apologetic resources may be brought to bear upon the situation. An essential part of his or her task is that of gaining the dialogue partner's confidence.

For, as we have stressed, the obstacles that prevent some people from coming to faith are not merely academic difficulties. Often, there are deeply personal barriers to faith. One might think of the business executive who is having an affair with his secretary and feels that the guilt of the situation prevents him from ever relating to God. Or one might think of the woman who has been alienated from her local church through the personal failings of her pastor or because of strongly negative associations dating from her childhood. The apologist must be one who is prepared to gain that person's trust, listen, and be able to bring the full resources of the gospel to bear on what is uncovered during the dialogue.

The medical model allows for another insight. Carl Jung once penned the following words: "Only the wounded physician can heal." A friend of mine has asthma. He always makes a point of seeing the same doctor. "Everyone else treats me as if I am making a lot of fuss about nothing," he said. "But this guy understands me." Why? Because he too is an asthma sufferer! He can be sure of a sympathetic reception, genuine compassion, and a real awareness of the possibilities for treatment. If you have had a problem yourself, it is very easy to relate to the needs of others going through the same thing.

There is a real piece of apologetic insight in that observation. Effective apologetics at a personal level rests on an ability to relate to the problems faced by others as they contemplate Christianity. It helps if you yourself went through a period of wrestling with similar issues before you became a Christian. Not only will you have worked through the issues yourself, you will be able to appreciate the mental state of people in this position of indecision.

But even if you have not been through this kind of experience, you can enhance your effectiveness as an apologist by talking to people who have come to faith through wrestling with difficulties. Ask them how they overcame their barriers to faith. Ask them to tell you how they felt at every stage in this process of turning to Christianity. This will help you to think yourself into the situation of people who are close to faith yet are held back by an obstacle—an obstacle they hope you will be able to remove.

It is one thing to tailor your apologetic approach to individuals. But what about larger audiences, such as congregations?

B. APOLOGETICS AND PREACHING

How is apologetics related to preaching? It is helpful to make a distinction between evangelistic preaching, often linked to special events and occasions, and the regular preaching ministry in a congregation. Apologetics has a significant, yet different, role to play in each context. We may begin by considering its role in evangelistic preaching.

The role of effective apologetics in evangelistic preaching may be summarized as follows:

a. to identify points of contact for the gospel (discussed in detail at pp. 30–47);

b. to allow the preacher to lodge the gospel proclamation in the experiential world of his or her audience (see pp. 26–29);

c. to anticipate and answer some of the obstacles to faith that are experienced within the audience (pp. 94–143);

d. to challenge the existing non-Christian worldviews present within that audience (pp. 144–86);

e. to create an intellectual and imaginative atmosphere favorable to faith (pp. 48–56); and

f. to explain how assent to Christianity becomes faith in Christ (pp. 56–60).

The evangelist is thus basically an apologist who preaches with passion and power, bringing the science and art of apologetics to bear on his or her audiences.

Evangelism, it is widely agreed, holds the key to the future well-being of the Christian church. The centrality of apologetics to evangelistic preaching is inescapable. But is it of value in other preaching contexts? What of those who are already converted? Is apologetics an irrelevance to them? Certainly not.

The sermon is unquestionably one of the most important resources of the Christian church. Here, week by week, the preacher has the opportunity to challenge and nurture the faith of the people of God. The sermon can be the key to enhanced levels of Christian understanding, new depths of commitment, and a renewed sense of vision in the Christian life. (On the other hand, it can be mindlessly boring.) The simple fact is that apologetics must become a regular part of the preaching program of the Christian churches. It is necessary for the growth and upbuilding of the people of God. Apologetic material should be incorporated into the regular preaching rhythm of the church. What would an apologetic sermon look like?

My concern is not to commend the preaching of entire sermons dedicated to the identification of problems that members of your congregation may be having, with eminently worthy and competent titles, such as "Some Difficulties Experienced Concerning the Christian Faith." It is rather to draw attention to the fact that apologetic material can easily be incorporated, in small doses, into the regular course of preaching. How?

The preacher must *anticipate* the difficulties that will be experienced by ordinary Christians and indicate how they may be handled. The sermon must *explain* basic ideas and concepts of the Christian faith in order that Christian congregations can achieve new depths of understanding. And finally, the sermon must *reassure* Christians of the credentials of their faith. Let us look at each of these in more detail.

a. Anticipate. In the course of their day-to-day lives, Christians come across things that bother and puzzle them. It may be the questions posed by non-Christians. It may be anxiety about the goodness of God. The preacher can and ought to anticipate such difficulties and provide responses in advance. Make a list of difficulties, potential or real, and try to work through them over the course of a year or so. These apologetic threads can easily be woven into the fabric of a sermon.

For example, a sermon on Easter Day would naturally concentrate on the reality of the resurrection of Christ and all that it means and implies for believers. But some apologetic material could easily be integrated into the sermon. "Of course, there will be those who say that the Resurrection never happened. That it was some kind of cover-up job. Let's just look at those points. . . ." In this way, real questions and difficulties—which may be experienced inside, as well as outside, the Christian church—can be handled, with appropriate responses and strategies being placed in the hands of those who hear such sermons.

b. Explain. The best defense of Christianity lies in its explanation. Often, people reject caricatures or parodies of the gospel, not realizing that they are doing so. Take time to explain the gospel, not taking anything for granted. Remember Augustine's remarks about Christianity after hearing Ambrose of Milan preach: "I had yet to discover that it taught the truth, but I did discover that it did not teach the things I had accused it of."

But there is another dimension to this—a real need to explain key Christian beliefs to ordinary Christians, who often become discouraged and confused about them and even begin to have doubts about their credibility. Take time to explain, not just what Christians believe about the Trinity or the divinity of Christ, but *why* they believe them. Not only will they be encouraged about the solidity of the foundations of their faith and be better able to explain and justify aspects of that faith to others, but they also will be enabled to attain new depths in their personal lives of faith.[1]

c. Reassure. Apologetics functions within the church at two quite different levels, which may be conveniently described as "objective" and "subjective." Objectively, apologetics reassures those inside the church of the credentials of the Christian faith—of the historical reliability of the Gospels, the historical reality of the death and resurrection of Christ, and of the interpretation of these events in Christian doctrines such as the divinity of Christ. Subjectively, it creates a climate of credibility in which believers come to "feel good" about their faith in its broad totality. Apologetics builds up confidence in the total package of the Christian gospel and thus creates an atmosphere of confidence within the church—an atmosphere that in turn nourishes evangelism and church growth.

C. THE APPEAL TO THE IMAGINATION

Effective apologetics does not so much impose Christian truth on people as draw them into that truth in such a way that they can appreciate and appropriate it. One of the saddest features of some modern apologetic writing is that it makes its appeal purely to reason and neglects the human imagination—perhaps one of the most powerful allies at the disposal of the apologist.

"A picture is worth a thousand words." We spend billions every year on television sets, video recorders, and photographic equipment—all to capture images. Television news editors often rate the importance of their stories in terms of the images that accompany the text. We live in an age of "the humiliation of the word" (Jacques Ellul). Commercial advertising discovered many years ago that it was not a closely reasoned and justified argument that sold products—it was superbly crafted images, making a direct and powerful appeal to the human imagination. Classical apologetics often seems blissfully unaware of this development and approaches the defense of the faith in the modern world with all the imagination of a dead duck. Instead of a picture, it gives us a thousand words—often, it must be said, deadly dull and unimaginative words.

Argument will always have its place in Christian apologetics. But it urgently needs to be supplemented by an appeal to imagery. "Imagination is not to be divorced from the facts; it is a way of illuminating the facts" (A. N. Whitehead).[2] Arguments are precise; images are suggestive. We need to meditate on those remarkable words of some Greeks who came to Philip: "Sir, we wish to see Jesus" (John 12:21). Here is our task: to help people see Jesus Christ with their own eyes. Let us learn from Christ, who opened his parables, not with a definition ("The kingdom of God is . . ."), but with an image ("The kingdom of God is like . . ."). The parables themselves are remarkably effective in inviting their hearers to step inside their narrative worlds and in stirring the imagination. The parables excite; too often, arguments dull.

Or suppose I was trying to commend to you the merits of nectarines—a fruit you have not yet tasted. One way would be to tell you that it has pinkish-red skin and sweet, yellowish flesh. That is better than nothing—but not that much better. Or I could appeal to your imagination. I would get you to imagine what a nectarine might be like. Imagine a peach. It's like that—only better. How? Well, imagine an apricot. It's like that as well. Try to imagine the consistency, the fragrance, the taste of both; taste them in your mind, and savour their sweetness. Good apologetics is like that—a creative imaginative appeal to what your audience already knows, in order to get them interested in, even excited about, what they have yet to discover.

Definitions are closed off and imprison people in formulas; images are open-ended and invite their hearers to imagine them and be captured by them. We must avoid sounding like theological dictionaries and instead be able to appeal to the imaginations of those to whom we speak. The well-honed and carefully chosen word must be used to convey images of grace to our hearers. We need to shift our language from the abstract to the concrete. But how?

One of the most powerful ways of appealing to the imagination is through stories. The story is one of the least appreciated resources available to the apologist. In listening to a story, we enter into an imaginary narrative world in which we are carried along by the sheer impetus of the story itself. It is not like an argument, in which every stage of a complex network of interrelated ideas can be probed and dissected. An argument proceeds in stages, and the move to each successive stage is dependent on an understanding of earlier stages. A story propels us forward into a willing suspension of disbelief. Our natural tendency to want to know what happens next allows the stages of the narrative to be presented without interruption. We want to know how it ends.

It is this sense of intrigue, even of mystery, that so artfully leads us to pay attention to a story. It is perhaps only afterward that we begin to reflect on the implications of everything that has been said. We are, so to speak, captured by the narrative. Joseph Conrad expressed this feeling well: "Yet even then I hesitated, as if warned by the instinct of self-preservation, from venturing on a distant and toilsome journey into a land of intrigue and resolutions. But it had to be done." And during the course of that narrative, our imaginations are engaged, ideas are explored, images are unfolded, and potential difficulties are neutralized or evaded—all within the course of the telling of a story.

Perhaps the finest example of the use of a story as an apologetic device is found in C. S. Lewis's *Chronicles of Narnia*. Outwardly an entertaining series of imaginative adventure novels aimed at teenagers, the seven volumes weave together into a coherent narrative, a remarkable assortment of apologetic arguments. Unlike the straightforward allegorical style of John Bunyan's *Pilgrim's Progress* (used earlier by Lewis in *The Pilgrim's Regress*), in which every event and incident has some recognizable and direct connection with Christian doctrine, the *Narnia* works center around adventure stories and subtle theological associations. The gentle apologetics are absorbed along with the narrative, sustained and supported by the strength of the plot and characterization, itself a remarkable tribute to Lewis's celebrated knowledge of English literature. That narrative character is obvious from the first moment of *The Lion, the Witch and the Wardrobe:*

> Once there were four children whose names were Peter, Susan, Edmund and Lucy. This story is about something that happened to them when they were sent away from London during the war on account of the air raids. They were sent to the house of an old Professor who lived in the heart of the country, ten miles from the nearest railway station and two miles from the nearest post office.[3]

Immediately, our imaginations are activated. What sort of house? What did the old professor look like? What starts off as a jolly adventure story set amid rummaging around in old houses soon turns into a theological journey of discovery, as the power of the human imagination is harnessed to enter an imaginary world in which theology subtly comes to life.

Consider the knotty theological problem that often surfaces as a real difficulty for apologetics. Are our images of God simply projections of human values and aspirations (see pp. 94–100)? Do we simply create God in our imaginations, using ourselves as models? Perhaps, God having created us in his image, we have simply returned the compliment?

As we noted earlier, this position is especially associated with the German Hegelian philosopher Ludwig Feuerbach (1804–72), especially his *Essence of Christianity* (1841).[4] According to Feuerbach, the idea of "God" is basically a projection of human needs and aspirations onto an imaginary transcendental plane. God is not there, but we are. And we "project" or "objectify" our human feelings, and by doing so, create God in our own image. A series of "projectionist" theories of religion, including those of Sigmund Freud and Karl Marx, have their intellectual roots in this analysis of the notion of God. All the content of our ideas of God derives directly from human experience.

How can we counter this view? One approach might be to mount a sustained challenge to the Hegelian analysis of objectification on which this view ultimately rests. Such a challenge has already been presented, in conceptual form, earlier in this work (pp. 94–97). In other words, we could argue. We could write thousands of words, countering Feuerbach point by point. It would be intellectually convincing, but it would also be deadly dull.

Happily, Lewis uses another, totally different approach, considerably more effective in its impact. He tells a story. He plants a series of powerful images in our imaginations and leaves them there to bear their theological fruit. In *The Silver Chair* (an obvious, but exceptionally creative, reworking of Plato's image of men in a cave), two children (Eustace Scrubb and Jill Pole) find themselves trapped with a Narnian prince in an underground kingdom. They have no direct knowledge of the world above the ground, save their memories. They are confronted with a witch, one of whose chief aims it is to convince the children that there is no outside world. The dialogue proceeds as follows:

> "What is this *sun* you speak of? Do you mean anything by the word?" . . . asked the Witch. . . .
>
> "Please it, your grace," said the Prince, very coldly and politely. "You see that lamp? It is round and yellow and gives light to the whole room; and hangeth moreover from the roof. Now that thing which we call the sun is like the lamp, only far greater and brighter. It giveth light to the whole Overworld and hangeth in the sky."
>
> "Hangeth from what, my Lord?" asked the Witch; and then, while they were all still thinking how to answer her, she added, with another of her soft, silver laughs, "You see? When you try to think out clearly what this *sun* must be, you cannot tell me. You can only tell me that it is like the lamp. Your *sun* is a dream; and there is nothing in that dream that was not copied from the lamp. The lamp is the real thing; the *sun* is but a tale, a children's story."[5]

How does this approach work? Lewis relies on his readers seeing the stupidity of the witch's argument. They know all about the sun. They can easily enter into the story and see that there is no way that anyone can disprove the witch's argument unless he or she has direct access to the "Overworld." And they can see that, despite her fine logic and rhetoric, the witch is simply wrong. The sun may look like a lamp. A lamp may indeed be a convenient visual aid for the sun, allowing something that, by the nature of things, cannot be seen to be described in terms of things that can be seen. But that does not mean that there is no sun. The flaw in the argument is exposed, not through relentless demolition of the Hegelian notion of objectification, but through a simple and subtle appeal to the world of experience of a child. It lacks philosophical rigor, but it more than makes up for it by its appeal to the imagination and to common human experience.

By the end of the witch's exposition, we are left with a smile on our face. There seems to be something built into human nature that allows us to enjoy seeing a sophisticated argument deflated. The reader is left with a faint sense of smugness. We know something that the witch doesn't. And that knowledge exposes her argument as superficial and flawed. Yet how does this insight arise? By telling a story. By appealing to the imagination. Point taken?

Art and literature abound in images—images that can make a deep and evocative appeal to the imagination. Obviously, you need to know your audience. There is no point in appealing to Fyodor Dostoyevsky or Marcel Proust if you are speaking to a group of steelworkers from Pittsburgh. A central task here is ascertaining what reading or viewing you may have in common with your audience. If you are going to use appeals to the arts or literature, you are going to have to take risks. Happily, the rewards often enormously outweigh those risks. They are profoundly worth taking. But they must be taken on the basis of information, not guesswork. This point is so important that it needs further illustration.

D. APOLOGETICS AND LITERARY FORMS

Most people read. What they read varies enormously—in frequency, in volume, in level, and in seriousness. Literature can embrace just about anything from Dante's *Divine Comedy* to newspaper cartoons. What people read gives you openings, ways in which you can begin to make contact with their worlds of thought.

As we saw in the previous section, stories have a disarming ability to get around the "watchful dragons" (C. S. Lewis) of rational prejudice against Christianity. When you argue with someone, you have to go through stage after stage before you finally come to your conclusion—that Christianity makes sense, and is something greatly to be desired. It is like touching the bases in baseball. You cannot get to second base without getting to first. Telling a story does not bypass those stages; it simply takes us through them, without interruption. It allows us to tell the entire story, rather than having to tell it piecemeal.

But what specific types of story are appropriate? We have noted how imaginative fantasies of the C. S. Lewis or J. R. R. Tolkien type have considerable value in relation to apologetics. But what of other types of narrative? Let's look at one type that has enormous (if neglected) potential for the Christian apologist. I refer to the detective novel. Television networks have long known about the enormous appeal of mysteries to their viewers. It is time that Christian apologists woke up to the possibilities that this genre offers us. Apologetics may present itself as the science of the detection of God, and, by doing so, make a deep-rooted appeal to one of the most popular modern literary genres. The apologetic possibilities of this literary genre first impressed me some time ago.

The place—one of Oxford University's seminar rooms on a hot summer's afternoon. It was the end of a long day of teaching, and I had been up late the night before marking examination papers. The seminar was on some aspect of New Testament scholarship—I have long since forgotten what. The speaker was probably one of the most distinguished scholars in his field. He was also deadly dull. If a Nobel prize were ever to be given in the field of utterly tedious ways of delivering lectures, this gentleman would have been shortlisted by acclamation.

As he droned on, I began to drop off. It wasn't entirely his fault. I was tired, and it was a hot day—but then, he hardly encouraged me to remain awake and alert! Only half-awake, I caught occasional phrases of his lecture. Some of these lingered in my mind. "The messianic secret" and "the mystery of the messiah" were two of them. And as my mind wandered aimlessly, searching for something more interesting to think about than the lecture itself, a ridiculous thought passed through my mind. "He might as well be talking about detective fiction, using phrases like that." And an additional thought passed through my mind—"Surely Raymond Chandler or Agatha Christie could make a better job of his material than he ever could." Looking briefly around the remainder of the seminar audience, I came to the reassuring conclusion that some related thought may have been passing through at least some of their minds. Those who were still awake, anyway.

That thought remained in my mind long after the main business of that afternoon was forgotten. Were there not quite a few parallels between the Gospels and detective novels? Might not this cast fresh light on familiar material? And so my mind began to work.

Detective fiction appeals to our basic feeling that the world is ordered. The natural scientist, like the criminologist, believes that the world is structured. The biblical writers noticed this ordering as well. The great Old Testament theme of "wisdom" echoes this observation. Things do not just happen at random. The world is not some kind of accident. Its incredibly detailed structuring is itself a witness to the creative power and providence of God. Just as the plot of a crime novel links events together, so the knowledge that God is creator brings together the incredible workings of the universe in a single pattern and process. The plot is the thread of continuity linking events; the creatorship of God is the bond coupling the events of the vast panorama of the world.

But how is this ordering uncovered? How do the great sleuths of the printed page realize what has been going on? How do they detect the common strands that explain the way things happened? The answer, of course, is *clues*. A clue is something that opens the way to understanding a mystery. But how do you recognize a clue when you see one?

A clue is something that may at first sight seem utterly insignificant. It could easily be missed. But to someone who knows what to look for, it can speak volumes. It points to a possible explanation of events. It suggests ways of making sense of a jumble of seemingly unrelated things. Clues set us on the right trail, allowing us to make sense of hitherto puzzling events and eventually disclosing the identity of the murderer.

The essence of every good detective novel lies in engaging the reader in the detective's search for the murderer. The reader is set alongside Miss Marple or Philip Marlowe as she or he uncovers clues and gradually builds up an understanding of events. It is only at this point that we, the readers, find out whether we have noticed all the clues and worked out their significance.

In certain vital respects the Gospels parallel the type of writing found in detective fiction. The reader of the Gospels is set alongside the disciples as they listen to Jesus preach, as they watch him in action, and as they finally see him die and rise again. But detective novels are "whodunits"; the Gospels are "whowasits."

The gospel writers allow us to see and hear what the disciples heard and force us to ask much the same questions they themselves must have asked before us. Who is this man? And just as the writers of detective novels single out, or draw our attention to, significant things (in other words, clues) we might otherwise have overlooked, so the gospel writers do the same.

The difference, of course, is that we already have the outcome. But the Gospels take on a freshness when we are willing to suspend our after-the-fact knowledge of who Jesus is and read the Gospels as if we do not know—when we evaluate the clues the gospel writers provide and see if the story is convincing. For example, read Matthew's gospel as "The Mystery of the Murdered Messiah." It is evident that Matthew initially wants us to draw the conclusion that Jesus was the Messiah, the long-expected descendant of King David who was expected to usher in a new era in the history of Israel. The first part of his gospel is therefore littered with clues pointing to this conclusion. Thus the gospel opens with a list of Jesus' forebears (Matt. 1:1–17) which establishes that Jesus was legally the son of David. And immediately we are confronted with a clue. Isn't the Messiah meant to have been the son of David? We are then given an account of the birth of Jesus in which Matthew makes sure that we notice the remarkable parallels between the circumstances of that birth and certain key prophecies of the Old Testament. Matthew draws our attention to this point no less than five times in his first two chapters (1:22–23; 2:5–7, 16, 17–18, 23).

Mark's gospel, on the other hand, opens by establishing the credentials of John the Baptist. John is the long-expected messenger who prepares the way for the coming of the Lord (Mark 1:2–3). Immediately our suspicions are aroused: is the Lord about to arrive? Having aroused our interest, Mark then records John's statement that someone even more significant will come after him (1:7–8). We are even more attentive now. Who is it whom Mark immediately introduces to us? Jesus of Nazareth suddenly appears on the scene (1:9). The conclusion Mark wishes us to draw is obvious.

Although some of the clues concerning the identity and significance of Jesus are pointed out with some force, others are left to the readers to pick up for themselves. For example, Jesus regularly addresses God as "Father" in his prayers—a very presumptuous practice by the standards of the time. At one point, Mark even gives us the Aramaic original of the word for "Father"—*Abba,* a remarkably familiar term impossible to translate into English ("Papa," "Dad," "Daddy," are often suggested as the nearest equivalents). The gospel writers do not bring out the full significance of this practice, which clearly points to Jesus understanding himself to have a remarkably intimate relationship with God.

Equally, the parallels between the "righteous sufferer" of Psalm 22 and the accounts of Christ's passion are not made explicit but are left unsaid. Jesus' words "My God, my God, why have you forsaken me?" (Matt. 27:46; the only point, incidentally, at which Jesus does not address God as "Father") draw our attention to this mysterious figure, who is mocked by those who watch him die (Ps. 22:6–8)—as is Jesus (Matt. 27:39–44). The "righteous sufferer" has his hands and feet pierced (Ps. 22:16)—as would most victims of crucifixion, including Jesus. The "righteous sufferer" sees his tormentors casting lots for his clothes (Ps. 22:18)—as does Jesus (Matt. 27:35).

Another remarkable parallel exists between the crucifixion of Jesus Christ and the account of the "suffering servant" of Isaiah 53, which only Luke notes explicitly (Luke 22:37). This famous Old Testament prophecy speaks of a suffering servant of God, who was "wounded for our transgressions, and bruised for our iniquities" (Isa.

53:5). Perhaps the most significant part of this prophecy relates to the fact that the servant is "numbered with sinners" (Isa. 53:12), which is clearly understood by the gospel writers to be fulfilled in the death of Christ, in two ways. First, Christ died by crucifixion, which was a form of execution reserved for criminals. In other words, Christ was identified with sinners by the manner of his death. Second, Christ was not crucified alone, but along with two criminals (Matt. 27:38), one on either side of him. Jesus was thus surrounded by sinners at the moment of his death. In both ways, Christ's death was recognized as a parallel of an important Old Testament figure. In fact, it seems that the first Christians could not help but notice the obvious connections between the life and death of Jesus and certain significant prophecies of the Old Testament and take a certain degree of delight in pointing them out to their readers, or allowing them to discover them for themselves.

Let's develop the idea of a clue slightly further by looking at two points. First, it is not always obvious at the time that an event is a clue. Thus in Arthur Conan Doyle's story *Silver Blaze,* the full significance of the fact that the dog did not bark during the night becomes evident only at a late stage. The fact was observed, but its significance becomes apparent only when Sherlock Holmes has begun to make connections between seemingly unrelated happenings of the night as to the horse's disappearance.

There is every reason to suppose that something similar has happened in the case of the Gospels. The first Christians appear not to have realized the full significance of some of the things Jesus said or did until after his resurrection, when they suddenly saw things in a completely new light. An apparently insignificant fact thus assumed a new meaning once its full significance was realized. Thus in John's gospel, we find an explicit reference to this process. Jesus makes a remark that appears to refer to the temple at Jerusalem, whereas after the Resurrection his disciples realized that it referred to Jesus himself (John 2:18–22).

It is clear that some clues concerning the identity and significance of Jesus were impossible to overlook—the Resurrection itself being the most obvious example. Others, however, appear to have been more subtle. They were recognized for what they really were only after the Resurrection. This point serves to remind us that the gospel accounts are meant to be read in the light of faith in the Resurrection, which the early Christians evidently took as fundamental to their beliefs about Jesus.

Second, a clue can be just as much about something *not*

happening, as about something that *did* happen. Let's take up the *Silver Blaze* mystery once more. The horse had been guarded by a dog. Yet the dog didn't bark in the night when it should have as the racehorse Silver Blaze was stolen. Holmes notes this fact and realizes its significance—that the dog knew the intruder and did not feel threatened by his presence.

The same sort of clue emerges in the Gospels. For example, Mark notes that Jesus was silent before his accusers (Mark 14:61). But why? Surely Jesus would have been expected to defend himself. The significance of this silence can be seen in the light of the silence of the suffering servant (Isa. 53:7) before his accusers. Mark appears to want us to pick up this clue and lead us on to see other parallels between Jesus and this mysterious Old Testament figure.

So the literary genre of the detective novel can be invaluable to the task of Christian apologetics. It allows the Gospels to be read in a new light. It allows connections and discoveries to be made. The reader can be taken up into the gospel narrative and be allowed to capture the sense of mystery—and rejoice when that mystery is gloriously resolved.

I give this simply as one example. There are many other types of literature available: the novel, the tragedy, or the personal journal. Each of these has considerable potential for the apologist. I refer to the detective novel because it is one I happen to like myself and which I know is liked by many of my friends—and so has proved invaluable in my own experience as a way of making sense of at least some aspects of Christianity to an audience open to having its imagination stimulated. It is up to individual apologists, knowing their audiences, to work out what literary forms are most helpful for them.

E. THE APPEAL TO CULTURE

Know your audience! If this theme is becoming tediously familiar in this book, it is simply because of its importance. The effective apologist must be able to identify with and enter into the experiential world of his or her audience. We have already explored the enormous apologetic importance of points of contact, which allow the apologist to correlate the gospel with human experience. In one sense, however, this only begins to tap the enormous resources available to the intelligent and creative apologist. One such resource is the cultural milieu of the audience. If apologetics is concerned with the creation and fostering of an imaginative and intellectual climate favorable to faith, then contemporary culture provides resources for the creation of such a climate which the apologist dare not neglect.

The word "culture" has overtones of intellectual elitism which some will understandably find offensive. But the word is used here in its broad sense, meaning the literature, art forms, and music with which people find they can identify. As far as the apologist is concerned, "culture" designates whatever his or her audience may enjoy reading, watching, or listening to, irrespective of whether this can be regarded as "cultured" in the narrow sense of the word. The words of a popular song; some lines from a much-read contemporary novel; a scene from a top-rated television movie; some lines from a major box-office hit—all have potential in the hands of the sensitive and intelligent apologist.

The most effective defense and communication of the gospel is not likely to come from the lips of a stranger to the culture in which the gospel is to be proclaimed. The indigenous apologist, familiar with his or her own situation, is in the best position to identify and exploit the hints and clues provided by that cultural milieu. The gospel is too easily made to appear a stranger to a culture; the apologist must ensure it is seen as a friend, interlocking with the ideas and values of that culture wherever possible. Before the gospel can transform a culture, it must first take root within it.

So how can this be done? Some practical hints are worth infinitely more than theoretical analysis.

a. Keep talking to people in known or anticipated audiences. Get to know their ways of speaking, what they like reading or watching, and their hopes and fears. Aim to bring out how the gospel is—or can become—an insider to their culture. Take care to use language that naturally relates to that audience rather than a way of speaking that instantly marks you—and your message—as an outsider. Os Guinness is among the most practiced exponents of this approach, and his books are worth reading for hints and pointers.

b. The words of popular songs often bring to conscious expression some of the feelings that are common in potential audiences. Listen to them, or get someone to listen to them for you. Those words often identify a felt need (such as hopelessness or the fear of meaninglessness) to which the gospel can relate. Michael Green is an especially skilled practitioner of this apologetic art; explore his writings, especially those aimed at students.

c. Become aware of the tensions and perceived inadequacies of the culture. Can you discern a sense of frustration with the way things are and a feeling of powerlessness to change them? The writings of

Francis Schaeffer are especially illuminating here, indicating how cultural developments often show up the incapacity of secular worldviews to satisfy human longings. A sensitive critic of modern Western culture can often discern chinks in a secular cultural armor and allow the gospel to gain cultural credibility as a result.

F. WE HAVE TIME FOR A FEW QUESTIONS . . .

I preach sermons and give talks worldwide, in about equal proportions. People sometimes ask about the difference between a sermon and a talk. Theoretically, there are all kinds of differences, which homileticians write endlessly about; pragmatically, the difference is quite simple—after a talk, you are asked questions. And you have to make sure you answer them well. You may be a first-rate speaker, but you can lose your credibility instantly if you handle a question badly. It is a central, and neglected, aspect of practical apologetics. Learn to field questions well. My own experience could be distilled in nine points.

1. Anticipate Questions

Many of the questions you will be asked are predictable. Take time to plan out in advance answers to possible questions, perhaps jotting down outlines of those answers on index cards. The more speaking you do, the more confident you will become through exposure to the key questions. It helps to try out your answers on a sympathetic audience—perhaps some friends or colleagues—to get reactions. Talk through possible questions and answers, and spot strengths and weaknesses in advance.

At Oxford recently, I organized an "apologetics workshop" in which students were each given a commonly asked question relating to the Christian faith in advance—for example, "Can you prove that God exists?" Simulating the conditions of a lecture room, they were each allowed three or four minutes to answer the questions. The group then debated the quality and effectiveness of the response, making suggestions for improvements. The collective wisdom of the group often resulted in marked improvement of the quality of the reply.

2. If It's a Good Question—Say So!

Be affirmative of the questioner. It's no substitute for a good answer, but it helps create a good atmosphere. It also buys a few precious seconds of time to help you frame your answer better.

3. Take a Few Seconds to Think Before Replying

Picture a small gathering of people, perhaps seven or eight, being addressed by a speaker. The talk comes to an end. The speaker remains standing to take questions. Now hear someone ask a question. The speaker replies (a) immediately—that is, less than a second after the question has been put; (b) after a pause of three or four seconds.

Which of those two response times creates the better impression? You might feel that the first would create much the superior impact in that it demonstrates intellectual brilliance. In fact, it does not. It creates the impression of an unthinking, mechanical response. It suggests that the questioner has simply triggered a preprogrammed response on the speaker's part. A pause of a few seconds is perfectly acceptable and creates the impression of a thoughtful response to the question. Even if you can give an answer to a question without the need for much thought, take those few seconds.

4. If the Question Is Difficult, Buy Time

Important, difficult, or unanticipated questions need careful responses. And that may mean that you need a little space to think up a good answer. But audiences become anxious, perhaps even suspicious, if you take more than about four seconds to respond to a question. For this reason, you need to be able to buy time. Former Soviet President Leonid Brezhnev was rumored to speak English perfectly well. But at international press conferences, he would always wait for his interpreter to translate questions from English into Russian before replying. Why? Because it gave him more time to think about his answer.

All speakers develop ways of buying precious time in order to give better answers to those hard questions. Here are some of them.

a. Sit down after answering each question. The physical action of standing up to answer the question will buy you three or four seconds.

b. Thank the questioner for raising the issue. This buys you up to five seconds.

c. Repeat the question for the benefit of those who did not hear it. This is often a necessity if you have a large audience and the only microphone is at the speaker's podium. This can buy you as much as thirty or forty seconds.

But be warned: if you cannot think on your feet, buying time will just delay the inevitable—a bad answer. Learn to think quickly, jotting down in your mind—or on some paper in front of you—the main points you want to make. And be encouraged: most people get better at answering questions as they gain in experience and confidence.

5. Don't Be Iffy

Imagine that you are a member of an audience that has just heard a distinguished speaker talk about the Christian faith. Let your mind build up a picture of the scene, creating images of the auditorium (large? small? a church? a lecture room? a theater?), the audience (how large? how are they dressed? what age range?), and the speaker (male or female? how old? what sort of voice did he or she have? what did he or she wear?). Now hear a member of that audience ask this question: "Do you really believe that Jesus Christ was the Son of God?" And now imagine the following responses, and try to understand how they *feel* to that audience.

1. Well, it all depends what you mean by "the Son of God." [The speaker then outlines a few options before finally indicating that he or she believes it in one specific sense.]

2. Yes, I certainly do. Let me just clarify what that phrase means. [The speaker then outlines the same options as above, making it clear which specific sense he or she believes to be right—the same choice being made as above.]

How would you characterize each reply? What kind of *impression* does each create? The first option gives an impression of uncertainty and hesitation; the second projects a much more positive note. Yet, in terms of their substance, both replies are the same. Both recognize that the phrase can mean several things; both accept that Jesus is the Son of God in the same sense of the term. Yet the first reply is "iffy"; its opening almost leads its audience to think that the speaker does not believe that Jesus is the Son of God. It is the form of the reply, not its substance, that has registered.

If you are asked questions that genuinely demand clarification of terms, try to avoid the "well-it-all-depends-what-you-mean" kind of reply. It is unnecessary. You can introduce qualifications and explanations in the course of the reply after giving a firm and positive response with your opening words.

6. Don't Give Hostages to Fortune

Your answer to a question may well raise far more serious questions in the minds of your audience. A crucial skill is that of giving concise answers that raise new issues only if you want them to raise new issues. An unskilled answer can quickly lead you into a minefield for which you are unprepared. Again, imagine a situation in which a speaker has been asked this question: "Why do some people seem to react more positively to Christianity than others?" Now try to sense how non-Christians in the audience would react if the speaker included the following in his reply:

> Of course, there's always the issue of predestination here. God predestines some to respond favorably to the gospel and others to reject it. So the reason why some seem to react more positively than others is basically that God determines their reactions to the gospel. And that is a fairly central theme of Christian theology in the Reformed tradition.

This is a classic example of a "hostage to fortune"—an unnecessary weak point that allows critics an immediate advantage. What has been said is fair enough, but it shifts the ground of debate to a quite different area. Predestination makes sense only within the context of faith; there is little point in trying to explain it to an audience of outsiders who will find it baffling and probably offensive.

The rule is simple: if you want to open up fresh ground—fine. You can develop the question in such a way that you move on to this ground. But do not get sidetracked unless you can handle the new ground.

7. Go Out on an Upbeat

When you answer questions from people in the audience, feel free to give them more than they asked for. They may want to tackle you over a difficulty; answer the difficulty and add in some extra helpful material. The impression you create will be positive and affirmative. A positive aftertaste is left behind by your answer.

Imagine that the following question has been asked: "How can God allow suffering?" That is a big question. It puts you on the defensive. You want to deal with the difficulties. You will probably feel the need to concede that, in the final analysis, we cannot give a watertight explanation of why there is suffering in the world. If you end your answer there, you will leave behind an impression of uncertainty and unconviction. You will have been heard to say "I don't know." That is the kind of loose end that cannot be left dangling. Tie it up. Try to imagine how a concluding section like this would sound:

> So in the end, I am not sure why there is suffering in the world. Nobody is. But what I am sure of is this. The God who gave his Son to suffer and die on the cross is a God of love. He is a caring God. He is committed to us. He suffered in Christ. So I am prepared to trust that there is some loving purpose behind the

suffering that we see. The God we're talking about just isn't the kind of God who would allow suffering without reason.

That section would add about thirty seconds to your reply. But it will transform the way in which your reply is seen because you end positively, with conviction and commitment. You still have every opportunity to talk about the issues suffering raises, but you make sure that your audience knows that such difficulties can coexist with faith and hope.

8. Be Prepared to Challenge Assumptions Lying Behind Questions

Often, it helps to explore some of the assumptions lurking in the background of a question. Unstated assumptions often prejudice people against faith; by identifying and engaging with them, a question can often be robbed of its force. Take the following question: "How can you ask us to believe in God when we can't be absolutely certain that he exists?" How would you respond?

One approach might be to take the questioner on a little ramble through Thomas Aquinas's Five Ways. But that does not really answer the question; it might also bore the remainder of the audience to tears. A more creative approach would be to note the assumption lying behind the question: *we need to be absolutely certain about things*. You could provide a very effective response to the question along the following lines.

> Now you seem to think that we need to be absolutely certain about something before we can accept it. But let me ask whether this is really true. After all, we can be absolutely certain about very few things indeed. Two and two make four, sure, and we can be absolutely certain about that. But so what? What about the really big things in life? I can't be absolutely certain that democracy is better than a dictatorship—but I will still fight for democracy any day! Anyway, let's just think about atheists for a minute. They can't be absolutely certain that God doesn't exist either. Nobody really knows. But I can tell you, from where I am standing, God is for real . . . (and you might go on to explore the implications of the resurrection and personal experience, to name but two obvious resources at this point).

The real issue may lie in the assumptions behind the question, not necessarily in the specific question itself. Be prepared to explore behind the question.

9. Appeal to Authorities

I once had to give a talk to a group of students at Oxford on the relationship between Marxism and Christianity. We had gathered in a lecture room at Magdalen College. The lecture had been accepted well, and I had not had real difficulties with any of the questions afterward. The chairman looked at his watch. "I think we have time for just *one* more question," he announced. A young man stood up. He asked his question. And as he asked it, I thought, "I have not the slightest idea how to answer this." Panic began to set in. I thought, "C. S. Lewis used to teach here at Magdalen. I bet he could have answered that question." And even as that thought died, it was replaced by another: *"He did!"* And the basic features of his answer came to mind. So I waited for the young man to finish asking his question. I smiled, waited three seconds, and replied: "That's a difficult question. But the answer is really quite simple. . . ."

Knowing the resources available to you can be very helpful, as I discovered on that occasion. But knowing about the key ideas and arguments of leading writers can be helpful for another reason: it lends weight and authority to your replies. It helps to appeal to authorities. It sounds far more impressive and convincing to declare that "the Oxford philosopher Austin Farrer says that . . ." than to say "*I* think that . . ."—even if the opinion happens to be the same! Immerse yourself in authorities. Pick up some key quotes and commit them to memory. Note arguments and be prepared to use them, making sure that they are supported by credible authorities. But what is meant by that word *credible?* Know your audience. Know whom they take seriously or whom they are likely to admire. If you don't know, ask.

Some of the most powerful arguments you can use in fielding questions come from anti-Christian writers. For example, suppose you are asked the following question: "Our problem is that we feel alienated from God. It's just a subjective impression. So why all this nonsense about the cross and objective ideas of alienation?" This view may be countered by appealing to the writings of Karl Marx, specifically the *Economic and Philosophical Manuscripts of 1844.* Marx argues that the human situation is characterized by *alienation.*[6] He distinguishes two different kinds of alienation. The first is alienation from your rights and your property—a sort of *objective* alienation. You are alienated. The second is *subjective*, a more psychological or existential idea of alienation. You feel alienated from yourself. Marx's insight is quite simple: you *feel* alienated because you *are* alienated. If your social and economic situation is disastrous, you are going to feel bad about it.

Marx then goes on to argue the case for a social and economic revolution. Part of his argument is of interest to us. No amount of tinkering around with our feelings, he declares, is going to solve our problems. They are but symptoms of a deeper problem that remains unresolved by emotional therapy. If you are oppressed and exploited, you are going to feel alienated. The only way you are going to get rid of this feeling of alienation is by changing your social and economic situation. An objective change will result in a subjective change. And so, you would argue, it is with the cross. Our feeling of alienation from God rests on an objective alienation from him—and thus the feeling of alienation can be abolished only by dealing with its root cause.

So get to know your authorities. Read widely; listen hard; and talk to people.

G. CONCLUDING REMARKS

An ancient Greek proverb says (translated somewhat freely), "A big book is a big bore." The time has come for this book to end. It has aimed to provide a creative approach to apologetics, suited for modern use, that is firmly grounded in the Christian doctrines of creation and redemption and remains anchored within the great Christian tradition of taking rational trouble over our faith—not least for the benefit of outsiders.

We have stressed that apologetics is both a science and an art. It is an academic discipline, rigorously grounded in Christian theology and passionately concerned to demonstrate and defend the truth of Christianity. But it is also a craft, a creative attempt to ensure that the gospel proclamation meshes as closely as possible with the needs and concerns of human existence. Like an ellipse, Christian apologetics centers on twin foci: on the one hand the truth and reliability of the Christian revelation, and on the other the need to relate it to, and demonstrate its transformative potential for, the human situation. It is a vital and necessary part of the equipment of all Christians, above all those concerned with preaching and evangelism. To repeat the closing statement of the introduction, "Apologetics is not about winning arguments—it is about winning people."

APPENDIX A

The Point of Contact in Classical Evangelical Thought: John Calvin

Calvin is nothing if not a biblical theologian. In his preface to the 1559 edition of his classic theological text the *Institutes of the Christian Religion*,[1] he indicates that he conceived it as a volume of Christian doctrine that will aid its readers as they try to understand Scripture in its totality:

> Although the Holy Scriptures contain a perfect doctrine, to which nothing can be added (our Lord having been pleased to unfold the infinite treasures of his wisdom therein), every person who is not intimately acquainted with them needs some sort of guidance and direction, as to what he or she ought to look for in them. . . . Hence it is the duty of those who have received from God more light than others to assist the simple in this manner and, as it were, give them a helping hand to guide and assist them to find everything that God has been pleased to teach us in his word. Now, the best way of doing this is to deal systematically with all the main themes of Christian philosophy.

The *Institutes* is thus like a pair of spectacles through which Scripture may be properly read. It stresses the unity of Scripture, which might otherwise seem like a series of unconnected narratives and statements.

A helpful way of thinking of the relationship between Calvin's *Institutes* and its foundations in Scripture (probably suggested by a growing Victorian public interest in botanical gardens) was put forward by the nineteenth-century Scottish writer Thomas Guthrie. Guthrie argued that Scripture was like nature, in which flowers and plants grow freely in their natural habitat, unordered by human hands. The human desire for orderliness leads to these same plants being collected and arranged in botanical gardens according to their species, in order that they can be individually studied in more detail. The same plants are found in different contexts—one of which is natural, the other of which is the result of human ordering. Doctrine represents the human attempt to order the ideas of Scripture, arranging them in a logical manner so that their mutual relation can be better understood.

The 1559 edition of Calvin's *Institutes* opens with a sustained discussion of the vital issue of how we can know anything about God. Calvin's doctrine of the knowledge of God is grounded in the dialectic he establishes between this knowledge in its natural and revealed forms. The first book of the *Institutes* opens with discussion of precisely this matter.[2] Even before turning to discuss this question, however, Calvin stresses that "knowledge of God and of ourselves are connected" (*Institutes* I.i.1). Without a knowledge of God, we cannot truly know ourselves; without knowing ourselves, we cannot know God. The two forms of knowledge are "joined together by many bonds"; although they are distinct, they cannot be separated. It is impossible to have either in isolation. This principle is of fundamental importance to an understanding of Calvin's strongly world-affirming theology: knowledge of God cannot be detached from, nor allowed to merge with, knowledge of human nature or of the world. A dialectic is constructed, resting upon a delicately balanced interplay between God and the world, between the Creator and his creation.

In dealing with our knowledge of God as the "creator and sovereign ruler of the world," Calvin affirms that a general knowledge of God may be discerned throughout his creation—in humanity, in the natural order, and in the historical process itself. Two main grounds of such knowledge are identified, one subjective, the other objective. The first ground is a "sense of divinity (*sensus divinitatis*)" or a "seed of religion (*semen religionis*)," implanted within every human being by God (I.iii.1; I.v.1). God himself has endowed human beings with an inbuilt sense or presentiment of his existence. It is as if something about God has been engraved in the hearts of every human being (I.x.3). Calvin identifies three consequences of this inbuilt awareness of divinity: the universality of religion (which, if uninformed by the Christian revelation, degenerates into idolatry: I.iii.1), a troubled conscience (I.iii.2), and a servile fear of God (I.iv.4). All of these, Calvin suggests, may serve as points of contact for the Christian proclamation.

The second such ground lies in experience of and reflection upon the ordering of the world. The fact that God is creator, together with an appreciation of his wisdom and justice, may be gained from an inspection of the created order, culminating in humanity itself (I.v.1–15). "God has revealed himself in such a beautiful and elegant construction of heaven and earth, showing and presenting himself there every day, that human beings cannot open their eyes without having to notice him" (I.v.1).

It is important to stress that Calvin makes no suggestion whatsoever that this knowledge of God from the created order is peculiar to, or restricted to, Christian believers. It is perhaps at this point that both Karl Barth and Cornelius van Til find themselves unable to endorse thoroughly Calvinian insights. For Calvin asserts that *anyone*, by intelligent and rational reflection upon the created order, should be able to arrive at the idea of God. The created order is a "theater" (I.v.5) or a "mirror" (I.v.11) for the displaying of the divine presence, nature, and attributes. Although God is himself invisible and incomprehensible, he makes himself known under the form of created and visible things (I.v.1). Although we cannot know God's essence, we can know him through his created works (I.v.9).

Calvin further insists that the orderliness of creation is a vital witness to God, discernible to even the unbelieving human eye. Both the physical world and the human body testify to the wisdom and character of God.

> In order that no one might be excluded from the means of obtaining happiness, God has been pleased, not only to place in our minds the seeds of religion of which we have already spoken, but to make known his perfection in the whole structure of the universe, and daily place himself in our view, in such a manner that we cannot open our eyes without being compelled to observe him. . . .
> Hence the author of the Letter to the Hebrews elegantly describes the visible world as images of the invisible, the elegant structure of the world serving as a kind of mirror in which we may see God, who is otherwise invisible. . . . To prove his remarkable wisdom, both the heavens and the earth present us with countless simple proofs—not just those more advanced proofs which astronomy, medicine and all the other natural sciences are designed to illustrate, but proofs which force themselves on the attention of the most illiterate peasant, who cannot open his eyes without seeing them (I.v.1–2).

Calvin thus commends both astronomy and medicine—indeed, he even confesses to being slightly jealous of them—in that they are able to probe more deeply into the natural world, and thus uncover further evidence of the orderliness of the creation and the wisdom of its creator. Significantly, however, Calvin makes no appeal to specifically *Christian* sources of revelation in this entire analysis. His argument is based on empirical observation and ratiocination. If Calvin introduces scriptural quotations, it is to consolidate a general natural knowledge of God, rather than to establish that knowledge in the first place. There is, he stresses, a way of discerning God which is common to those inside and outside the Christian community (*exteris et domesticis communem:* I.v.6).

Having thus laid the foundations for a general knowledge of God, Calvin stresses its shortcomings; his dialogue partner here is Cicero, whose work *de natura deorum*, "on the nature of the gods," is perhaps one of the most influential classical expositions of a natural knowledge of God.[3] The epistemic distance between God and humanity, already of enormous magnitude, is increased still further on account of human sin. Our natural knowledge of God is imperfect and confused, even to the point of contradiction on occasion. A natural knowledge of God serves to deprive humanity of any excuse for ignoring him; nevertheless, it is inadequate as the basis of a full-fledged portrayal of the nature, character, and purposes of God. Calvin thus introduces the notion of biblical revelation; Scripture reiterates what may be known of God through nature, while simultaneously clarifying this general revelation and enhancing it (I.x.1). "The knowledge of God, which is clearly shown in the ordering of the world and in all creatures, is still more clearly and familiarly explained in the Word" (I.x.1). It is only through Scripture that the believer has access to knowledge of the redeeming actions of God in history, culminating in the life, death, and resurrection of Jesus Christ (I.vi.1–4). For Calvin, revelation is focused on the person of Jesus Christ; our knowledge of God is mediated through him (I.vi.1).

In that Jesus Christ is known only through the scriptural record, the centrality and indispensability of Scripture to theologian and believer alike is assured. Calvin adds, however, that Scripture can only be properly read and understood through the inspiration of the Holy Spirit (I.vii.1). Nevertheless, Calvin does not develop a mechanical or literal understanding of the inspiration of Scripture. It is certainly true that Calvin occasionally uses images that might suggest a mechanical view of inspiration—for example, referring to the biblical authors as "clerks" or "scribes," or speaking of the Holy Spirit "dictating." These images, however, are almost certainly to be understood metaphorically, as accommodations or visual figures. The content of

Scripture is indeed divine—yet the form in which that content is embodied is human. Scripture is the *verbum Dei,* not the *verba Dei.* There is unquestionably an implicit parallel with the Incarnation at this point, as at so many other points in Calvin's thought: divine and human coexist, without compromising or destroying each other. Scripture represents the Word of God mediated through the form of human words, weighted with divine authority on account of their origin.

God may thus be fully known only through Jesus Christ, who may in turn be known only through Scripture; the created order, however, provides important points of contact for, and partial resonances of, this revelation. Having thus identified the manner in which God may be known, Calvin proceeds to consider what may be known concerning him. At this point, nature is left behind. The doctrine of the Trinity, the first major aspect of his understanding of the nature of God to be expounded, is treated as a biblical doctrine resting on special revelation, rather than an insight which may be gained from general revelation or nature.

Let us summarize Calvin's teaching. A distinction is drawn between "knowledge of God the creator" and "knowledge of God the redeemer." A "knowledge of God the creator" may be had from both nature and Scripture, with the latter endorsing, extending, and clarifying what may be gleaned from the former. But this is not saving knowledge. "Knowledge of God the redeemer" may be found only through Jesus Christ, in Scripture. Nature thus points to Scripture, as Scripture points to Christ. A cascade of witnesses allows us to proceed from the creation to the Creator and thus to the Redeemer. A natural knowledge of God is thus foundational to Calvin's apologetic. It is no accident that this vigorous defense of a natural knowledge of God, accompanied by a rigorous analysis of its apologetic implications, should open the pages of Calvin's definitive 1559 *Institutes.*

Calvin's views on the created order as a point of contact for divine revelation may be said to dominate the Reformed tradition until the nineteenth century. Nourished by such sources as Butler's *Analogy of Religion,* this tradition had a distinguished history of use within Western Christianity. In the present century, however, it has faced a significant challenge from the approach to apologetics associated with Cornelius van Til, which we will discuss in Appendix B.

A Critique of Presuppositionalism: Cornelius van Til

In the late 1920s, the Presbyterian Church in the United States of America was shaken by a series of controversies between conservatives and liberals. Eventually, these controversies led to one of the most important shake-ups in religious higher education: the departure of four members of the Princeton Theological Seminary faculty to form Westminster Seminary, Philadelphia.[1] Convinced that Princeton had abandoned its commitment to the "old theology," J. Gresham Machen and three Princeton colleagues (including Cornelius van Til) became the nucleus of the faculty of the new seminary, dedicated to maintaining the tradition from which Princeton now seemed to have departed. Yet paradoxically, the approach to apologetics that has come to be closely linked with Westminster Seminary bears little relation to the "old Princeton school" of apologetics, which had dominated American reformed thought until the 1920s. The apologetic system of Cornelius van Til, generally designated "presuppositionalism,"[2] represents a conscious and deliberate move away from the position of writers such as Benjamin B. Warfield toward a position more similar to that associated with later Dutch Reformed writers such as Abraham Kuyper.

One of the central presuppositions of presuppositionalism (for our purposes here, *the* central presupposition) is a critique of "autonomy." For van Til, the logical starting point of apologetics must be the biblical notion of God. Yet classical evangelical apologetics, as found in the writings of Calvin or Edwards, begins its thinking without the presupposition of God, on the basis of the pedagogical assumption that one proceeds from the known (such as nature or human experience) to the unknown (the existence of God). To rework a turn of phrase deriving from Anselm of Canterbury's *Cur Deus homo,* traditional apologetics begins *remoto Deo,* "apart from God," and aims to end up showing that God is the most reasonable explanation of the way the world is. Van Til summarizes this approach, as it is found in the Old Princeton theology:

> According to this method, natural man was assumed to be able:
> a. to work up a natural theology that would show theism to be more probably true than any other theory of reality, and
> b. to show that Christianity is more probably true than any other theory of sin and redemption.[3]

Van Til argues that this approach can lead only to human beings creating God in their own image and using human criteria of rationality and evidence instead of divinely authorized criteria. They are guilty of idolatry—the creation and worship of a god made in their own image.

Why? Van Til's reply is somewhat complex and often couched in rather tortuous English. The basic structure of his argument, however, appears to be as follows. If we begin our thinking about God without presupposing his existence, we are, in effect, already precommitted to a nonbiblical worldview from which God is excluded, or which will conceive of him in purely human terms. We have begun our thinking from an autonomous starting point—and that very starting point, in effect, predetermines our conclusions. The only valid starting point is the presupposition of the existence of God—not just any idea of God, however, but the view of God explicitly set forth in Scripture. Apologetics must therefore, according to van Til, begin from above (with God), rather than from below (with the everyday world of experience and events).

Van Til thus declares that the possibility of a dialogue with those outside the Christian faith is excluded. There is no common ground. If you accept the presupposition of God, with all that this entails, you are already Christian; if you do not, then you cannot even begin to see the merits of the Christian case. Only by total surrender to the presupposition of God can the non-Christian see the merits of the Christian case.

Yet van Til is confronted by an arsenal of texts, from Scripture and the reformed tradition, which affirms that sinful human beings do have access to knowledge of God from creation—that is to say, from below. Van Til recognizes this point:

The Apostle Paul speaks of the natural man as actually possessing the knowledge of God (Romans 1:19–21). The greatness of his sin lies precisely in the fact that "when they knew God, they glorified him not as God. No man can escape knowing God. It is indelibly involved in his awareness of anything whatsoever. Man *ought*, therefore, as Calvin puts it, to recognize God. There is no excuse for him if he does not. The reason for his failure to recognize God lies exclusively in him.[4]

This is an admirable summary of the situation. But where does van Til take us next? He declares that "all men, due to the sin within them, always and in all relationships seek to 'suppress' this knowledge of God. The natural man constantly throws water on a fire he cannot quench. He has yielded to the temptation of Satan and has become his bondservant."[5] It is this notion of the deliberate and systematic suppression of a natural knowledge of God that requires critical examination.

The theology of this position is exceptionally vulnerable. Its apologetic implications are as disastrous as they are unwarranted. Dialogue with the world is excluded. Yet there is a curious inconsistency in van Til's approach. Conceding that all have access to knowledge of God, he insists that all (apparently without exception) suppress that knowledge. Yet if there exists a real, yet suppressed, knowledge of God outside the Christian community, the apologist has the opportunity to uncover this knowledge and raise it to the level of articulated consciousness. Van Til seems to refuse to recognize the apologetic propriety of this approach, apparently believing that it represents a capitulation on the part of the apologist to the presuppositions of an agnostic audience. Yet this is not the case; the apologist is merely maneuvering for position—*reculer pour mieux sauter,* as it were. Those who have not suppressed such knowledge of God can, by judicious use of an arsenal of apologetic techniques, bring out the memory of this repressed knowledge of God.

Van Til's point is that a natural knowledge of God, which arises from human autonomy, leads to idolatry. But the sixteenth-century reformers, such as Luther and Calvin, were perfectly aware of this danger. Calvin stresses that a natural knowledge of God can easily degenerate into idolatry. Such a knowledge of God is inadequate; it must be supplemented by revelation. Yet, rightly understood, a natural knowledge of God is a starting point—and nothing more—for the full richness of God's self-revelation.

The error in question is not *making use* of a natural knowledge of God, but making *improper* use of such knowledge. If a starting point (natural knowledge of God the Creator) is confused with the end point (revealed knowledge of God the Redeemer), a serious distortion of the kind feared by van Til will result. But, as Calvin stresses, it need not. It is up to the apologist to uncover—that is to say, raise to explicit consciousness—and to make the best use of that "suppressed knowledge" and allow it to lead on to greater and better things.

As we noted earlier, the dangers of abusing a natural knowledge of God are well known in classical apologetics. Van Til, like Barth, reminds us of the need to be responsible and scriptural in our apologetic appeal to nature and human experience; yet neither of these writers succeeds in undermining the foundations that give theological justification to a limited and informed appeal to nature.

Van Til's position is thus seriously vulnerable, both historically and theologically. We have already explored the importance of these points and indicated our anxieties concerning the type of approach advocated by van Til. Theologically, it fails to integrate the Christian doctrines of creation and redemption. Historically, van Til's position is not characteristic of the reformed tradition as a whole.

Van Til claims to represent the integrity of the reformed tradition. But does Calvin himself, who may reasonably be argued to be the *fons et origo* of this distinguished school, actually endorse van Til's position? Surely not. Is not Benjamin B. Warfield, whose distrust of Abraham Kuyper is well documented, a more faithful representative of this school? It is difficult to see how van Til can claim Calvin as a representative of the presuppositionalist position. Warfield seems to summarize Calvin's position on the relation of general and special revelation superbly when he writes:

> Each is incomplete without the other. . . . Without general revelation, special revelation would lack that basis in the fundamental knowledge of God as the mighty and wise, righteous and good, maker and ruler of all things, apart from which special revelation of this great God's intervention in the world for the salvation of sinners could not either be intelligible, credible or operative.[6]

General revelation provides the point of contact for special revelation, this latter alone being saving knowledge of God.

Further, the attitude that van Til espouses does not appear to be characteristic of post-Calvinian reformed theology. The basic difficulty here can be illustrated from a study by my Oxford colleague, Dr. John Platt, into the function of arguments for the existence of God within Dutch reformed theology during the period 1575–1650.[7] If van Til is correct in his presentation and application of the reformed tradition (especially, one might add, *Dutch* reformed theology), one would expect its leading writers to explicitly disavow a rational apologetic. In fact, one finds nothing of the sort. There is no suggestion that a rational apologetic amounts to a crude and irresponsible human declaration of autonomy. Nowhere is rational apologetics treated as a gesture of defiance against God; rather, it is treated as an entirely proper and natural means of laying a reliable and persuasive rational foundation for the reformed doctrine of God.

My own modest studies in the history of apologetics suggest that van Til's ideas may be reasonably suggested to rest upon a later school of thought, grounded in the writings of the noted Amsterdam theologian and philosopher Abraham Kuyper, rather than in the classical reformed tradition itself. The "Old Princeton" apologetic, as developed in the writings of Warfield and others, has a far greater claim to be considered as the most faithful representative of the reformed tradition. The approach to apologetics that is developed in this book reverts to the central insights of this older tradition, believing—with the greatest reluctance—that the approach developed by van Til fails to make the maximum use of God-given resources for apologetics.

But whatever our criticisms of van Til might be, there can be no doubt that he has shown the necessity of grounding apologetics in a sound theological foundation. Indeed, it might be fair to suggest that it is van Til's theological rigor in itself, rather than the specific results of its application, that gives him a place of honor among contemporary apologists.

Notes

Introduction

[1]For an excellent survey, see Avery Dulles, *A History of Apologetics* (Philadelphia: Westminster, 1971).

[2]A distinguished exception is R. C. Sproul, *If There Is a God, Why Are There Atheists?* (Minneapolis: Bethany House, 1974).

[3]A recent survey among students uncovered the following as the two top reasons for rejecting Christianity: "Christians are hypocrites"; "Christians are too exclusive." Neither of these reasons are "academic" or "intellectual." Robert M. Kachur, "Why I'm Not a Christian," *HIS* (February 1986), 7–10.

Chapter 1: The Theological Foundations of Effective Apologetics

[1]This consideration has a distinguished history of use within the Christian tradition. Augustine's careful analysis of the theme of "the clouded mind" is especially important in this connection, in that it shows that he is aware of potential limitations on our natural knowledge of God, on account of human sin. Calvin and Luther expressed reservations of a related kind. There was every danger, they argued, that what can be known of God from nature might, on account of human sin, be argued to be *all* that can be known of God. In this way, nature could easily become idolized, with the creation being worshiped in place of the Creator. Calvin's response to this difficulty was to construct a sophisticated theological framework by which the value of the creation could be affirmed while in no way confusing it with the God who brought it into being.

[2]Calvin, *Institutes*, I.v.9.

[3]Karl Barth, *Dogmatics in Outline* (London: SCM Press, 1949), 23.

[4]The theme of an especially powerful section in Barth's *Church Dogmatics*, 8 vols. (Edinburgh: T. & T. Clark, 1956–75), IV/1, 157–210.

[5]John L. McKenzie, "The Word of God in the Old Testament," *Theological Studies* 21 (1960), 205.

[6]See Ford Lewis Battles, "God Was Accommodating Himself to Human Capacity," *Interpretation* 31 (1977), 19–38.

[7]This point is brought out clearly by A. N. Wilder, *Early Christian Rhetoric: The Language of the Gospel* (London: SCM Press, 1964).

[8]*Opera Calvini* (Corpus Reformatorum edition) 26.387-8 'Dieu s'est fait quasi semblable une nourrice, qui neparlera point à un petit enfant selon qu'elle feroit à un homme . . . nostre Seigneur s'est ainsi familièrement accommodé nous."

[9]E.g., OC29.70, 356; 36.134; 43.161.

[10]OC32.364–5.

[11]*Institutes*, I.xiii.1.

[12]A point brought out superbly by W. Balke, "The Word of God and Experientia According to Calvin," in W. H. Neuser, ed., *Calvinus ecclesiae doctor* (Kampen: de Groot, 1978), 19–31.

[13]C. S. Lewis, *Surprised by Joy* (London: Collins, 1959), 20.

[14]C. S. Lewis, "The Language of Religion," in *Christian Reflections* (London: Collins, 1981), 169.

[15]*Westminster Shorter Catechism*, question 31.

[16]See further Alister McGrath, *Making Sense of the Cross* (Leicester: Inter-Varsity Press, 1992), 45–86.

[17]Hendrik Kraemer, *The Christian Message in a Non-Christian World* (London: Edinburgh House Press, 1938), 303.

[18]See Basil Mitchell, "Contemporary Challenges to Christian Apologetics," in *How to Play Theological Ping-Pong* (London: Hodder & Stoughton, 1990), 25–41, esp. 25.

[19]C. S. Lewis, *God in the Dock* (Grand Rapids: Eerdmans, 1970), 96.

[20]See Kenneth E. Bailey, *Poet and Peasant* (Grand Rapids: Eerdmans, 1976); Joachim Jeremias, *The Parables of Jesus* (London: SCM Press, 1963); David Wenham, *The Parables of Jesus* (London: Hodder & Stoughton, 1989).

[21]Kenneth E. Bailey, *Through Peasant Eyes* (Grand Rapids: Eerdmans, 1980), xv.

[22]J. A. Baird, *Audience Criticism and the Historical Jesus* (Philadelphia: Westminster, 1969).

[23]See Paul Collart, *Philippes: ville de Macedoine depuis ses origines jusqu'à la fin de l'époque romaine* (Paris: Boccard, 1937).

[24]See Bertil Gartner, *The Areopagus Speech and Natural Revelation* (Uppsala: Gleerup, 1955).

[25]See F. F. Bruce, *The Defense of the Gospel in the New Testament* (Grand Rapids: Eerdmans, 1959).

Chapter 2: Points of Contact

[1]*Georgias*, 493b–d.

[2]Diogenes Allen, *The Traces of God* (Cambridge, Mass.: Cowley Publications, 1981), 19.

[3]Paul Elmer Moore, *Pages from an Oxford Diary* (Princeton: Princeton University Press, 1937), sec. XVIII.

[4]Augustine, *Confessions*, I.i.1, translated by H. Chadwick (Oxford: Oxford University Press, 1991), 3.

[5]For a superb presentation of Augustine's thoughts on this tension, see John Burnaby, *Amor Dei: A Study in the Religion of St. Augustine* (London: Hodder & Stoughton, 1938), 52–73.

[6]*Confessions* XII.xvi.23; Chadwick, 257.

[7]C. S. Lewis, *Surprised by Joy* (London: Collins, 1959), 20.

[8]Ibid., 19.

[9]C. S. Lewis, *Screwtape Proposes a Toast* (London: Collins, 1965), 97–98.

[10]Simone Weil, *Waiting for God* (New York: Putnam, 1951), 210.

[11]Lewis, *Screwtape Proposes a Toast* (London: Collins, 1965), 99.

[12]Extract from a sermon preached by the author at Ridley College, University of Melbourne, Australia, 16 July 1991.

[13]John Polkinghorne, *Science and Creation: The Search for Understanding* (London: SPCK, 1988), 20–21.

[14]C. S. Lewis, *Mere Christianity* (New York: Macmillan, 1952), 31–32.

[15]On these, see Colin Brown, *Philosophy and the Christian Faith* (Leicester: Inter-Varsity Press, 1986), 20–32; Keith E. Yandell, *Christianity and Philosophy* (Grand Rapids: Eerdmans, 1984), 48–97.

[16]Francis Schaeffer, *Trilogy* (Leicester: Inter-Varsity Press, 1990), 262–63.

[17]Pp. 147-55.

[18]Perhaps the most accessible exploitation of this approach is to be found in the writings of John Polkinghorne. The following of his works should be consulted: *The Way the World Is* (London: SPCK, 1983); *One World* (London: SPCK, 1986); *Science and Creation* (London: SPCK, 1988); *Science and Providence* (London: SPCK, 1989). Those wishing to explore his potential as a communicator of key aspects of modern quantum theory should explore his *The Quantum World* (London: Longman, 1986).

[19]Polkinghorne, *The Way the World Is*, 12.

[20]Jeffrey Stout, *Ethics After Babel* (Princeton: Princeton University Press, 1988), 109–23.

[21]Lewis, *Mere Christianity*, 16.

[22]For the distinction, see Alister E. McGrath, *Luther's Theology of the Cross* (Oxford: Blackwell, 1985), 164–69.

[23]Austin Farrer, *Said or Sung* (London: Faith Press, 1960), 13.

[24]Extract from a talk given to an audience of students drawn from tertiary educational institutions throughout the Melbourne area, 24 July 1991.

Chapter 3: From Assent to Commitment

[1]Ludwig Wittgenstein, *Philosophical Investigations*, 2d ed. (Oxford: Basil Blackwell, 1958), secs. 19, 23. More generally, see D. M. High, *Language, Persons and Belief: Studies in Wittgenstein's Philosophical Investigations* (Oxford: Oxford University Press, 1967); William Hodern, *Speaking of God: The Nature and Purposes of Theological Language* (London: Epworth, 1965).

[2]Ferdinand de Saussure, *Cours de linguistique générale* (Wiesbaden: Harassowitz, 1967), 146–57; S. Ullmann, *Semantics: An Introduction to the Science of Meaning* (Oxford: Blackwell, 1962), 80–115.

[3]See A. Grabner-Haider, *Semiotik und Theologie: religiose Rade zwischen analytischer und hermeneutischer Philosophie* (Munich: Kosel Verlag, 1973), 51–143.

[4]See J. Trier, *Der deutsche Wortschaft im Sinnbesinn des Verstandes* (Heidelberg: Winter Verlag, 1931).

[5]For its occurrence, see Melanchthon, *Loci Communes* (1521 ed.), preface.

[6]*Luther's Works, The Liberty of a Christian*, 54 vols. (Minneapolis: Augsburg, 1974–90), 31:351.

[7]Raymond Aron, *Dimensions de la conscience historique* (Paris: Gallimard, 1961), 52; cf. the remark of Sartre on the French Revolution: "We already knew the biography of Robespierre . . . as a succession of well-established

facts. These facts appear concrete because they are known in detail, but they lack *reality* since we can no longer connect them to the totalizing movement." Jean-Paul Sartre, *Critique de la raison dialectique*, 2 vols. (Paris: Gallimard, 1960), 1:86.

[8]See 35–37.

[9]See Appendix B, 'A Critique of Presuppositionalism: Cornelius van Til.'

[10]The point will be familiar to readers of works such as Alasdair MacIntyre's *Whose Justice? Which Rationality?* which stresses the variety of rationalities available in the intellectual marketplace.

[11]For a good account, see R. C. Sproul et al, *Classical Apologetics* (Grand Rapids: Zondervan, 1984), 243–52.

[12]See Sheldon Vanauken, *A Severe Mercy* (London: Hodder & Stoughton, 1977), 75–100.

[13]Ibid., 98–99.

[14]Ibid., 99.

Chapter 4: What Keeps People from Becoming Christians?

[1]Michael Green, *Evangelism Through the Local Church* (London: Hodder & Stoughton, 1990), 144–45. The point is developed further at 260–64.

[2]Cited by E. E. Evans-Pritchard, *Theories of Primitive Religion* (Oxford: Clarendon, 1965), 100.

[3]See Alister E. McGrath, *A Life of John Calvin* (Oxford/Cambridge, Mass.: Blackwell, 1990), 12–21.

[4]D. R. Davies, *On to Orthodoxy* (London: Hodder & Stoughton, 1939).

[5]Ibid., 27. The reference to the "Great War" reminds us that Davies wrote before the outbreak of the Second World War.

[6]Ibid., 13.

[7]Ibid., 207.

[8]Richard Holloway, *Another Country, Another King* (London: Collins, 1991), 112.

[9]Ibid., 113.

[10]Pp. 48-52.

[11]Basil Mitchell, *How to Play Theological Ping-Pong* (London: Hodder & Stoughton, 1990), 56. See also Alister E. McGrath, "Doctrine and Ethics," *Journal of the Evangelical Theological Society* 34 (1991): 145–56.

[12]See J. H. Harvey and C. Weary, eds., *Perspectives on Attributional Processes* (Iowa: University of Iowa Press, 1981).

[13]Full details in Peter Brown, *Augustine of Hippo* (London: Faber & Faber, 1967).

[14]Augustine, *Confessions*, V.xiii.23–xiv.25, trans. H. Chadwick (Oxford: Oxford University Press, 1991), 88.

[15]Two resources here are Os Guinness, *Doubt: Faith in Two Minds* (Oxford/Batavia, Ill.: Lion, 1979); Alister McGrath, *Doubt: Handling It Honestly* (Leicester: Inter-Varsity Press, 1990), U.S. ed., *The Sunnier Side of Doubt* (Grand Rapids: Zondervan, 1990).

[16]See M. J. Ferreira, *Scepticism and Reasonable Doubt* (Oxford: Clarendon, 1986).

[17]Nancy Cartwright, *How the Laws of Physics Lie* (Oxford: Clarendon, 1989).

[18]See the exposition in Rom Harré, *The Philosophies of Science* (Oxford: Oxford University Press, 1974), 42–43.

[19]Harré, *Philosophies of Science*, 43. For a point-by-point refutation of these three principles, see 43–48.

[20]There is a vast literature. Wilfred Sellars, *Science, Perception and Reality* (New York: Humanities Press, 1963), provides an excellent starting point.

[21]Willard van Orman Quine, *From a Logical Point of View*, 2d ed. (New York: Harper & Row, 2d ed., 1963), 42–43.

[22]Willard van Orman Quine, *Methods of Logic* (London: Routledge & Kegan Paul, 1952), xiii.

[23]Karl Popper, *The Poverty of Historicism*, 2d corrected ed. (London: Routledge & Kegan Paul, 1961). The unusual title of the work alludes to the title of Marx's book *The Poverty of Philosophy*, which was in turn an allusion to Proudhon's *Philosophy of Poverty*.

[24]Francis Schaeffer, *Trilogy* (Leicester: Inter-Varsity Press, 1990), 132–33.

[25]Ibid., 110.

[26]Ibid., 58.

[27]Ibid., 134.

[28]Ibid., 140.

[29]Its most widely used publication to date is Roger Fisher and William Ury, *Getting to Yes: Negotiating Agreement Without Giving In* (London: Hutchinson, 1984).

[30]Ibid., 29–30.

Chapter 5: Intellectual Barriers to Faith

[1]See Max W. Wartofsky, *Feuerbach* (Cambridge: Cambridge University Press, 1982), 252–340.

[2]I use the English word *projection* to translate the German term *Vergegenständigung*. An alternative translation might be "objectification." See Wartofsky, *Feuerbach*, 206–10.

[3]See 156-60.

[4]For a helpful introduction, see Martin Redeker, *Schleiermacher: Life and Thought* (Philadelphia: Fortress, 1973).

[5]See J. Glasse, "Barth on Feuerbach," *Harvard Theological Review* 57 (1964), 69–96.

[6]Eduard von Hartmann, *Geschichte der Logik*, 2 vols. (Leipzig, 1900), 2:444.

[7]We have already explored the theological foundations and consequences of this notion of a "point of contact" in Chapter 1 and examined it further in relation to the Christian resolution of the Euthyphro dilemma in ethics (39-42).

[8]For a biography, see Ernest Jones, *Sigmund Freud: Life and Work*, 3 vols. (London: Hogarth, 1953–57).

[9]See Fraser Watts and Mark Williams, *The Psychology of Religious Knowing* (Cambridge: Cambridge University Press, 1988), 24–37.

[10]Sigmund Freud, *The Future of an Illusion* in *Complete Psychological Works*, 24 vols. (London: Hogarth, 1953–), 21:30.

[11]See Paul Ricoeur, *Freud and Philosophy: An Essay on Interpretation* (New Haven: Yale University Press, 1970).

[12]For what follows, see A.-M. Rizzuto, *The Birth of the Living God: A Psychoanalytical Study* (Chicago: University of Chicago Press, 1979); W. W. Meissner, *Psychoanalysis and Religious Experience* (New Haven: Yale University Press, 1984).

[13]Sigmund Freud, "Leonardo da Vinci and a Memory of His Childhood," in *Complete Psychological Works*, 11:123.

[14]Jones, *Sigmund Freud*, 2:394.

[15]See B. Spilka, R. W. Hood, and R. L. Gorsuch, *The Psychology of Religion: An Empirical Approach* (Englewood Cliffs, N.J.: Prentice-Hall, 1985).

[16]See Michael J. Buckley, *At the Origins of Modern Atheism* (New Haven/London: Yale University Press, 1987).

[17]Buckley, *Origins of Modern Atheism*, 67.

[18]Alasdair MacIntyre and Paul Ricoeur, *The Religious Significance of Atheism* (New York: Columbia University Press, 1969), 14.

[19]Alasdair MacIntyre, "Is Understanding Religion Compatible with Believing?" in B. R. Wilson, ed., *Rationality* (Oxford: Blackwell, 1974), 73.

[20]For a more detailed discussion, see 147-55.

[21]For these points, see J. L. Mackie, "Evil and Omnipotence," in B. Mitchell, ed., *The Philosophy of Religion* (Oxford: Oxford University Press, 1970), 92–104; Basil Mitchell, *The Justification of Religious Belief* (London: Macmillan, 1970), 15–16.

[22]Hume's original point was that, having experience only of this world, we cannot declare that it is "the best of all possible worlds." For precisely the same reasons, we cannot know that it is *not* the best of all possible worlds. That judgment requires access to information that we do not possess and can never possess.

[23]C. S. Lewis, *The Problem of Pain* (London: Geoffrey Bles, 1940), 14.

[24]Ibid., 16.

[25]Ibid., 22.

[26]Ibid., 35.

[27]Ibid., 36.

[28]See 45-46.

[29]C. S. Lewis, *Problem of Pain*, 83.

[30]Ibid., 81.

[31]For what follows, see Alister McGrath, *Suffering* (London: Hodder & Stoughton, forthcoming).

[32]We explore and evaluate Marx's views on the nature of Christianity later: see 156-60.

[33]Lesslie Newbigin, *The Gospel in a Pluralist Society* (Grand Rapids: Eerdmans, 1989), 1. The following works should also be consulted: Norman Anderson, *Christianity and Comparative Religion* (Leicester: Inter-Varsity Press, 1970); Gavin D'Costa, *Theology and Religious Pluralism* (Oxford: Blackwell, 1986); Stephen Neill, *Christian Faith and Other Faiths* (Oxford: Oxford University Press, 1970); Lesslie Newbigin, *The Finality of Christ* (London: SCM Press, 1969). These last two works are by leading writers with

long experience of the complex Indian situation, and are especially recommended.

[34]Diogenes Allen, *Christian Belief in a Postmodern World* (Louisville: Westminster/John Knox Press, 1989), 9.

[35]John Milbank, "The End of Dialogue," in G. D'Costa, ed., *Christian Uniqueness Reconsidered: The Myth of a Pluralistic Theology of Religions* (Maryknoll, N.Y.: Orbis, 1990), 174–91; quote at 176. This essay merits detailed reading.

[36]John Hick, *Truth and Dialogue* (London: Sheldon Press, 1974), 148.

[37]John Hick, *God and the Universe of Faiths* (London: Collins, 1977), 146.

[38]Hugo Meynell, "On the Idea of a World Theology," *Modern Theology* 1 (1985), 149–63.

[39]Richard Rorty, *The Consequences of Pragmatism* (Minneapolis: University of Minnesota Press, 1982), 166.

[40]Newbigin, *Gospel in a Pluralist Society*, 9–10.

[41]John Hick, *The Second Christianity* (London: SCM Press, 1983), 86.

[42]Michael Green, *Evangelism and the Local Church* (London: Hodder & Stoughton, 1990), 61.

[43]For full analysis of the issues, see Peter Carnley, *The Structure of Resurrection Belief* (Oxford: Clarendon, 1987), with full bibliography.

[44]See Gary R. Habermas, "Resurrection Claims in Non-Christian Religions," *Religious Studies* 25 (1989), 167–77.

[45]For demonstration that paradox does not require a break with classical logic, see D. Elton Trueblood, *Philosophy of Religion* (New York: Harper & Row, 1957), 25–26.

[46]John Hick, ed., *The Myth of God Incarnate* (London: SCM Press, 1977), 167–85.

[47]See Alister E. McGrath, *"Homo assumptus?* A Study in the Christology of the *Via Moderna,* with Particular Reference to William of Ockham," *Ephemerides Theologicae Lovanienses* 60 (1984), 283–97. See further Alfred J. Fredoso, "Human Nature, Potency and the Incarnation," *Faith and Philosophy* 3 (1986): 27–53; Richard Cross, "Nature and Personality in the Incarnation," *Downside Review* 107 (1989): 237–54.

[48]Ithaca/London: Cornell University Press, 1986. See also the excellent earlier study of R. T. Herbert, *Paradox and Identity in Theology* (Ithaca/London: Cornell University Press, 1979). For a rather wooden and unpersuasive response, see J. Hick, "The Logic of God Incarnate," *Religious Studies* 25 (1989), 409–23.

[49]See the excellent discussion of the views of Spinoza and others in G. R. Lewis and B. A. Demarest, *Integrative Theology* (Grand Rapids: Zondervan, 1987–92), 2:347–51.

[50]Gerhard O. Forde, *Theology Is for Proclamation* (Minneapolis: Fortress, 1990), 70–71.

[51]C. S. Lewis, letter to Arthur Greeves, 11 December 1944, in W. Hooper, ed., *They Stand Together* (London: Colins, 1979), 503.

[52]Thomas C. Oden, *After Modernity . . . What? Agenda for Theology* (Grand Rapids: Zondervan, 1989), 168–69.

[53]See 44–46.

[54]See 30–34.

⁵⁵For a detailed discussion of the idea of a "model," see Alister E. McGrath, *Understanding the Trinity* (Grand Rapids: Zondervan, 1990), 45–77.
⁵⁶See 139–41.
⁵⁷See 42–43.
⁵⁸For a full account of its potential here, see Alister E. McGrath, *Justification by Faith* (Grand Rapids: Zondervan, 1990), 77–95.
⁵⁹A useful little study is Lesslie Newbigin, *Sin and Salvation* (London: SCM Press, 1956).
⁶⁰G. K. Chesterton, *The Everlasting Man* (London: Hodder & Stoughton, 1934), 4–5.
⁶¹See Alister E. McGrath, *Luther's Theology of the Cross* (Oxford: Blackwell, 1985), for details.
⁶²See 123–33.

Chapter 6: A Clash of Worldviews

¹Diogenes Allen, *Christian Belief in a Postmodern World* (Louisville: Westminster/John Knox Press, 1989), 2.
²For an excellent introduction by a leading philosopher of religion, see Allen, *Christian Belief in a Postmodern World*, 1–19. For more specialized studies, see Frederick Ferré, *Shaping the Future: Resources for the Post-Modern World* (New York: Harper & Row, 1976); David R. Griffin, *God and Religion in the Postmodern World* (Albany, N.Y.: State University of New York, 1988); Houston Smith, *Beyond the Post-Modern Mind* (New York: Crossroad, 1982); Harvey Cox, *Religion in the Secular City: Towards a Postmodern Theology* (New York: Simon & Schuster, 1984).
³This is explored in Alister E. McGrath, *The Genesis of Doctrine* (Oxford/Cambridge, Mass.: Blackwell, 1990), 172–200.
⁴Basil Mitchell, *Morality, Religious and Secular* (Oxford: Clarendon, 1980); Alasdair MacIntyre, *Whose Justice, Which Rationality?* (Notre Dame, Ind.: University of Notre Dame, 1988).
⁵We explored this question briefly at 63–65.
⁶Thomas C. Oden, *After Modernity . . . What? Agenda for Theology* (Grand Rapids: Zondervan, 1989), 75.
⁷See 181–86. ???
⁸See Alister E. McGrath, *The Making of Modern German Christology* (Oxford: Blackwell, 1986); new ed. in preparation (Leicester: Inter-Varsity Press, and Grand Rapids: Zondervan, forthcoming).
⁹Albert Schweitzer, *The Quest of the Historical Jesus* (London: Black, 1954).
¹⁰Iris Murdoch, *The Sovereignty of the Good* (London: Collins, 1970), 80.
¹¹A useful introduction may be found in Gottfried Martin, *Kant's Metaphysics and Theory of Science* (Manchester: Manchester University Press, 1955), 16–20.
¹²MacIntyre, *Whose Justice? Which Rationality?* 6.
¹³Hans-Georg Gadamer, *Truth and Method* (London: Sheed & Ward, 1975), 271.
¹⁴Rudolf Carnap, "Intellectual Autobiography," in P. A. Schilpp, ed., *The Philosophy of Rudolf Carnap* (La Salle, Ill.: Open Court, 1963), 57.
¹⁵Allen, *Christian Belief in a Postmodern World*, 132.

[16]Wilfrid Sellars, *Science, Perception and Reality* (New York: Humanities, 1963).

[17]N. R. Hanson, *Perception and Discovery* (Cambridge: Cambridge University Press, 1961), 169.

[18]Ibid., 246–47.

[19]Ibid., 216.

[20]Ibid., 234.

[21]For a thoughtful and sympathetic study of the theological side of things, see Nicholas Lash, *A Matter of Hope* (London: Darton, Longman & Todd, 1981). More generally, see David McLellan, *Karl Marx: His Life and Thought* (London: Macmillan, 1973); Delos B. McKown, *The Classical Marxist Critiques of Religion* (The Hague: Nijhoff, 1975).

[22]V. I. Lenin, *Religion* (London: Lawrence and Wishart, 1932), 11–12.

[23]Karl Marx, *Das Kapital* 3 vols. (Moscow: Progress Publishers, 1958–59), 1:79.

[24]See 94–100.

[25]Karl Marx, "Zur Kritik der hegelschen Rechtsphilosophie," in *Werke*, 4 vols. (Berlin, 1959–61), 1:379.

[26]Marx, "Kritik," in *Werke*, 1:488.

[27]This is an extremely difficult notion to analyze in English, not least on account of the subtle interaction between the two German words Marx uses (*Entäusserung* and *Entfremdung*) to describe the phenomenon. The reader is referred to Bertell Ollman, *Alienation: Marx's Conception of Man in Capitalist Society* (Cambridge: Cambridge University Press, 1977), for a full analysis.

[28]Marx, "Kritik," in *Werke*, 1:488.

[29]Ibid.

[30]Marx, *Das Kapital*, 1:79.

[31]Marx, "Thesen über Feuerbach," in *Werke*, 2:4.

[32]This point is explored further on 94–97.

[33]We noted the same fatal weakness concerning the "genus of religion" in relation to the crudely homogenizing approaches of liberal approaches to the religions: see 148–60. This issue is increasingly being recognized as one of the most serious obstacles in the path of responsible Christian approaches to this question.

[34]A. J. Ayer, "What I Believe," in George Unwin, ed., *What I Believe* (London: Allen & Unwin, 1966), 13.

[35]Such as Andrew Dickson White's vigorously polemical, and at times grossly inaccurate, *History of the Warfare of Science with Theology in Christendom*, 2 vols. (New York: Appleton, 1896). The influence of this work may be detected in page after page of Bertrand Russell's hastily written *History of Western Philosophy*.

[36]See the pioneering study of Adrian Desmond and James Moore, *Darwin* (London: Michael Joseph, 1991).

[37]Alister E. McGrath, *The Genesis of Doctrine* (Oxford/Cambridge, Mass.: Blackwell, 1990), 77–79.

[38]See McGrath, *The Genesis of Doctrine*, 72–80.

[39]John Henry Newman, *The Idea of a University* (Oxford: Oxford University Press, 1960), 343–61. For an excellent analysis, see M. Jamie Ferreira, *Doubt and Religious Commitment* (Oxford: Clarendon, 1980), 116–23.

[40]Norwood Hanson, *Perception and Discovery* (San Francisco: Freeman and Cooper, 1969).
[41]Ibid., 408.
[42]A. Flew and A. MacIntyre, *New Essays in Philosophical Theology* (London: SCM Press, 1955), 96–99. Note the reply by Basil Mitchell at 103–5.
[43]Karl Popper, "Autobiography," in P. A. Schilpp, ed., *The Philosophy of Karl Popper* (La Salle, Ill.: Open Court, 1974), 28–29.
[44]Karl Popper, *The Logic of Scientific Discovery* (New York: Basic Books, 1959), 50.
[45]*On Certainty* (New York: Harper & Row, 1969), no. 94, p. 15.
[46]See 38–39.
[47]Mary Daly, *Beyond God the Father: Towards a Philosophy of Women's Liberation* (Boston: Beacon, 1973); Daphne Hampson, *Theology and Feminism* (Oxford: Blackwell, 1990).
[48]Carol P. Christ, *Laughter of Aphrodite: Reflections on a Journey to the Goddess* (San Francisco: Harper & Row, 1987); Naomi Ruth Goldenberg, *Changing of the Gods: Feminism and the End of Traditional Religions* (Boston: Beacon, 1979).
[49]See Rosemary Radford Ruether and Eleanor McLaughlin, eds., *Women of Spirit: Female Leadership in the Jewish and Christian Traditions* (New York: Simon and Schuster, 1979).
[50]Richard Holloway, *Another Country, Another King* (London: Collins, 1991), 118.
[51]See Elizabeth Schüssler-Fiorenza, *In Memory of Her: A Feminist Reconstruction of Christian Origins* (New York: Crossroad, 1983). More generally, see Ben Witherington III, *Women in the Ministry of Jesus* (Cambridge: Cambridge University Press, 1988).
[52]Mary Evans, *Women in the Bible* (Exeter: Paternoster Press, 1983), 51.
[53]Ben Witherington III, *Women and the Genesis of Christianity* (Cambridge: Cambridge University Press, 1990), 246.
[54]Alister McGrath, *Roots That Refresh: A Celebration of Reformation Spirituality* (London: Hodder & Stoughton, 1992), 26–29.
[55]Roland H. Bainton, *Women of the Reformation*, 3 vols. (Minneapolis: Augsburg, 1971–77).
[56]See Alister McGrath, *Understanding the Trinity* (Grand Rapids: Zondervan, 1990), 45–77, for details and discussion.
[57]G. B. Caird, *The Language and Imagery of the Bible* (London: Duckworth, 1980), 80.
[58]See 94–100; 156-60.
[59]Mary Hayter, *The New Eve in Christ* (London: SPCK, 1983), 38.
[60]Ibid., 41.
[61]Ibid.
[62]On these general themes, see Diogenes Allen, *Christian Belief in a Postmodern World;* Thomas C. Oden, *After Modernity . . . What? Agenda for Theology.*
[63]David Kolb, *Critique of Pure Modernity;* cited in Oden, *After Modernity,* 76.
[64]Oden, *After Modernity,* 77.

⁶⁵The following works are helpful: Matei Calinescu, *Five Faces of Modernity* (Durham, N.C.: Duke University Press, 1987); Terry Eagleton, *The Ideology of the Aesthetic* (Oxford: Blackwell, 1990); Kevin Hart, *The Trespass of the Sign* (Cambridge: Cambridge University Press, 1989); David Harvey, *The Condition of Postmodernity* (Oxford: Blackwell, 1989); Christopher Norris, *What's Wrong with Postmodernism?* (Baltimore: Johns Hopkins Press, 1990).

⁶⁶For an excellent analysis, see David Lehman, *Signs of the Times* (London: André Deutsch, 1991).

⁶⁷Allen, *Christian Belief in a Postmodern World*, 5–6.

⁶⁸This point can be developed by considering the "paradox of hedonism," the feeling of "divine dissatisfaction," and the sense of yearning for something undefinable—all pointing to the human need for God, discussed in detail on pp. 30–34. The reader is referred to this section for further details.

⁶⁹See 73–75.

⁷⁰The most important writings are his *Order of Things: An Archaeology of the Human Sciences* (New York: Vintage Books, 1973); *Power/Knowledge: Selected Interviews and Other Writings, 1972–1977* (New York: Pantheon Books, 1980); *Histoire de la folie à l'âge classique* (Paris: Gallimard, 1972).

⁷¹See 86–87.

⁷²Stanley Rosen, *Hermeneutics as Politics* (Oxford: Oxford University Press, 1987), 189–90.

⁷³Richard Rorty, *Consequences of Pragmatism* (Minneapolis: University of Minneapolis Press, 1982), xlii.

⁷⁴Ibid.

⁷⁵For useful introductions, see Russell Chandler, *Understanding the New Age* (Waco: Word, 1988); Douglas Groothuis, *Unmasking the New Age* (Leicester: Inter-Varsity Press, 1992).

⁷⁶A point stressed by Ted Peters, *The Cosmic Self: A Penetrating Look at Today's New Age Movement* (San Francisco: Harper Collins, 1991).

⁷⁷Reported in *Time*, 7 December 1987, 64.

⁷⁸A trend documented and evaluated by Harvey Cox, *Turning East: The Promise and Peril of the New Orientalism* (New York: Simon & Schuster, 1977).

⁷⁹David K. Clark and Norman L. Geisler, *Apologetics in the New Age* (Grand Rapids: Baker, 1990), 7.

⁸⁰The best account is Clark and Geisler, *Apologetics in the New Age*, 117–221.

⁸¹Marilyn Ferguson, *The Aquarian Conspiracy* (Los Angeles: Tarcher, 1981), 176.

⁸²Cited in Chandler, *Understanding the New Age*, 38.

⁸³See 19-23.

Chapter 7: From Textbook to Real Life

¹I try to do something along these lines in my books *Understanding Jesus* (Grand Rapids: Zondervan, 1990), *Understanding the Trinity* (Grand Rapids: Zondervan, 1990), and *Justification by Faith* (Grand Rapids: Zondervan, 1990).

²A. N. Whitehead, *The Aims of Education* (New York: Macmillan, 1929), 139.

³C. S. Lewis, *The Lion, the Witch, and the Wardrobe* (New York: Collier, 1970), 1.

[4]For the points at issue, see Max W. Wartofsky, *Feuerbach* (Cambridge: Cambridge University Press, 1982), 293–386.

[5]C. S. Lewis, *The Silver Chair* (New York: Macmillan, 1956), 155–56.

[6]Bertell Ollman, *Alienation* (Cambridge: Cambridge University Press, 1976).

Appendix A: John Calvin

[1]For details of this work, see Alister E. McGrath, *A Life of John Calvin* (Oxford/Cambridge, Mass.: Blackwell, 1990), 136–42.

[2]On this question, see E. A. Dowey, *The Knowledge of God in Calvin's Theology* (New York: Columbia University Press, 1952); T.H.L. Parker, *Calvin's Doctrine of the Knowledge of God* (Edinburgh: Oliver & Boyd, rev. ed. 1969.)

[3]See Egli Grislis, "Calvin's Use of Cicero in the Institutes I:1–5—A Case Study in Theological Method," *Archiv für Reformationsgeschichte* 62 (1971), 5–37.

Appendix B: Cornelius van Til

[1]For the details, see Bradley J. Longfield, *The Presbyterian Controversy: Fundamentalists, Modernists and Moderates* (Oxford: Oxford University Press, 1991), 28–53; 162–80.

[2]The central work to be considered is Cornelius van Til, *The Defense of the Faith*, 3d ed. (Nutley, N.J.: Presbyterian and Reformed, 1967). For useful analyses and evaluations, see R. C. Sproul, John Gerstner, and Arthur Lindsley, *Classical Apologetics* (Grand Rapids: Zondervan, 1984), 183–338; E. R. Geehan, ed., *Jerusalem and Athens* (Phillipsburg, N.J.: Presbyterian and Reformed, 1971); Mark Hanna, *Crucial Questions in Apologetics* (Grand Rapids: Baker, 1981).

[3]Van Til, *Defense of the Faith*, 260.

[4]Ibid., 92.

[5]Ibid.

[6]Benjamin B. Warfield, *The Inspiration and Authority of the Bible* (Philadelphia: Presbyterian and Reformed, 1948), 210. See further K. R. Trembath, *Evangelical Theories of Biblical Inspiration* (Oxford: Oxford University Press, 1987), 20–27; David H. Kelsey, *The Uses of Scripture in Recent Theology* (Philadelphia: Fortress, 1975), 17–24.

[7]John Platt, *Reformed Thought and Scholasticism: The Arguments for the Existence of God in Dutch Theology, 1575–1670* (Leiden: Brill, 1982).

For Further Reading

Material directly relevant to the questions discussed in this work is presented in the notes to the appropriate sections. This section aims to identify works of interest to the theme of apologetics in general.

General Works on Apologetics

Allison, Brian. *Analytical Studies in Apologetics* (Unionville, Ont.: Brice & Bensa, 1990).

Blamires, Harry. *A Defence of Dogmatism* (London: SPCK, 1965).

Brown, Colin. *Philosophy and the Christian Faith* (Leicester: Inter-Varsity Press, 1969).

Bruce, F. F. *The Apologetic Defense of the Gospel* (Wheaton: InterVarsity Press, 1959).

Casserley, J.V.L. *Apologetics and Evangelism* (Philadelphia: Westminster Press, 1962).

Christiani, Leon. *Why We Believe* (New York: Hawthorne, 1959).

Clark, Gordon H. "Apologetics," in C.F.H. Henry, ed., *Contemporary Evangelical Thought* (Great Neck, N.Y.: Channel, 1957), 137–61.

Clark, Kelly James. *Return to Reason* (Grand Rapids: Eerdmans, 1990).

DeWolf, L. Harold. *The Religious Revolt Against Reason* (New York: Harper & Row, 1949).

Dulles, Avery. *A History of Apologetics* (Philadelphia: Westminster Press, 1971).

Dyrness, William. *Christian Apologetics in a World Community* (Wheaton: InterVarsity Press, 1983).

Evans, C. Stephen. *The Quest for Faith* (Wheaton/Leicester: InterVarsity Press, 1986).

Lewis, Gordon R. *Testing Christianity's Truth Claims: Approaches to Christian Apologetics* (Chicago: Moody Press, 1976).

Mitchell, Basil. *The Justification of Religious Belief* (Oxford: Oxford University Press, 1981).

Morey, Robert A. *A Christian Handbook for Defending the Faith* (Nutley, N.J.: Presbyterian and Reformed, 1979).

Morrison, Frank. *Who Moved the Stone?* (London: Faber & Faber, 1930).

Mouw, Richard. *Distorted Truth: What Every Christian Needs to Know About the Battle for the Mind* (San Francisco: Harper & Row, 1989).

Neill, Stephen C. *Christian Faith and Other Faiths* (Oxford: Oxford University Press, 1970).

Newport, John. *Life's Ultimate Questions* (Waco: Word, 1989).

Oden, Thomas C. *After Modernity . . . What? Agenda for Theology* (Grand Rapids: Zondervan, 1990).
Pinnock, Clark. *Reason Enough* (Wheaton: InterVarsity Press, 1980).
Purtill, Richard L. *Reason to Believe* (Grand Rapids: Eerdmans, 1974).
Ramm, Bernard. *Varieties of Christian Apologetics* (Grand Rapids: Baker, 1965).
Trueblood, David Elton. *Philosophy of Religion* (New York: Harper & Row, 1957).
Warfield, Benjamin B. "Apologetics," in *Studies in Theology* (New York: Oxford University Press, 1932), 3–21.
Wolterstorff, Nicholas. *Reason Within the Bounds of Religion* (Grand Rapids: Eerdmans, 1976).

Specific Approaches to Apologetics

Barrett, Earl E. *A Christian Perspective of Knowing* (Kansas City, Mo.: Beacon Hill, 1965).
Buswell, J. Oliver. *A Christian View of Being and Knowing* (Grand Rapids: Zondervan, 1960).
————. *A Systematic Theology of the Christian Religion*, vol. 1 (Grand Rapids: Zondervan, 1962).
Carnell, Edward J. *An Introduction to Christian Apologetics* (Grand Rapids: Eerdmans, 1948).
Casserley, J.V.L. *Graceful Reason: The Contribution of Reason to Theology* (Greenwich, Conn.: Seabury, 1954).
————. *The Case for Orthodox Theology* (Philadelphia: Westminster Press, 1959).
Clark, Gordon H. *A Christian View of Men and Things* (Grand Rapids: Eerdmans, 1952).
————. *Religion, Reason and Revelation* (Nutley, N.J.: Presbyterian and Reformed, 1964).
Geisler, Norman. *Christian Apologetics* (Grand Rapids: Baker, 1976).
Gerstner, John H. *Reasons for Faith* (New York: Harper & Row, 1960).
Grounds, Vernon C. *The Reason for Our Hope* (Chicago: Moody Press, 1945).
Hackett, Stuart C. *The Resurrection of Theism* (Chicago: Moody Press, 1957).
Hamilton, Floyd E. *The Basis of Christian Faith* (New York: Harper & Row, 1964).
Hanna, M. *Crucial Questions in Apologetics* (Grand Rapids: Baker, 1981).
Holmes, Arthur F. *Faith Seeks Understanding* (Grand Rapids: Eerdmans, 1971).
Lewis, C. S. *Mere Christianity* (New York: Macmillan, 1948).
————. "Christian Apologetics," in *God in the Dock* (Grand Rapids: Eerdmans, 1970), 89–103.
Lewis, Gordon R. "Schaeffer's Apologetic Method," in Ronald W. Ruegsegger, ed., *Reflections on Francis Schaeffer* (Grand Rapids: Zondervan, 1986), 69–104.
Mascall, E. L. *He Who Is: A Study in Traditional Theism* (London: Longmans, 1948).
Michalson, Carl. *The Rationality of Faith* (New York: Scribners, 1963).
Pinnock, Clark. *Set Forth Your Case* (Nutley, N.J.: Craig, 1967).

————. "Cultural Apologetics: An Evangelical Standpoint," *Bibliotheca Sacra* 12 (January 1970), 58–63.

Reymond, Robert L. *The Justification of Knowledge* (Nutley, N.J.: Presbyterian and Reformed, 1976).

Rushdoony, Rousas J. *By What Standard? An Analysis of the Philosophy of Cornelius van Til* (Nutley, N.J.: Presbyterian and Reformed, 1959).

Schaeffer, Francis A. *Trilogy* (Leicester: Inter-Varsity Press, 1990).

Sproul, R. C.; Gerstner, John; and Lindsley, Arthur. *Classical Apologetics: A Rational Defense of the Christian Faith and a Critique of Presuppositional Apologetics* (Grand Rapids: Zondervan, 1984).

van Til, Cornelius. *The Defense of the Faith* (Nutley, N.J.: Presbyterian and Reformed, 1955).

————. *A Christian Theory of Knowledge* (Nutley, N.J.: Presbyterian and Reformed, 1969).

Wolfe, David L. *Epistemology: The Justification of Knowledge* (Downers Grove: InterVarsity, 1982).

Yandell, Keith E. *Christianity and Philosophy* (Grand Rapids: Eerdmans, 1984).

Young, Warren C., *A Christian Approach to Philosophy* (Wheaton: Van Kampen, 1954).

Index

Murdoch, Iris, 151
Music, 204
Mystery, 199–200; sense of, 195, 203
Myth of Christian Uniqueness, The
    (Hick and Knitter), 118
Myth of God Incarnate, The (Hick),
    66, 123–24, 128
Mythology, Greek, 178
Myths, pagan, 121

Narnia, Chronicles of, 195–96, 197
Natural theology, 18
Nature, 18, 163–64, 165; religion of,
    118
Nazism, 111, 146, 175, 176, 179, 181
Neitzsche, Friedrich, 144–45
Neopaganism, 88, 182, 185
New Age movement, 88, 181–86
Newbigin, Lesslie, 108, 114
Newman, John Henry, 162
Newton, Isaac, 23, 24
Niebuhr, Reinhold, 71, 139
Nielsen, Kai, 39
Nihilism, 87

O'Hair, Madalyn Murray, 182
"Objectification," 196–97, 226n2
Objectivity, 153–54
Observation, theory of, 153–54
Ockham. *See* William of Ockham
Oden, Thomas C., 134, 146
Orderedness, 34, 38–39
Original sin, 138

Pain. *See* Suffering
Panentheism, 183
Pannenberg, Wolfhart, 122–23, 124
Pantheism, 183
Parables of Jesus, 20, 27, 172, 194
Paradox, 33, 124, 165
"Paradox of hedonism," 33, 232n68
Parallels in Gospels, 200–202
Pascal, Blaise, 55
Pasternak, Boris, 80
Paul, the apostle, 105, 120, 136, 182,
    219
Pauline writings, 27–28
Pelagianism, 150
Penicillin, analogy of, 54
Perfectibility, human, 69–70, 139
Plato, 30, 41, 101
Platonism, 127
Platt, John, 220
Pluralism, religious, 108–119, 113–14,
    175
Point of contact, 11, 30–47, 191–92,
    203, 212, 220, 226n7

Polkinghorne, John, 39, 224n18
Polytheism vs. monotheism, 111
Pope, Alexander, 75
Popper, Karl, 83, 85, 164–65
Positivism, 162–63
Postmodernism, 88, 144, 147, 175–81
Preaching, 46, 190–93
Presuppositionalism, 56–58, 217–21
Presuppositions, 40, 86, 123, 132–33,
    162, 180, 209
Princeton theology, 217–18, 221
"Principle of analogy," 17
Prism, analogy of, 23–24
Probability, 79
Projection theory, 95–96, 100, 196
"Proofs" for existence of God, 35–37
Prophecy, biblical, 83, 141, 201–2
Proudhon, Pierre Joseph, 226n23
Proust, Marcel, 198
Psychoanalysis, 97–98, 100
Psychogenesis, 98–99

Quadrilateral of faith, 81
"Quest of the historical Jesus," 150–
    51
Questions, dealing with, 205–211
Quine, Willard van Orman, 82

Rastafarianism, 115
Rationalism, Enlightenment, 147–55,
    184
Rationality, universal, 145, 152, 181
Realism, Scottish common sense, 152
Reality, perception of, 124
Reason, 34–38, 56; limits of, 17. *See*
    also Rationalism, Enlightenment
Reassurance, 193
Redemption, 45, 116, 138, 148
Reformation, the, 66–67, 170
Reformed doctrine, 220–21
"Reforming" church, 170–71
Relativism, 109, 175, 178
Relevance, problem of, 73–75
Religion, 94–95, 158; and Marxism,
    159–60; origin of, 98; vs. cul-
    ture, 110
"Religion," 109–110, 230n33
Religions, world, 110–11, 114
Repression, theory of, 97
Resurrection, the, 66, 89, 95, 105,
    119–23, 124, 127, 129, 133,
    169, 181, 185–86, 193, 202
Revelation: divine, 147, 211; general
    and special, 216, 220
Righteousness, 142
Robinson, John, 131
Roman Catholicism, 72